Leading Educational Networks

Also Available from Bloomsbury

System Leadership, *Susan Cousin*
Foucault and School Leadership Research, *Denise Mifsud*
A New Theory of Organizational Ecology, and its Implications for Educational Leadership, *Christopher M. Branson and Maureen Marra*
Education Governance and Social Theory, *edited by Andrew Wilkins and Antonio Olmedo*
Exploring Consensual Leadership in Higher Education, *edited by Lynne Gornall, Brychan Thomas and Lucy Sweetman*
Leadership for Sustainability in Higher Education, *Janet Haddock-Fraser, Peter Rands and Stephen Scoffham*
Leadership in Higher Education from a Transrelational Perspective, *Christopher M. Branson, Maureen Marra, Margaret Franken and Dawn Penney*
Global-National Networks in Education Policy, *Rino Wiseman Adhikary, Bob Lingard and Ian Hardy*

Leading Educational Networks

Theory, Policy and Practice

Toby Greany and Annelies Kamp

BLOOMSBURY ACADEMIC
LONDON • NEW YORK • OXFORD • NEW DELHI • SYDNEY

BLOOMSBURY ACADEMIC
Bloomsbury Publishing Plc
50 Bedford Square, London, WC1B 3DP, UK
1385 Broadway, New York, NY 10018, USA
29 Earlsfort Terrace, Dublin 2, Ireland

BLOOMSBURY, BLOOMSBURY ACADEMIC and the Diana logo are
trademarks of Bloomsbury Publishing Plc

First published in Great Britain 2022
This paperback edition published 2024

Copyright © Toby Greany and Annelies Kamp, 2022

Toby Greany and Annelies Kamp have asserted their right under the Copyright,
Designs and Patents Act, 1988, to be identified as Author of this work.

For legal purposes the Acknowledgements on p. ix constitute an
extension of this copyright page.

Cover design: Charlotte James
Cover image © sharply_done/ Getty Images

All rights reserved. No part of this publication may be reproduced or transmitted
in any form or by any means, electronic or mechanical, including photocopying,
recording, or any information storage or retrieval system, without prior
permission in writing from the publishers.

Bloomsbury Publishing Plc does not have any control over, or responsibility for, any
third-party websites referred to or in this book. All internet addresses given in this
book were correct at the time of going to press. The author and publisher regret any
inconvenience caused if addresses have changed or sites have ceased
to exist, but can accept no responsibility for any such changes.

A catalogue record for this book is available from the British Library.

Library of Congress Cataloging-in-Publication Data
Names: Greany, Toby, author. | Kamp, Annelies, author.
Title: Leading educational networks : theory, policy and practice /
Toby Greany and Annelies Kamp.
Description: First Edition. | New York : Bloomsbury Academic, 2022. |
Includes bibliographical references and index.
Identifiers: LCCN 2022004200 (print) | LCCN 2022004201 (ebook) |
ISBN 9781350178878 (Hardback) | ISBN 9781350226814 (Paperback) |
ISBN 9781350178861 (PDF) | ISBN 9781350178885 (ePub)
Subjects: LCSH: Education–Research. | Education–Information services. |
Information networks.
Classification: LCC LB1028 .G689 2022 (print) | LCC LB1028 (ebook) |
DDC 370.72–dc23/eng/20220225
LC record available at https://lccn.loc.gov/2022004200
LC ebook record available at https://lccn.loc.gov/2022004201

ISBN:	HB:	978-1-3501-7887-8
	PB:	978-1-3502-2681-4
	ePDF:	978-1-3501-7886-1
	eBook:	978-1-3501-7888-5

Typeset by Integra Software Services Pvt. Ltd.

To find out more about our authors and books visit www.bloomsbury.com
and sign up for our newsletters.

Annelies – to the memory of Jon Leitch, former Principal of Hillcrest High School.

Toby – to the memory of Denis Mongon, former teacher, visiting professor and 'next practice' mentor and collaborator.

Contents

List of Tables	viii
Acknowledgements	ix
Publishers Note	x
About the Authors	xi
List of Abbreviations	xii
Introduction	1
1 Understanding Networks in Contemporary Education Systems	7
2 Four Theoretical Lenses	31
3 Networks in England	55
4 Networks in Aotearoa New Zealand	73
5 Analysing Networks through the Lens of School Effectiveness and School Improvement	93
6 Analysing Networks through the Lens of Governance Theory	109
7 Analysing Networks through the Lens of Complexity Theory	127
8 Analysing Networks through the Lens of Actor-Network Theory	145
9 The Theory and Practice of Network Leadership	161
10 Leading Networks: Implications for Policy and Practice	179
Concluding Thoughts	199
Notes	202
References	209
Index	238

Tables

1.1	Four theoretical perspectives on school networking, adapted from Muijs, West and Ainscow (2010) and Muijs et al. (2011)	11
1.2	Vignette – the Learning Links Network (England)	16
4.1	Ethnic identity of school-aged children as per cent of total school-aged population (Tomorrow's Schools Independent Taskforce 2018: 24)	75
6.1	Hierarchical strategies for fostering networks	115
9.1	Eight core features of networks and their leadership implications	176
10.1	Synthesis of key concepts, arguments and implications from the four theoretical lenses	181

Acknowledgements

We are hugely grateful to the many leaders in Bampton and various Kāhui Ako in Christchurch who contributed to the research for this book and to all the many leaders and colleagues we have learnt from and with over the years. To Dr Vicente Reyes and Dr Mauricio Pino Yancovic for their comments on the Singaporean and Chilean case studies. In England, particular thanks to Jane Creasy for her collaborative wisdom and support. At Bloomsbury, thanks to Alison Baker and Evangeline Stanford for their patience and understanding through the pandemic.

Publishers Note

Every effort has been made to acknowledge any copyrighted materials reprinted herein. However, if any copyright owners have not been located and contacted at the time of publication, the publishers will be pleased to make the necessary arrangements at the first opportunity.

About the Authors

Toby Greany has been researching and working with educational leaders and their networks for more than two decades. He is currently Professor of Education and Convener of the Centre for Research in Education Leadership and Management (CRELM) at the University of Nottingham, UK. Former roles include Professor of Leadership and Innovation, UCL Institute of Education; Director – Research and Policy, National College for School Leadership (England); and Special Adviser, House of Commons Education and Skills Select Committee. He has significant international experience, including spending time in New Zealand (as an Erskine Scholar based at the University of Canterbury in 2018) and Singapore (on the National Institute of Education's Distinguished Visitors Programme in 2016). He has written more than fifty articles, chapters and reports on issues relating to educational leadership and networks, including *School Leadership and Education System Reform (2nd edition)* (co-edited with Peter Earley, 2021) and *Hierarchy, Markets and Networks: Analysing the 'Self-Improving, School-Led System' Reforms in England and the Implications for Schools* (with Rob Higham, 2018).

Annelies Kamp is Associate Professor in Leadership, Head of the School of Educational Studies and Leadership and Deputy Pro-Vice Chancellor of the College of Education, Health and Human Development at the University of Canterbury, New Zealand. She has over twenty-five years of experience in senior leadership roles in Crown agencies, industry training and the not-for-profit sector. She has been a Ministerial Board appointment in the post-compulsory education sector in both Australia and Aotearoa New Zealand, and Deputy Director at the Higher Education Research Centre at Dublin City University in Ireland. Her books include *Rethinking Learning Networks: Collaborative Possibilities for a Deleuzian Century* (Peter Lang, 2013), *A Critical Youth Studies for the 21st Century* (Brill, 2015), *Re/Assembling the Pregnant and Parenting Teenager: Narratives from the field(s)* (Peter Lang, 2017) and *Education Studies in Aotearoa: Key Disciplines and New Directions* (NZCER, 2019).

Abbreviations

ANT	Actor-Network Theory
AST	Academy of Singapore Teachers (Singapore)
CPD	Continuing Professional Development
DfE	Department for Education (England)
ERA	Education Reform Act (1988) (England)
ERO	Education Review Office (NZ)
FSM	Free School Meals
GCSE	General Certificate of Secondary Education
ICT	Information Communications Technology
IES	Investing in Educational Success (NZ)
LA	Local Authority
LCN	Learning and Change Networks (NZ)
LMS	Local Management of Schools (England)
MAT	Multi-Academy Trust
MAT CEO	Multi-Academy Trust Chief Executive Officer
MoE	Ministry of Education
NCEA	National Certificate of Educational Achievement (NZ)
NCSL	National College for School Leadership (England)
NIE	National Institute of Education (Singapore)
NLC	National Certificate of Educational Achievement (NZ/Singapore)
NLE	National Leader of Education (England)

NPM	New Public Management
NPQH	National Professional Qualification for Headship (England)
OA	Opportunity Area (England)
OECD	Organisation for Economic Co-operation and Development
Ofsted	Office for Standards in Education (England)
PISA	Programme of International Student Assessment
PLC	Professional Learning Community
SEM	School Excellence Model (Singapore)
SEND	Special Educational Needs or Disabilities
SESI	School Effectiveness and School Improvement
SIN	School Improvement Network (Chile)
SISS	Self-Improving, School-led System (England)
SLEs	Local Public Education Services (Chile)
TIMSS	Trends in International Maths and Science Study
TLP	Transnational Leadership Package
TSA	Teaching School Alliance (England)

Introduction

Imagine a leader...

Imagine a school leader who works in the education system you are most familiar with. Picture them in their office, at school. Now imagine that they are facing an issue they have never encountered before, or a challenge they have been trying to address for some time, without success. Who do they turn to for ideas and support? Depending on the particular country and system they are in, the chair of the school's governing body, an expert trainer or coach or their supervisor at the district office may be ideal for supporting on some issues, but less so on others. For example, a school principal might not want to reveal they are struggling to the person who is also responsible for assessing their performance. Or the challenge might not be something that anyone not currently working in a school can really help with. The COVID-19 pandemic certainly presented multiple new challenges for school leaders but, in England at least, the advice and support provided to them by the national Department for Education was woefully inadequate (Greany et al. 2021). As a result, in many situations, our imaginary school leader will turn to their networks for support. Such networks might be reliant on individual relationships, or they might operate at an organizational level, for example if the school is part of a local cluster or a wider membership organization.

Four points are significant here, each of which we revisit and develop throughout this book. First, if our imaginary school leader does not have such networks to turn to, if they and their school operate in 'splendid isolation', then there will be limited opportunities for them and their staff to learn from practices in other schools or other parts of their educational system, or to get emotional or practical support from their peers when they face challenges. Second, if the networks our imaginary leader engages with are all informal and organic, with no coherent ways of working or supporting infrastructure, then there is a risk that they could disintegrate when key members leave, or if network members are faced with more significant challenges that distract their time and attention. Third, while 'network' can be a noun, networking is also a verb and a skill – by which we mean that our imaginary leader must actively choose whether and how to participate in networks and the level of investment they want to make, and also that leaders can learn to become better networkers in the process of net-work. Fourth, networks develop in dynamic interaction with the context, structures and cultures within which they exist: they shift and change in line with the agency of participants, the historic, geographic and wider environmental conditions in which they are embedded, the resources they can draw upon and the objectives they pursue, as the case studies in this book clearly illustrate.

One implication of these points is that networks do not develop automatically or in consistent ways; networks always operate on a continuum, or perhaps more accurately a set of continua, reflecting the strength, length, breadth and depth of the relationships and activities that develop within and through the network. A second implication is that networks can operate at multiple levels, often simultaneously – between individual leaders and teachers, between schools, and/or across different parts and levels of an educational system, for example where they connect schools with other education providers, with employers, or with district, regional and/or national policymakers. A third implication is that some individuals and organizations will have better opportunities to access and benefit from networks than others, so networks have important implications for equity and wider educational outcomes for students as well as for the professional and career development of the educationalists involved.

In view of these points, this book has two overarching aims: firstly, to draw on a range of theoretical perspectives and on examples from different international contexts in order to deepen our understanding of how and why educational networks develop and function, and the kinds of leadership involved; and, secondly, to draw out the implications of this analysis for policy, practice and research. However, to be clear, we do not aim to provide a 'recipe' for successful networks, or to suggest that networks and networking are inherently positive. Indeed, although we do conclude that networking does have benefits, we also show that networks are not a panacea and that making the most of them requires new ways of thinking about leaders and leadership – as well as wider aspects of policy and practice – in education.

Outline of the book

This book provides a global perspective on inter-school networks and their leadership. It focuses in particular on evidence and practice in four school systems – Aotearoa New Zealand, Chile, England and Singapore. The core empirical evidence we draw on is from two detailed case studies – from England and New Zealand – which we have researched specifically for this book. The evidence from Chile and Singapore is drawn from the literature, informed by the experience that one of us has in Singapore and enriched by advice from two expert colleagues (Dr Vicente Reyes and Dr Mauricio Pino Yancovic); we are immensely grateful for their insights.

We examine this evidence through four distinct theoretical lenses – educational effectiveness and improvement, governance theory, complexity theory and Actor-Network Theory. We selected these lenses deliberately, but also pragmatically: they are not the only possible tools for examining networks, but they allow us to unpick the diversity and complexity of networks and to develop a more multifaceted and holistic understanding than has been attempted thus far. The lenses allow us to explore networks at different levels and from different angles: moving from the level of the individual school, to the local and national systems that schools operate within, to the wider environmental factors that shape, and are shaped by, network activity in education. That said, the lenses are not intended to be seamless or even neatly interlocking: at times our analysis through one lens disrupts or problematizes an implication we have drawn from another lens. In our view, these disruptions validate our approach, revealing how networks can develop and be experienced differently, depending on the standpoint of the observer. We hope that readers will value the breadth of the analysis, and agree that it supports a valid and important set of insights and implications for policy, practice and further research.

The structure of the book is as follows:

Chapter 1 explores existing theory, evidence and practice in relation to educational networks and their leadership and defines eight core features of networks. It starts by setting out definitions of the key terms and concepts that underpin the book, for example clarifying that our focus is on inter-organizational networks involving publicly funded schools and that we adopt Provan and Kenis' definition of a 'network' as involving three or more 'legally autonomous organizations that work together to achieve not only their own goals but also a collective goal' (2008: 231). It then reviews existing theories of why schools and school leaders engage in networks and evidence on the impact of networks. It also identifies the 'dark side' of networks and considers common barriers to networking in education. It synthesizes evidence from education and wider sectors to support the eight features, while acknowledging that these are by no means comprehensive. The last part of the chapter looks at global developments in this area, first by briefly reviewing evidence in relation to countries worldwide and then by describing network policies and practices in Singapore and Chile in greater detail.

Chapter 2 introduces the four theoretical lenses that we then draw on in later chapters to analyse our network cases. The chapter starts by citing Varpio et al. (2020) who argue that theories can offer a combination of descriptive, explanatory, emancipatory, disruptive and, potentially, predictive power. Each theory is then introduced in two sections. The first provides a brief overview of the theory itself and of the key debates or issues that have characterized its development. The second 'key concepts' section sets out a selection of concepts or models that are commonly used by researchers in that particular area. We draw on these 'key concepts' in the later chapters as a structure to assess the networks we examine across the four countries.

Chapters 3 and 4 describe the educational context and network landscape of England and Aotearoa New Zealand, respectively, before setting out the primary case studies – Bampton Alliance in England and Aupaki Kāhui Ako in New Zealand. Each chapter adopts a similar structure, first introducing the national context, then reviewing the educational policy context and particularly how policymakers have sought to incentivize and support inter-organizational networks, then moving on to provide an evidence-based overview of the state of play on educational networks in practice, before introducing the case study itself. The Bampton Alliance is a newly formed partnership which brings together multiple schools and school groups (Multi-Academy Trusts) to address shared priorities across one locality that had become increasingly fragmented as a result of recent government reforms. Aupaki Kāhui Ako is funded by government and brings together eight schools and eleven early childhood education providers in one area of Christchurch, a city facing continuing educational disruption following the earthquakes of 2010 and 2011.

Chapters 5–8 arguably form the heart of the book. Each chapter takes one theoretical lens and uses this to interrogate and deepen our analysis of networks and network leadership across the four systems. In Chapter 5, we focus on educational effectiveness and improvement, drawing on key concepts developed by David Hargreaves. We examine how leaders work to influence teaching, assessment and curriculum and to make a difference to children's learning and wider outcomes, and the ways in which inter-organizational networks can facilitate these efforts. In Chapter 6 we draw on governance theory to assess the ways in which hierarchy, market, network and community forms of co-ordination operate separately and together to influence the work of schools and school leaders, including how they operate in networks. Chapter 7 draws on complexity theories and particularly the four complexity conditions identified by Davis and Sumara (2008) – internal diversity, internal redundancy, neighbour interactions and decentralized control – to assess how networks operate to support emergence and innovation. Finally, Chapter 8 draws on Actor-Network Theory, and particularly the concepts taken up by Landri (2021) in his recent ANTian analysis of educational leadership and management in Italy – symmetry, translation, network and network stabilization. This allows us a close-up focus on the micro-practices by which leaders and other actors – both local and distant, human and non-human – seek to 'translate' the possibilities for action, including through inter-organizational networks.

Chapters 9 and 10 draw out key learning and implications from these analyses for policy and practice. Chapter 9 focuses on network leadership. It argues that the dominant global paradigm has focused on leadership within single schools, rather than networks, although two concepts have emerged – distributed and system leadership – which begin to grapple with the more complex and adaptive forms of leadership required in networks. It then sets out three areas which we see as key to successful network leadership in our case study contexts, precisely because these practices offer the potential to span the issues we identify through the four conceptual lenses: working productively with tensions and paradox, collective sense-making and adopting an ecological approach. The chapter concludes by identifying implications, presenting these in relation to the eight core features of networks identified in Chapter 1. Finally, Chapter 10 starts with a synthesis of the key messages that emerge from Chapters 5–8, identifying and discussing the implications that flow from this. It then addresses two themes in greater depth. Firstly, the nature and role of the place-based 'middle tier' which operates between central governments and individual schools in most systems, because this is the critical space in which networks are generally forged and operate. The second theme is leadership development, where attention globally is largely focused on individual leaders and the leadership of individual schools. The chapter argues that a parallel focus on developing collective, network and place-based leadership is required.

This can be achieved through embedded, co-design approaches which work to build local collaborative capacity and social learning systems.

Finally, in the Concluding Thoughts section, we reflect briefly on the implications of this book for future research, its theoretical and empirical contribution to the knowledge base, and on the process of writing this book across a twelve-hour time difference during the global pandemic.

1

Understanding Networks in Contemporary Education Systems

Introduction

The Introduction to this book asked you to imagine a school leader and to consider why and how they might need to draw on their networks to help them address the personal and professional challenges they confront in their daily work. In addition, the Introduction began to examine the complex and elusive nature of networks, for example by highlighting that they do not develop automatically or in consistent ways, that they can operate at multiple levels, and that some individuals and organizations have better opportunities to access and benefit from networks than others. This complexity has meant that the importance of networks has not always been recognized, but this situation has begun to change in recent years and networks are now becoming more central to policy, practice and research in education (Grimaldi 2011).

One reason for the increased focus on networks in education is the set of shifts taking place in wider societies. For example, Castells (2009) argues that we now live in a 'network society', resulting from transformations such as the spread of digital information and communications technologies together with wider developments, such as globalization, which are changing norms, expectations, cultural dynamics and the ways in which individuals and organizations connect to one another (Urry 2005; Giddens 2002; Beck 1992). These transformations directly affect education, meaning that contemporary leaders must deal with issues that are more complex and adaptive than the issues their predecessors faced. For example, how can a school best support a newly arrived, refugee student who has faced significant personal trauma and does not speak the local language? How can that same school best equip every child to thrive in a world faced with massive and seemingly continual change (Hannon and Peterson 2020)?

Reflecting these shifts, policymakers in many contexts have come to see networks between schools and between different parts of their education systems as an important mechanism for sharing knowledge and expertise, improving pupil outcomes, addressing equity challenges, making schools more responsive to parental and community needs and/or securing wider innovations (Ehren and Baxter 2021; Burns and Koster 2016). However, the implications of this 'network turn' are not straightforward, as Theisens (2016: 61–2) indicates:

> One of the problems of the network concept is that we understand relatively little about how interactions in networks lead to systems that are sufficiently organised to function … horizontal networks [operate] between all kinds of different stakeholders in the education system, the ministry, the inspectorate, teacher unions, all kinds of interest organisations, advisory groups and schools themselves. These horizontal networks lack the clarity of the vertical, hierarchical line but they are indispensable in the fragmented governance systems that decentralisation, privatisation and deregulation have led to.

This chapter begins by exploring evidence and practice in relation to educational networks around the world and is structured in two main parts. The first starts by setting out definitions of the key terms and concepts that underpin the book and then goes on to explore existing theories and evidence of why schools and school leaders engage in networks. It also draws together evidence on the impact of networks and defines eight core features of networks, which we return to in Chapter 9. The second section starts by reviewing the development of policy and practice on educational networks in countries around the world. It then goes on to describe network policies and practices in Singapore and Chile: two contrasting systems that have worked in different ways to foster networks and network leadership in recent years. These examples complement the extended case studies of networks in England and Aotearoa New Zealand (Chapters 3 and 4) and thus inform our analysis in subsequent chapters.

Why networks? – existing research and theory

This section starts by setting out definitions of the key terms and concepts that underpin the book. It goes on to explore existing theory around why policymakers and school leaders seek to develop networks and the evidence that such networks can support the achievement of desired outcomes. It also highlights parallel evidence on the 'dark side' of networks, showing that partnerships are never a straightforward panacea. It concludes by drawing together evidence from education and wider sectors to set out eight core features of networks and by summarizing the most common barriers to networking around the world.

Defining networks and network leadership

This book is rooted in an understanding of the broad 'network society' shifts outlined in the opening section, but its focus within this landscape is more specific – we are interested in the nature of leadership across partnerships and networks involving publicly funded schools. This means that we focus mainly on inter-organizational networks, although we recognize that organizations are made up of individuals and it is those individuals who actually engage in network activity, as we highlighted in the Introduction. Within this scope, we focus on both lateral (i.e. school to school) partnerships and also meta-networks that involve schools and wider groups, such as policymakers, early childhood and/or tertiary education providers. For example, the case studies of networks in both England and New Zealand include both types of network. We focus less on school partnerships with organizations in different sectors, such as employers, universities or private schools, although we reference such activity where relevant and our analysis is informed by our research and work in these areas (for example Lucas et al. 2017; Greany et al. 2014; Greany and Brown 2015; Kamp 2013b).

Popp et al. (2014: 18) explain that 'at their base, networks consist of the structure of relationships between actors (individuals and organizations) and the meaning of the linkages that constitute those relationships'. The focus is thus on 'social ties and interactions, rather than individual actors' (Perry, Pescosolido and Borgatti 2020: 4), as a means of understanding behaviour. Given our focus on school partnerships, we adopt here Provan and Kenis' definition of a 'network' as involving three or more 'legally autonomous organizations that work together to achieve not only their own goals but also a collective goal' (2008: 231).[1] As we explore throughout this book, this definition can encompass many types of partnership, including arrangements that are more and less formalized. In practice, policymakers and practitioners frequently use other terms, such as partnerships, communities of learning, collaboration, cluster or alliance, that can fit this definition and so we too use these terms where appropriate.[2] However, Provan and Kenis' definition does exclude certain types of inter-organizational networks, including partnerships between two schools, non-goal-directed networks and structures (such as Multi-Academy Trusts in England) that incorporate multiple schools into a single organizational framework. That said, we seek to explore the dynamic and permeable nature of networks, one aspect of which is that they often traverse apparently fixed definitional boundaries: for example, an informal, non-goal-directed network can quickly become goal-directed, while an existing network of autonomous schools can choose to amalgamate into a single organizational entity, for example to secure funding or enhance legitimacy, but may still retain many network features.

Just as it is challenging to define networks, leadership can be equally hard to pin down, with as many as 65 different classification systems developed to define the field (Fleishman et al. 1991) and over 300 definitions of leadership available (Bush and Glover 2014). Much of this work focuses on leadership within organizations, where traditional, hierarchical structures tend to shape the exercise of leadership. In contrast, leadership across networks is widely perceived to require different skillsets (Williams 2012; Milward and Provan 2006; Huxham and Vangen 2003) and a growing number of studies provide empirical evidence to support these claims (Paquin and Howard-Grenville 2013; Silvia and McGuire 2010). This work highlights the distinct issues that leaders must attend to in what Crosby and Bryson (2005) call the 'shared-power world' of networks, including power, control, agency, ownership, values and trust. We return to these issues below and in Chapters 9 and 10, but at this stage we adopt Northouse's (2009: 3) broad definition of leadership as 'a process whereby an individual influences a group of individuals to achieve a common goal' as our starting point.

Network theories, rationales and benefits

This section reviews existing literature to identify common aims and purposes for networks. It then surveys the evidence that networks can impact on desired outcomes in education and more widely. Not surprisingly, given the 'network society' shifts referenced above, networks have become a central focus for research across many different disciplines, including anthropology, economics, sociology and political science. Academics in each discipline tend to adopt different theoretical perspectives, creating a 'cacophony of heterogeneous concepts, theories and research results' (Oliver and Ebers 1998: 549). The development of network science in recent years, specifically through Social Network Analysis (SNA) and Egocentric Network analysis, has helped to bring greater coherence in how we conceptualize and analyse networks (Bidart, Degenne and Grossetti 2020; Perry, Pescosolido and Borgatti 2020; Kadushin 2012). Much of this work focuses on ego – that is, individual, rather than inter-organizational – networks, so clearly there are risks in assuming that concepts and findings transfer. However, our approach is to draw on this body of work in ways which enrich our analysis whilst highlighting differences.

Muijs, West and Ainscow (2010), building on a more extensive review (Muijs et al. 2011),[3] helpfully narrow down the range of potential theoretical perspectives on networking in education, always with a focus on how these help to illuminate aspects of school effectiveness and improvement. The four perspectives they focus on – constructivist theory, social capital theory, new social movements and Durkheimian theory – are summarized in Table 1.1.

Table 1.1 Four theoretical perspectives on school networking, adapted from Muijs, West and Ainscow (2010) and Muijs et al. (2011)

Theory	Rationale for why schools might choose to engage in networks
Constructivist theory	Organizations are sense-making systems creating shared perceptions and interpretations of reality. Each organization has its own unique perception of reality. This risks myopia if the organization is closed to external influences, but this can be addressed through networking through which external partners can provide complementary cognition. The more uncertainty and complexity that exist in the environment, the more there is a need for collaboration to ensure that organizations are able to adopt the necessary competence to cope with the complexity that surrounds and impacts on them.
Social capital theory	Networking allows organizations to harness resources held by other actors, in particular knowledge and information that an individual organization might require in order to be effective. A network can also exert more influence on its social and political surroundings than individual actors and can help spread innovations. A key issue is whether the gains from networking accrue mainly to the individual school, the network as a whole, society or a combination of these. In cases where the benefits are seen as entirely societal or at network level, the motivation of individual actors (schools) may be limited.
New social movements	New social movements, such as the environmental movement, are not built on traditional identities, such as class, but develop their own collective identity. New social movements are typically diverse and diffuse but are often built around and dominated by activist leaders. Hadfield (2007) claims that bottom-up networks of schools display transience, complexity and a need to build up new network identities that are distinct from their constituent schools. Furthermore, like new social movements bottom-up school networks are often shaped by charismatic head teachers.

Durkheimian theory	This perspective sees networking as key to combatting anomie, a malaise in individuals characterized by feelings of alienation and purposelessness. Anomie commonly occurs when society is undergoing rapid change, and when there is a significant discrepancy between the ideological theories and values individuals and society hold and their actual practices. According to Durkheim (1972), anomie results from a lack of strong ties and the regulation and integration that they bring. Muijs and Ainscow suggest that schools facing challenging circumstances, and particularly failing schools, may seek to alleviate organizational anomie by engaging in networks which offer shared values and moral purpose as well as opportunities for integration and regulation.

It is important to elaborate the concept of social capital, given its centrality to many assessments of networks, including Muijs et al.'s work. While social capital can be explored at individual and/or group level, our focus is on the group level and thus draws on the heritage of Putnam (1993), Bourdieu (1990) and Coleman (1988). The importance of social capital is commonly related to three roles: facilitating information flow, enabling influence to be exerted on actors through group norms and social 'credentialing' whereby transaction costs can be lowered, for example through the development of trust. Lin (1999) argues for a fourth role – recognition:

> Social relations are expected to reinforce identity and recognition. Being assured and recognized of one's worthiness as an individual and a member of a social group sharing similar interests and resources not only provides emotional support but also public acknowledgment of one's claim to certain resources. These *reinforcements* are essential for the maintenance of mental health and the entitlement to resources.
>
> (Lin 1999: 31)

A central aspect of using social capital as a concept is not on network structures but on *action*: the flows that occur through the network and the investments made by network members in pursuit of expected returns. In this, social capital requires an 'apparently gratuitous expenditure of time, attention, care, [and] concern' that requires a 'very specific labour' (Bourdieu 1986: 253) by network members. Muijs, West and Ainscow (2010: 11) suggest that motivation for this labour lies in the potential, within 'successful' networking, for both individual and collective benefit.

The four perspectives detailed by Muijs, West and Ainscow (2010) highlight a range of motivations for, and potential benefits from, networking for school effectiveness, as well as some of the ways in which networks might operate to secure impact. So, for example, while constructivist theory emphasizes the role of networks in co-designing new knowledge and ways of working, social capital theory – in their interpretation – focuses on more instrumental aspects of knowledge exchange to address organizational gaps and needs. New social movements suggests that schools might network in order to affirm a particular identity or belief system and/or to achieve a wider outcome, such as impact on policy, while Durkheimian theory highlights the need for solidarity with other schools in the context of rapid external change, such as all that we have witnessed in the context of COVID-19.

This range of motivations and potential benefits from networking is broadly supported by research beyond education. For example, Popp et al. (2014) illustrate the benefits of networking in a number of areas, including information sharing, knowledge generation and exchange, individual and organizational learning, capacity building, service coordination, problem-solving, innovation and policy influencing and development. Similarly, Provan and Kenis (2008: 240) explain that organizations might join or form networks for a variety of reasons, including the need to gain legitimacy, to serve clients more effectively, to attract more resources or to address complex problems, but that regardless of the specific reason, at a general level, all network organizations are seeking to achieve some end that they could not have achieved independently.

In the education sphere, the importance of professional learning is widely recognized (Révai 2020) and networks are positioned as ideal contexts for such learning to take place, as Leithwood (2019: 176–7) explains:

> Networks provide a context for learning closely reflecting accounts of human learning found in a cluster of overlapping theoretical conceptions ... Sociocultural theory posits that learning occurs through interaction with others (especially with more skilled others) and the circumstances or culture in which they are located. According to conceptions of situated cognition, what is learned is strongly influenced by the circumstances in which it is learned, helping to reduce the gap between abstract knowledge and knowledge that can be used in practice. Informal learning ... is non-didactic, is embedded in meaningful activity, builds on the learner's initiative, interest, or choice ... and does not involve assessment external to the activity.

In addition to providing a rich context for professional learning, networks are variously seen by policymakers, practitioners and researchers as offering wide potential. This potential includes providing emotional and practical support to leaders, teachers and schools, in particular those that are struggling or that are spread across dispersed rural areas, ensuring 'joined up' and inclusive provision that meets the needs of all children, offering a broader and more engaging curriculum than would be possible in an individual school and supporting innovation cultures and the diffusion of successful innovations (Suggett 2014; Hargreaves 2010, 2011, 2012a, 2012b). Other work has highlighted the potential for networks to contribute to local area improvement and to connect and cohere top-down and bottom-up improvement efforts through 'middle out' change (Munby and Fullan 2016), as well as reversing costly system-generated school isolation (Wylie 2012b). The OECD (2015: 73) concludes that 'well-functioning collaborative networks add high value and can enable the whole to become more than the sum of its parts'.

In practice, many of these outcomes have proved difficult to evaluate, in particular across more diffuse and dynamic partnerships (Janssens and Ehren 2016) and due to a lack of systematic evaluations across different countries and contexts (Révai 2020). As a result, the evidence that networks in education really do impact in ways that their proponents claim remains partial at best. The evidence is strongest in relation to partnerships that are more tightly structured and with more narrowly defined objectives, such as a common model in England in which successful schools are brokered to support lower-performing schools to improve (Muijs 2015a; Chapman, Muijs and Macallister 2011). Clearly, these school-to-school support partnerships in England are mandated by policy and tend to receive significant additional resources and support, making them very different from other kinds of voluntary collaboration. Nevertheless, the evidence that networking can add value remains persuasive, as Armstrong, Brown and Chapman (2020) conclude:

> Teachers, school leaders and other educational stakeholders all gain from working collaboratively with colleagues outside of their institutions and ... this is (indirectly) to the advantage of the educational experiences and outcomes of the young people within their schools and classrooms.

However, this does not mean that all networks are successful or that positive impact is guaranteed. Critics on the right have argued that the claims for networks in education are overstated, that they distract schools from their core purpose and represent a significant opportunity cost (i.e. because they use up time and energy that could usefully be focused elsewhere) (Croft 2015). Equally, critical theorists, such as Grimaldi (2011: 121), argue that networks have been presented as 'magical concepts' which promise 'modernity, neutrality, pragmatism and positivity', but that the reality is vastly more complex and uncertain, not least as a result of often 'unremarked' (Thrupp 2018) but important power differentials. Certainly, as we explore in subsequent chapters, networks are often messy and problematic, many do not succeed in their original aims, the process can eat up considerable amounts of busy leaders' time, and it can take a long time for benefits to emerge. Furthermore, there are significant barriers to collaboration in many school systems.

There can also be a 'dark side' to networks (Bidart, Degenne and Grossetti 2020). While networking can support equitable partnerships, it can also reproduce unequal power relations and internal hierarchies (Greany and Higham 2018; Kamp 2013b); networking can be open and inclusive, but also the reverse (Hatcher 2008); knowledge and expertise can be shared through networks, but there are also dangers, such as groupthink (Ehren and Perryman 2017), and while organizations can co-ordinate networks on the basis of trust, they can equally be motivated by risk, fear and suspicion and can collaborate without trust (Cook, Hardon and Levi 2007).

Eight core features of networks and barriers to their achievement

This section describes eight core features of networks as well as common barriers to their development. The evidence to support these features comes largely from our own research and observations (Greany and McGinity 2021; Greany 2020a; Greany 2018a; Greany and Higham 2018; Greany and Maxwell 2017; Greany and Allan 2014; Kamp 2013b; Kamp 2017; Kamp 2019b), but is also informed by various empirical and theoretical studies in education[4] as well as wider studies of partnerships and networks beyond education (as referenced).

Firstly, successful inter-organizational networks and partnerships generally reflect a shared goal or interest. In education, the partnerships that have the greatest discernible impact tend to focus on addressing shared and reasonably specific collaborative priorities around improving teachers' practice and/ or enhancing outcomes for specific groups of students or curriculum areas (see Table 1.2 Learning Links vignette for an example). However, in practice, individuals and organizations can have multiple motivations for engaging in networks, so the stated goal might not reflect the full picture. For example, Kadushin (2012) identifies three intrinsic needs which lead individuals to engage

Table 1.2 Vignette – the Learning Links network (England)

> Learning Links was started by four primary schools, all serving deprived communities in one Local Authority (LA) area in England. Over an eight-year period, five additional local primary schools in similarly deprived contexts were invited to join the network. Each school contributes funding (£3,000 annually) and releases senior leaders and (less regularly) teachers to engage in network activities. The funding pays for a retired head teacher to facilitate and chair the cluster. The original motivation for starting the network was to provide collective, school-based Continuing Professional Development (CPD) for new and existing teachers, because the existing programmes offered by the LA were seen as ineffective. Over time, additional activities had been introduced and layered on to this original focus, all of which aimed to improve student learning and the quality of teaching and leadership. These additional activities included moderating student work, appointing the same 'improvement partner' (i.e. external reviewer) for all member schools, holding annual shared governor meetings, undertaking peer-evaluations/reviews between schools (Greany 2020b) and sharing data on student progress with the aim of identifying good practice and areas for mutual support. However, network development had sometimes been challenging, with at least one significant 'dead end' that nearly caused some schools to leave, and difficulties with finding non-time-consuming ways for teachers to share and exchange their practice. In addition, some other local schools argued that the network was exclusive – an 'invitation only club' for schools judged Good and Outstanding by Ofsted.
>
> Adapted from Greany and Higham 2018: 72–3

in networks: i) *safety* – the desire for social support in dense, cohesive networks; ii) *effectiveness* – leading us to reach out beyond our current situation and comfort zone, in the process making connections across diverse networks; and iii) *status* – or 'keeping up with the Joneses', by accessing asymmetric networks which can advance our rank and level of social capital. Clearly, organizations are not the same as individuals, but the point is that network motives and goals are frequently multidimensional and one need (for example for safety) can be in tension with another (for example for effectiveness). This might explain findings from various evaluations which indicate that simply providing funding for new school networks and asking them to define some shared goals rarely leads to sustainable impact.

Second, network impact relates to the level of commitment and contribution – the investment – of network members. Such commitment requires a degree of shared ownership over decision-making, and therefore power, so that the contribution and expertise of different partners are equally valued regardless of their 'usual' positional role, and a sense that benefits are shared equally. However, in practice, a school's ability to commit to these networking processes is likely to relate to issues such as its size, socio-economic status and/or remoteness, and can wax and wane in line with its internal capacity, leadership commitment and external factors.

Third, successful networks generally share values, practices and attributes, such as solidarity, honesty, reciprocity and trust, which take time to build (for example, the Learning Links network had developed over eight years). Two points are important here: first, people with like characteristics tend to be connected (*homophily*, or 'birds of a feather') and this is often true of organizations (for example the Learning Links schools all serve deprived communities); second, the process of collaboration involves mutual influence (feedback), leading to a level of convergence in norms and behaviours over time (*isomorphism*) (Greany 2020b). The circumstances of network formation, for example whether or not schools are mandated to join a particular group, influence the development of share values, practices and attributes and their existence cannot be taken for granted. Furthermore, the exact nature and influence of these features on network functioning are not clear-cut. For example, Hargreaves (2010) argues that 'deep' (i.e. successful) partnerships require strong ties between staff at multiple levels across schools, with close and frequent interactions and high levels of relational trust and reciprocity, including an ability to give and receive formative and developmental feedback on aspects of practice. Yet research outside education has shown that strong ties in relatively closed networks can actually limit opportunities, whereas weak ties across distributed networks can allow new information to flow and problems to be innovatively solved even in the absence of high levels of trust (Wellman 1983; Granovetter 1973).

Fourth, inter-organizational partnerships are embedded within wider societal contexts and interact with the multiple social networks that operate within and, often, across the organizations involved. These social networks might be more and/or less formalized; for example, a partnership might decide to convene a formal network for subject leaders from each school, but a subset of these same subject leaders might also meet informally outside work. Organizational roles are also important: for example, the nature and content of networks involving school principals can be very different to networks involving classroom teachers. One way to make sense of this complexity comes from egocentric analyses, which see networks as having four dimensions – structure, function, strength and content (Perry, Pescosolido and Borgatti 2020) – which interact to influence individual and network-level outcomes and behaviours. *Structure* reflects the architecture of the network, including the presence and patterns of linkages between members. *Function* relates to the types of exchanges, services or supports made accessible through the network. *Strength* captures the intensity and duration of bonds between network members. *Content* refers to what flows to or from network members, which might include more tangible aspects, such as information, knowledge, money, skills or less tangible cultural aspects, such as attitudes, opinions and beliefs.

The fifth feature of networks is that many develop formalized governance and management structures over time as they grow, believing this will improve efficiency. However, such structures can risk reducing levels of ownership for (some) members. Pino-Yancovic et al. (2020) suggest that networks exist on a spectrum – from loose 'association', to 'emerging collaboration' focused on addressing short term tasks, to 'sustained collaboration' and, finally, 'collegiality' characterized by shared vision and values – with different formations serving different purposes and the potential to move from one model to another over time. Suggett's review (2014: 9) suggests that effective networks were, for the leaders studied, about minimal 'red-tape' and the absence of the 'constraints of structured approaches'. Provan and Kenis (2008) identify three typical models of governance: i) 'shared governance networks' are governed equally by all network members; ii) 'lead organization networks' are governed by one network member, acting as a centralized network broker; and iii) 'Network Administrative Organizations' (NAO) are networks governed externally by a separate administrative entity, often with a formal manager or CEO. Many networks begin with informal 'shared governance', but as they grow in size they commonly evolve towards a 'lead organization' or NAO structure because finding consensus and organizing activities become more complex in larger networks. However, Milward and Provan (2006: 22) acknowledge that these structures can lead to power imbalances, increased costs and/or decreased transparency, precipitating declining commitment from members. Many networks employ an external facilitator, which can help to reduce coordination demands and introduce wider expertise, but also carries the risk of reduced ownership.

Sixth, research indicates a number of design principles or features that are important for network effectiveness. In addition to the points above around shared goals and values, these include more specific aspects such as the availability of resources (including allocated time for network participation) and the use of shared protocols and routines that guide action and support impact, without pushing the network towards rule-following (Hargreaves, Parsley and Cox 2015; McCarthy, Miller and Skidmore 2004).

Seventh, networks in education are frequently focused on generating new knowledge (*exploration*) and diffusing innovations across schools (*exploitation*), but doing this successfully requires sophisticated skills backed by supportive processes, such as the collaborative enquiry approaches referenced below. David Hargreaves (2010, 2011, 2012a, 2012b) is one of several observers who argue that collaborative 'joint practice development' between teachers is the key to building trust, developing capacity and securing impact across networks. However, the challenge is not only to generate, articulate and diffuse knowledge and expertise, but to ensure that the resulting practices are actually more effective than what went before. Many networks identify 'lead practitioners' (aka boundary spanners) who are charged with facilitating these processes, but an approach that is founded on a one-way transfer of knowledge (i.e. from 'experts' to 'less expert' peers) can excite resistance and risks trying to 'drag and drop' practices without consideration of how they might need to be adapted for different contexts. Research on knowledge sharing (Hartley and Beningto 2006; Fielding et al. 2004) indicates that knowledge is not simply 'transferred' from one context to another, but rather continuously reviewed and transformed as it is taken into different settings, although the extent to which such knowledge benefits from formal codification or not is debated (Peurach and Glazer 2012; Holmqvist 2003), as is the most appropriate role of research evidence and data in these processes (Coldwell et al. 2017). Many networks adopt cycles of collaborative enquiry (such as action research, research and development, Learning and Change Networks, networked improvement communities and so on), informed by collective reflection on evidence and data and, sometimes, common quality frameworks, as a means of cumulatively building and sharing practice (Brown and Poortmen 2018; Greany and Maxwell 2017; Bryk 2015).

Eighth, leading and managing networks requires sophisticated skills and qualities – certainly from lead facilitators, but also from wider participants given that networks inevitably involve distributed and hybrid forms of leadership. Such leadership is not always successful and there is an argument that leading a single school is not a good preparation for leading across a network. Indeed, many appointed to school leadership roles lack training in organizational theory in general, or leading change in particular (Hargreaves 2011), but it seems that networking and network leadership can be learned and developed (Brown 2020). The role of network leadership is a nimble, influencing role concerned with leadership among leaders (Kamp 2019b) and so Popp et al. (2014: 33) argue that network leaders must nurture a culture that 'addresses competing interests, politics and power differentials; and that promotes trusting relationships, curiosity, conscious interest in gaining different perspectives, and respect for diversity of views among organizations.' However, according to Vangen and Huxham (2003), gaining and maintaining momentum in networks can require a degree of 'collaborative thuggery', where network leaders have to manipulate agendas or play the politics in order to overcome the risk of inertia and to move action forward.

These eight features of successful networks are not intended to be exhaustive. For example, Muijs et al. (2011) develop a typology of networks which considers additional issues, such as the time frames involved and the geographic spread of network members. We agree that these issues are important and touch on some of them in the subsequent chapters, but have kept to eight significant features emerging from multiple studies at this stage for the sake of parsimony.

Finally, we briefly highlight evidence on some common barriers to networks in education, although it is clear that the nature and impact of these barriers are context-specific. Paniagua and Istance (2018) undertook an international survey of network leaders and identified barriers that included: complacency and a lack of commitment from network members, the loss of central funding when policy priorities changed, lack of time, competition between schools and overly tight accountability requirements that hinder innovation. Similarly, Armstrong, Brown and Chapman (2020: 16) summarized the most common barriers in England in terms of: 'threats to school autonomy (and perceived power imbalances), capacity (including funding and resources), (staff) workload and a marketized national policy context that fosters and actively encourages competition.' Findings from other countries and contexts indicate overlaps with these findings, several of which we explore in more detail in subsequent chapters.

Educational networks in review – a global scan

This section is not intended to provide a comprehensive overview of school network policies and practices globally, which would require a book in its own right. Instead, we draw on published evidence to give a sense of how network policies have developed globally. In the following section, we provide short case studies of two jurisdictions – Chile and Singapore – to illustrate different approaches in more detail.

Revai (2020: 8) reports that 'more and more countries have been investing in establishing networks in education as forms of organization to facilitate change' and draws together vignettes from different countries, including Hungary, the Netherlands and France, as well a Europe-wide online network, to illustrate this claim. In a similar vein, Rincon-Gallardo and Fullan (2016) review examples and evidence from Canada (Ontario and Alberta), the United States, Mexico and Columbia as well as England and Aotearoa New Zealand. Paniagua and Istance (2018) set out to identify and survey educational networks focused on pedagogy and innovation globally, making a conscious effort to find examples from beyond Anglo-Saxon countries. They approached thirty-eight networks, of which twenty-seven completed the survey and are included in the report: eleven from nine different European countries, seven from the UK (England and Scotland), three from South America (Columbia, Peru and Chile), two from Canada, one from Japan and three with an international focus.[5] The size of these networks varies widely, from 8 to 1,000 member schools, as does the level of sustainability, with six of the twenty-seven having continued for more than ten years. Paniagua and Istance (2018) categorize the networks into three broad, non-exclusive groups, reflecting the dominant focus of their activity:

- pedagogical approach networks – includes networks implementing the same innovations and defined by common pedagogical principles
- innovation promotion networks – networks that share their different innovative pedagogies
- professional learning networks – focused on providing professional development to schools and teachers

These reviews suggest that networking policies and practices are most clearly developing in Anglo-Saxon, European and Latin American contexts. Our own reading of published research that focuses on individual networks and/or specific countries supports the same conclusion, with most focusing on one or more context in Australasia, Canada, Europe and/or the United States. For example, Suggett (2014) reviews findings from networking efforts in Australia (Victoria) and England, and references parallel work in British Columbia and New Zealand. Brown (2020) reports on networking initiatives in Germany and England, while Sartory (2017) focuses specifically on Germany. In the United States, there has been a rapid growth in networking initiatives as well as important academic work in this area in recent years, frequently with a focus on practical problem-solving informed by the principles of improvement science (Bryk 2015), design-based improvement (Mintrop 2017) and/or research-practice partnerships (Penuel and Gallagher 2017). Building on these foundations, The Carnegie Foundation for the Advancement of Teaching has promoted 'networked improvement communities' as a model for collective enquiry and improvement across groups of schools (Sherer et al. 2021).

However, the fact that most published evidence is weighted towards these contexts does not mean that educational networks are not a feature of policy and practice in other parts of the world. The apparent lack of evidence on networking from Africa, Asia and the Middle East might simply reflect the fact that education research from these areas has developed more recently and may be less likely to feature in English-language publications (Hallinger and Hammad 2017). Indeed, a focused search for evidence from a subset of these locations identified that networking and collaboration is commonly a feature, although it operates in different ways. For example, focusing only on research published in English from China and south-east Asia, we find clear evidence that many – perhaps most – schools do engage in networks (Harris, Zhao and Caldwell 2009; Wu 2005). Walker and Qian (2020: 13) interviewed 101 primary school principals from across different parts of China and report:

> (A) widely adopted policy of forming school networks or consortiums which allowed principals to share or seek resources from partner schools. Most networks are initiated or coordinated by local governments – the major purpose is to group strong and weak schools to narrow achievement gaps between schools … . The practice of forming networks has also spread to less developed regions. A Guizhou principal said his school was a member of a large consortium of thirteen partner schools. The schools provide each other mutual support as well as co-organizing events such as Arts Festivals and sports meetings.

Earlier research by the same authors (Qian and Walker 2019: 511) found that some of these partnerships involve extensive levels of collaboration and exchange between schools. For example, one principal reported sending thirty-six teachers to spend time in partner schools over the course of several years, sometimes staying for as long as an entire semester. However, the research from China and south-east Asia also stresses important differences as well as similarities in educational leadership when compared with findings from Western contexts, as a result of contextual and cultural differences (Hallinger 2018). For example, Hallinger and Walker (2017: 139) review accumulated findings on principal instructional leadership in five East Asian contexts (China, Taiwan, Malaysia, Singapore and Vietnam), and conclude that:

> Traditional values that honor hierarchy, seniority and status continue to shape perspectives toward power and staff involvement. Therefore, despite continuing

efforts to 'decentralize authority,' 'involve teachers in decision making,' 'empower teachers' and create cadres of 'middle-level leaders' in these societies, educational change and school improvement remain largely top-down enterprises.

These differences also influence the role and nature of networking for school principals. Such networking is certainly important – 'being able to effect instructional change in schools in some societies involves as much work outside as within schools' (2017: 138) – but this networking is more clearly focused on maintaining strong relations with government and/or party officials than might be the case in most Western contexts.

In conclusion, evidence on networks is undoubtedly more extensive in some contexts than others, but the brief exploration of evidence from China and southeast Asia indicates that networks are also widespread – if distinctive – there too. In the following section we offer more detailed overviews of networking policies and practices in Singapore and Chile, which complement the case studies of England and Aotearoa New Zealand in Chapters 3 and 4 and inform our theoretical analyses in the remainder of the book.

Case studies of two diverse systems

School networks in Singapore

Singapore's educational journey and success in international rankings such as PISA and TIMSS have been studied extensively by both national and international observers (Koh and Hung 2018; Greany 2018b; Tan, Low and Hung 2017; Ng 2010, 2017; Lee et al. 2014; Dimmock and Tan 2013; Barber and Mourshed 2007). These studies highlight important contextual features which can be seen to have facilitated Singapore's success, including its: small size (356 schools in total), tight central control exercised by a single political party and pragmatic focus on efficiency and effectiveness in the context of a need for rapid nation-building and economic development through human capital following independence in 1965.

Since the late 1990s, education policies in Singapore have sought to move away from top-down and standardized approaches and to encourage greater creativity and student-centred pedagogies, encapsulated in the Thinking Skills Learning Nation (TSLN) and Teach Less Learn More (TLLM) agendas. The resulting approach is often characterized in terms of 'centralized-decentralization'

(Ng 2010) or a 'tight-loose-tight' (Toh et al. 2016), involving a combination of tight central prescription over aspects such as the curriculum and required pupil outcomes (which include, but go beyond academic test scores), together with a looser level of control over how schools operate to achieve these outcomes.

Lee, Ho and Yong (2021) describe the development of school networks in Singapore, showing how these integrate with the wider reform strategy. The school cluster system was introduced in 1997 'to support the TSLN vision as a structure for coordinating capacity-building efforts and encouraging individual school innovations while ensuring schools align with the overall directives set by Ministry of Education (MOE)' (2021: 169). Schools are organized into four geographical zones with seven to nine clusters per zone and ten to thirteen schools per cluster. Each cluster is overseen by a cluster superintendent, described as 'senior or experienced principals whose role is to communicate MOE's policies and to guide and supervise school leadership teams to understand and implement MOE's policies' (2021: 169). In addition, the Academy of Singapore Teachers (AST) is an MOE-sponsored body that aims 'to build a teacher-led culture of professional learning and excellence', including through the facilitation of professional learning communities (PLCs) within individual schools and networked learning communities (NLCs) across schools (Bautista, Wong and Gopinathan 2015). Lee, Ho and Yung (2021: 173–4) explain that:

> While PLCs stress professional learning in communities of teachers within schools, NLCs involve teachers from different schools, promoting teachers to learn from one other, learn with one another and learn on behalf of each other ... These NLCs may be (1) subject based, like subject chapters under the AST; (2) role based, like an NLC for School Staff Developers and (3) interest based NLCs 'on any area that anyone is passionate about' ... As NLCs involve teachers across schools, it can function at the cluster, zonal or even national levels'.

Studies of networks in Singapore have mainly focused on their potential for developing and diffusing innovations (Hung et al. 2016; Toh et al. 2016; Toh et al. 2014). These innovations have generally been developed in pioneering 'nodal' schools with funding and support from the MOE. The 'nodal' schools and their staff generally lead the diffusion process across networks, but this work is actively supported by the MOE and its agencies, for example with cluster superintendents sometimes selecting the schools and individual teachers who are seen as best placed to benefit from the new learning. Toh et al. (2016) thus characterize school networks as part of a systemic – or ecosystem – approach to innovation, in which successful diffusion relies on a combination of structural, social-cultural, economic and epistemic carryovers. Critically, it is the epistemic carryovers – for example where networking leads to changes in teachers' values and beliefs about learning and the nature of knowledge – that appear to have greatest sustainable impact. Hung et al. (2016) draw on similar examples to characterize different types of innovation and different diffusion models, for example distinguishing between those that are 'designed deep' (i.e. tightly defined and requiring in-depth change) and those that are 'designed wide' (i.e. broadly defined, with less need for fundamental change). The 'designed deep' innovations were diffused across a smaller number of schools, and required more intensive apprenticeship-type learning between expert and novice teachers, backed by cross-school leadership and support from wider agencies. In contrast, the 'designed wide' innovations could be diffused across a wider network with less intensive levels of engagement and support, but also with less significant impact on the technical core of classroom teaching.

Networks thus form part of a carefully calibrated approach overseen by the MOE. On the one hand this remains a hierarchical model, with the clusters and cluster superintendents providing a mechanism for policy-driven reforms to be enacted, for school quality to be monitored and for professional development and learning to be shared across schools. However, within this model, schools have been given greater autonomy to make contextually appropriate decisions and the accountability system has been reformed to remove school rankings and to emphasize the centrality of school self-evaluation and improvement. Meanwhile, the PLCs and NLCs are explicitly aimed at building the capacity of teachers and leaders and encouraging school-led innovation, in particular in the context of the desired shift towards more creative, digitally enabled and student-centred pedagogies. However, despite – or perhaps even because of – the tight reform framework in Singapore, networking between schools can be challenging. For example, Lee, Ho and Yong (2021) acknowledge that existing cultural practices, such as heavy teacher workloads, fear of compromising students' test scores and a dependency culture in which teachers expect top-down guidance, all present challenges for networking that school and system leaders will need to overcome.

School networks in Chile

Networks involving public schools in rural areas and, separately, groups of private schools have existed in Chile for several decades, but the requirement for all publicly funded schools to engage in networks is a far more recent development (Montecinos, González and Ehren 2021; Pino-Yancovic et al.

2019, 2020; Pino-Yancovic and Ahumada 2020). The School Improvement Network (SIN) strategy was launched nationwide in 2015, when over 500 networks involving 5,500 schools across all fifteen regions of the country 'were created to support the improvement of municipal schools and, in some cases, private subsidized schools' (Pino-Yancovic et al. 2020: 16). A further reform, initiated in 2018 but continuing until 2025, involves the removal of Chile's 345 municipalities from school oversight, and their replacement with seventy Local Public Education Services (SLEs) charged with enhancing the quality of public education, including through the facilitation of school networks.

This investment in networks forms part of a wider set of reforms, introduced since 2008, which aim to address systemic weaknesses and high levels of inequality between schools in Chile. In the early 1980s the Pinochet regime introduced market mechanisms, such as vouchers for parents to use at private subsidized schools, which emphasized choice, competition and vertical accountability. Over time this had led to public municipal schools being seen by more affluent parents as the least attractive option for educating their children: thus, whereas, 'in 2000, over 54 per cent of elementary and secondary students in Chile were enrolled in municipal schools, by 2014 this had dropped to 36.8 per cent' (Montecinos, González and Ehren 2021: 202). The reforms introduced since 2008 have therefore increased levels of investment in deprived, municipal schools and reduced the emphasis on choice and competition across the system, for example by removing the ability of private subsidized schools to select students, to charge additional fees, or to generate profit. The existing, high-stakes national accountability framework has been reshaped, for example to emphasize the importance of school-level improvement planning and leadership, although it retains national student tests and school inspections and rankings, with sharp consequences for schools judged to be making 'insufficient' progress. Montecinos, González and Ehren (2021: 201) conclude that although the reforms represent 'a distinct break' from the past two decades of market-oriented reforms, they nevertheless combine a focus on networks with 'a managerial approach and hierarchical control by the Ministry of Education' through the SLEs and accountability framework. Furthermore, the introduction of networks into an historically competitive system is seen as problematic, especially given the continuing focus on school-level accountability.

Pino-Yancovic et al.'s (2020) government-funded evaluation studied the early development of SINs (i.e. 2016–17) through a national survey and a multi-site case study of fifteen SINs in five different regions of the country (see also Pino-Yancovic and Ahumada 2020; Pino-Yancovic et al. 2019). They explain that most SINs bring together between five and fifteen schools, each represented by the principal and curriculum coordinator, together with representatives from the municipality and the Ministry, with meetings occurring monthly throughout the school year. The law requires each SIN to have a coordination committee, made up of two school leaders and at least one representative from the municipality and Ministry. The Ministry provides guidance for SIN development, defining the objectives of the networks as follows:

> To develop a collaborative working culture among schools that are members of the School Improvement Network, with the purpose of generating individual and collective learning for networked improvement, and also for the improvement of the local communities where the network is embedded.
>
> (Pino-Yancovic et al. 2019: 28)

Pino-Yancovic et al. (2020) structure their evaluation by conceptualizing SINs in relation to a three-stage collaborative enquiry cycle, involving: i) the identification of common challenges, ii) inquiring and taking action and iii) monitoring and reflection. Not surprisingly, they identified a range of development trajectories and participant perspectives across the SINs studied. All of the networks had an initial and continuing focus on disseminating government policies, but most have moved beyond this to develop a sense of shared purpose based on common challenges and to engage in more systematic forms of knowledge-sharing across schools, although few have gone further to develop shared objectives and action. On this basis, they conclude that:

> SINs are a highly valued as a significant strategy to exchange pedagogical practices and professional experiences, reducing the isolation that traditionally school leaders have faced in Chile and building professional capital. However, participants have faced many difficulties to connect their work within SINs with their school practices.
>
> (2020: 9)

More recent studies (Montecinos, González and Ehren 2021; González, Ehren and Montecinos 2020) show how the SIN networks have begun to fit within a wider governance framework which is now being developed through the replacement of multiple small municipalities by the larger and more coherent SLEs. Each SLE has statutory responsibility for structuring and organizing support for the schools under its jurisdiction, meaning that it has clear hierarchical responsibilities (for example, for addressing underperformance) while also being required to facilitate the school networks. SLEs reflect a clear commitment to network governance in how they themselves operate, for example with a requirement to establish regional and local councils that give representatives from various constituencies (municipal authorities, students, teachers, parents, school leaders, school councils and tertiary education institutions) a voice in the development and monitoring of local education strategy.

As noted, SLEs must also facilitate networks of schools: for example, Montecinos, González and Ehren (2021: 214) explain that each SLE central office must 'decide on the type of collaboration between schools in the territory, such as by grade level, geographical proximity or how schools are assessed by the Quality Agency'. González, Ehren and Montecinos (2020) studied the early efforts of one newly formed SLE team to develop these networks across its constituent schools, starting initially with geographically zoned networks for three separate groups (principals, curriculum coordinators, school-climate coordinators), with an assumption that teacher networks might follow later. Building trust and ownership among schools had proved challenging, despite efforts by the SLE facilitators, and the research team conclude that, at least at this early stage:

> SLE professionals' leadership role in mandated network formation suggests a mindset where vertical and centralised coordination, associated with hierarchical governance, predominates over horizontal and distributed leadership, associated with network governance.
>
> (2020: 15)

In summary, policy and practice in Chile now emphasize networks and network governance as key features of a system that also includes a history of competition and an ongoing hierarchical framework. Early evidence on the networks that have formed indicates some positive aspects, but also some challenges to be overcome.

Conclusion

This chapter has explored and synthesized what is known from existing research into inter-organizational networks in education and more widely. We set out eight core features of networks which, together, provide a framework for assessing the networks that we examine throughout the book. We revisit these eight features in Chapter 9, drawing out more specific implications for network leadership. This chapter also acknowledges the 'dark side' of networks, including the risk that they can accentuate existing inequalities between schools, arguing that although they do offer benefits they are by no means a panacea.

Our review of evidence on the extent of networks globally shows that published evidence is skewed towards Europe, Australasia and North and South America, but that an assessment of research in China and south-east Asia indicates that networks are also common in these contexts. The short case studies of school networks in Singapore and Chile begin to reveal the distinctive nature of policy and practice in these diverse contexts and the ways in which this influences the purpose, cohesiveness and impact of the networks that emerge.

Leadership is also a theme throughout this chapter, even if sometimes implicit: we define this leadership broadly as a process of influence and acknowledge that networking requires distinctive, hybrid and distributed forms of leadership, which many school leaders are not well-equipped for, although we argue that networking is a skillset that can be learned and developed. We develop these observations further in subsequent chapters and draw the implications together in Chapters 9 and 10.

2

Four Theoretical Lenses

Introduction

In this chapter we introduce, necessarily briefly, the four theoretical lenses through which we will engage with the case studies in the chapters that follow. The premise of the chapter – and, indeed, the book – is that an array of theories facilitates a deeper exploration of the limits and possibilities for collaboration across diverse jurisdictions. In selecting our four lens – educational effectiveness and improvement, governance theory, complexity theory and Actor-Network Theory – we aim to both lengthen and broaden our perspective. The analysis proceeds from the level of the individual teacher or school, to the wider geopolitical factors and national and global systems that schools operate within and 'act back' on, and finally, through Actor-Network Theory, adopting a different sensibility that is attentive to the processes 'of the (more-than-) social world' (Michael 2017: 3), foregrounding how networks of human and non-human actants net-work in particular ways, with or without particular effect.

For Hargreaves (2001: 487–8), any educational model should:

> derive from a theory: it must be more than a set of measured variables. A useful theory contains a relatively small set of concepts in explicit relationships, and measured variables should be capable of being contained within the concepts. When integrated into a coherent whole, the concepts become a theory from which testable hypotheses can be derived.

Yet theory can be conceptualized otherwise: 'We see theory as a set of assumptions about how the world works. This breaks with the tradition in education of understanding theory as little more than a hypothesis, implying, therefore, that theories are something to be tested' (Gulson, Clarke and Bendix Petersen 2015: 3–4). In this, the authors argue that the role of scholarship is to move beyond one's own presuppositions, values and habituated ways of making sense. This involves comparing and juxtaposing diverse traditions of sense-making. Theory affords us this opportunity, and the opportunity to 'offend and interrupt … to block the reproduction of the bleeding obvious, and thereby, hopefully, open new possibilities for thinking and doing' (MacLure 2010: 277). Thomson and Heffernan (2021: 161) show how theory can provide a framework for research, offering coherence and focus, a structure, borders, a basis for connecting to other research and ways of seeing, and allowing for a level of generalization which moves beyond the particular and enables critical interrogation of the issues at play. Theory's value thus lies, at least partly, in its ability to 'get in the way'; it should not necessarily be simple, clear and transparent (Law 1999: 8). A theory can, but does not have to, derive from empirical data; a diversity of research can inform it.

In discussing the development of theories of educational effectiveness with which this chapter opens, Kyriakides, Creemers and Panayiotou (2020: 33–4) note there are important reasons for engaging with theory. First, the development of models as an intermediate step towards theory development allows researchers to explain previous empirical research 'parsimoniously'. Second, a model frees researchers from the risk of 're-inventing the wheel'; it also 'maps a series of avenues for future research', in the process expanding the knowledge base. Third, a model can provide 'a road map for practitioners'. In this, the authors note 'hints' that the absence of theory has hindered effective professional development supporting practitioner uptake of effectiveness knowledge (Creemers and Kyriakides 2015).

As we explained in the Introduction, our decision to focus on the four particular theoretical lenses set out below is both deliberate and pragmatic: deliberate in that we think they offer distinctive but complementary perspectives on networks and network leadership, but pragmatic in that we could, equally, have chosen other frameworks, given additional space and time. In the previous chapter, we synthesized much of the existing research into inter-organizational networks in education, including the work of Muijs, West and Ainscow (2010) which applies four alternative lenses to evidence of networking in England (constructivist theory, social capital theory, new social movements and Durkheimian theory). We see our work as complementary to these existing efforts, helping to broaden the range of lenses available and thereby illustrating that there is no one 'right' way to investigate networks and their leadership. However, by applying the four perspectives set out in this chapter across four diverse national contexts, we aim to develop a more multifaceted and holistic understanding of networks in education than has been attempted thus far. The theories we have selected thus aim to offer a combination of descriptive, explanatory, emancipatory, disruptive and, potentially, predictive power (Varpio et al. 2020).

In terms of the structure of the chapter, each theory is introduced in two sections. The first provides a necessarily brief overview of the theory itself and any key debates or issues that have characterized its development. The second 'key concepts' section sets out a selection of concepts or models that are commonly used by researchers in that particular area, which we then draw on in subsequent chapters to assess the networks we describe.

Educational effectiveness and improvement

Over the past five decades, education effectiveness and improvement have become a globally dominant field, if not an ideology, of educational improvement (Bogotch, Miron and Biesta 2007). As a field, it concerns itself with 'variation, quality and equity in education across schools, networks and systems, attending not only to "what works" but also how, for whom, when and why' (Hall, Lindorff and Sammons 2020: xii). If 'effectiveness' research is essentially a school's impact on its pupils and how this is measured, 'improvement' research focuses on the learning conditions, cultures and internal practices and processes which secure change. The two traditions thus have different roots, but have 'grown together over time and been reciprocally informative' (Lindorff, Sammons and Hall 2020: 10). Together, they do not 'invent new ideas' but, rather, 'concentrate[s] on understanding the lessons to be drawn from existing practices' (Creemers 2007: 223).

For Murphy (1991: 166–8) the legacy of the first two decades of work on effectiveness was fourfold. First, a fundamental acceptance that, given appropriate conditions, all children can learn. Second, a rejection of the thesis that the quality of a school can be judged by the socio-economic status of its location. Third, eschewing the practice of victim-blaming where poor outcomes or behaviour were deemed to reflect deviant children and problematic families. Fourth, acknowledging that effective schools are 'more tightly linked – structurally, symbolically and culturally'. In this, educational effectiveness and improvement offered a response to the 1960s sociological belief that socio-economic status determined life chances.

With a paradigmatic genesis in the field of scientific management (Thomson, Gunter and Blackmore 2021), the origins of the field are commonly acknowledged as a reaction to extensive input-output work in the United States, including *Equality of Educational Opportunity* (Coleman 1966) and *Inequality* (Jencks et al. 1972). These studies were unable to identify any measurable within-school variable that consistently made a difference to equity of student achievement, leading to an argument that 'education cannot compensate for society' (Bernstein 1970: 344). Contemporaneously, the RAND Corporation (Averch et al. 1972: ix–x) moved beyond a focus on input-output to include process, organization and experimental approaches. The RAND authors noted the limitations of the research to date, four of which were identified as major: the data were a 'crude measure' of what was happening, educational outcomes were almost exclusively measured by cognitive achievement; there was little examination of cost implications of results (making policy-relevant statements difficult), and few studies maintained adequate controls over what actually happens in classrooms.

Since that time, effectiveness and improvement researchers have sought to address these critiques and to generate evidence that accounts for variations between schools: how some schools do 'better' than might be expected. The first phase in the development of the field focused on economically oriented 'education production' models that assumed increased inputs would lead to incremental outcome improvement. These 'black box' models soon revealed that the relation between input and outcomes was more complex than originally anticipated (Kyriakides, Creemersa and Panayiotou 2020: 35–6). The second phase gave increasing focus to variables at the student level. Issues of equity emerged in focusing on the extent to which schools could mediate the educational background of students. The third phase reflected attempts to integrate school effectiveness research, teacher effectiveness research and input-output studies. This stage reflected the development of models that had a 'multi-level structure, where schools are nested in contexts, classrooms are nested in schools, and students are nested in classrooms or teachers' (Kyriakides, Creemersa and Panayiotou 2020: 36). Thus the trajectory moved from looking within individual schools at specific factors such as leadership, instructional focus, learning climate, high expectations and measures of student achievement (Edmonds 1979), to exploring schools' characteristics as social institutions (Reynolds 2010; Rutter et al. 1979) and, over time, to understanding schools in context (Townsend 2007). Some argue the need to go further still – to move 'away from the black box, nine to four, five day week, subject fragmented, eggbox school' (MacBeath 2007: 71) – not least in order to assess issues of equity and social justice given that disadvantaged children are often poorly served by traditional models of schooling (Kelly 2020: 71).

In tracing developments in the school improvement field from the 1960s, Hopkins (2015) illustrates how the research agenda has both informed and been informed by wider changes in policy and practice, especially in English-speaking countries. Thus, a focus on within-school factors in the research has driven an equivalent focus in policy frameworks, for example informing the design of school inspection and evaluation frameworks in many systems. However, Hopkins also notes the limited impact seen from various comprehensive school reform programmes that have sought to apply the findings from improvement research at scale. Partly as a result, he suggests that since the millennium, policy, practice and research has reoriented towards school networks, area-based approaches and a focus on whole system reform, alongside its continuing focus on within school processes and outcomes of change.

One example of how the School Effectiveness and School Improvement research has attempted to assess the range of variables that influence school operations and outcomes is the 'dynamic model' developed by Creemers and Kyriakides (2008). The model takes the process of teaching and learning as its starting point and analyses factors at four inter-linked levels – student, classroom, school and system. It seeks to assess both the presence and quality of specific, measurable variables in each area and to recognize the non-linear relationships that exist within and across the levels. Research undertaken using the dynamic model has highlighted the extent to which school-level factors are situational, meaning that in order to remain effective, schools must continue to adapt to changes in their context, suggesting that top-down improvement initiatives are unlikely to be successful unless they can be adapted in such ways (Creemers and Kyriakides 2009). For Scheerens (2013: 7), the dynamic model's sophistication was 'good news for recognising the complexity of educational effectiveness phenomena, but bad news for parsimony'.

Contemporary School Effectiveness and School Improvement research are intimately bound up with a wider body of educational effectiveness research, with significant literatures now available in each of the main areas of schooling. These include: the nature of effective teaching and learning in classrooms (and, increasingly, beyond classrooms, for example though digital technology), interventions which accelerate progress for disadvantaged learners, including those with Special Educational Needs or Disabilities, the most effective forms of professional development and learning for teachers, the design and content of the curriculum or the ways in which leadership influences school processes, cultures and outcomes.[1] What unites these research efforts is the dominance of their applied focus on assessing the nature of more and less effective schooling practices. In recent years many researchers in these areas have prioritized scientific 'what works' style methodologies, such as randomised controlled trials (RCTs), and have adopted sophisticated systematic and meta-review techniques in order to synthesize this evidence and identify the most effective and efficient approaches (Collins and Coleman 2021; Hattie 2008). On the back of these efforts, school and system leaders have been encouraged to become more 'evidence-informed' in their decision-making and daily practices (Gorard 2020). However, this evidence movement has also been critiqued, including by some within the School Effectiveness and School Improvement movement, who highlight the limitations of using RCTs to evaluate complex whole-school change processes across diverse contexts, the distortions that can develop in an evidence base that is focused solely on tightly specified and measurable change, and the risks to teacher professionalism and autonomy if practices become overly prescribed (Zhao 2017; Biesta 2007).

Finally, we acknowledge a long-standing critique of the School Effectiveness and School Improvement field, which is that most studies in this area remain 'atheoretical... mainly concerned with the establishment of statistical relationships between variables' (Kyriakides, Creemers and Panayiotou 2020: 38). For example, Scheerens (2013) reviewed 109 studies and categorized just six as significantly informed by wider theory. Debates continue around how far such research defines and pursues 'good' education in normative and technocratic terms using understandable, but arguably insufficient, measures and analysis (Gorard 2010; Thrupp 2001a). Critics thus argue that the approach reflects an overly narrow conceptualization of schooling and school outcomes, and an under-theorized understanding of how and why educational outcomes differ across different contexts (Trujillo 2013).

Key concepts in theories of school effectiveness and improvement

As outlined above, school effectiveness research has largely focused on the internal factors that make schools more or less successful in improving outcomes for learners. By contrast, some school improvement research does recognize the role of external networks, for example in terms of knowledge exchange and professional learning for staff, although the main focus has been on within school cultures and processes (Kools and Stoll 2016). The framework we outline here reflects work over more than a decade by David Hargreaves (2001, 2010, 2011, 2012a, b). We have selected this framework because it is both underpinned by theory and positions inter-organizational networks as a core mechanism for enhancing school improvement and effectiveness; however, we note that Hargreaves's intention was to challenge the 'conventional model' of school effectiveness and improvement, which he describes as 'relatively narrow and parochial, legitimising a highly limited view of the outcomes and processes of schooling' (2001: 497).

Hargreaves's 'capital theory' of school effectiveness and improvement (2001: 488) starts by arguing that the focus should be on schools' 'capacity for improvement', a concept that has since been captured in the axiom 'the best schools are the best at getting better' (NAHT 2020). Hargreaves sets out a series of master concepts[2]: intellectual capital, social capital and leverage, along with a fourth 'conventional concept' of institutional outputs. First, intellectual capital is defined as 'the sum of the knowledge and experience of the school's stakeholders that they could deploy to achieve the school's goals', which grows through 'the creation of new knowledge and the capacity to transfer knowledge between situations and people' (Hargreaves 2001: 487). Second, social capital enriches intellectual capital and develops through trust, reciprocity and networks. The third master concept – leverage – reflects the ways in which school and teacher actions influence educational outputs, or outcomes, which, in an Aristotelian sense, must include moral as well as intellectual gains. In this initial framework, Hargreaves was clear that inter-organizational networks could enrich teachers' knowledge and work, and thereby help build intellectual capital, but only if social capital norms of trust and reciprocity were in place.

Hargreaves's later work (2010, 2012b) positioned inter-organizational networks – characterized as 'families' of schools, or 'deep' partnerships – even more centrally as a mechanism for school and system-wide improvement. This argument reflected his view that 'families' of schools could meet a wider range of learner needs, and could thereby achieve a wider set of outcomes than is possible for a school working alone. However, Hargreaves argued that 'deep' partnerships would only develop and realize these benefits if they made 'joint practice development' – that is, 'school-based, peer-to-peer activities in which development is fused with routine practice (so that) professional development becomes a continuous, pervasive process' (2012b: 8) – the norm. Achieving this, Hargreaves argued, required sophisticated partnership-building skills and qualities from school and system leaders, including a commitment to co-creating new ways of working in order to build social capital and foster a shared commitment to improvement, expressed as 'collective moral purpose'. Furthermore, high levels of trust and reciprocity could ensure that schools and teachers engaged in robust peer evaluation and challenge, thereby supporting a process of continuous improvement.[3]

Governance theory

Governance is defined by Bevir (2011: 1) as the:

> theories and issues of social coordination and the nature of all patterns of rule. More specifically, governance refers to various new theories and practices of governing and the dilemmas to which they give rise. These new theories, practices, and dilemmas place less emphasis than did their predecessors on hierarchy and the state, and more on markets and networks.

These analyses draw from a range of theoretical traditions, including rational-choice theory, organizational theory and (neo)-institutional theory, with the aim of opening up the 'black box of the state' (2011: 1). The motivation for these efforts is arguably the shift, perceptible across many countries and over several decades, from 'government to governance' (Denters and Rose 2005). This shift reflects how traditional forms of hierarchical command and control are being replaced by models that enable steering at a distance (Hudson 2007). The changes are driven by multiple factors, most notably that governments around the world, and specifically advanced Western economies, have had to respond to forces unleashed by globalization and rapid technological innovation. These forces have reduced the ability of national governments to, for example, regulate their independent economic strategies, and have contributed to increasing levels of complexity in most policy areas. As a result, governments are frequently faced with what Rittel and Webber (1973: 160) call 'wicked problems', which can neither be clearly understood nor resolved by a single actor and so, inevitably, 'propel networks to centre stage' (Kickert, Klijn and Koppenjan 1997: 137) because central government must rely on other actors to achieve its policy goals. In this context, according to Bevir (2011: 2), governance theory:

> replaces a focus on the formal institutions of states and governments with recognition of the diverse activities that often blur the boundary of state and society ... [highlighting] phenomena that are *hybrid* and *multijurisdictional* with *plural stakeholders* who come together in *networks*.

These changes led to arguments that the state was being 'hollowed out' (Rhodes 1997), but more recently it has been seen to be adapting. Kapucu (2006: 887) argues that the shift is from 'the traditional bureaucratic paradigm to a post bureaucratic paradigm', where power is exercised through a 'plethora' of collaborative structures to 'consensually' work to produce 'more flexible, fluid, diverse and responsive forms of service delivery' (Ball 2009: 537). Jessop (2011) characterizes the new role of the state in these contexts as 'meta-governance', which involves seeking overarching authority by setting and adapting the conditions in which governance occurs, including by actively mixing and managing combinations of hierarchy, markets and networks to try to achieve its goals. This perspective can afford the state significant powers, although messiness, ad hocery and governance failure remain endemic (Ball 2011).

One common manifestation of these shifts has been reflected in the rise of New Public Management (NPM) (Hood 1991) – conceived of as 'deliberate policies and actions to alter organizational structures, process and behavior to improve administrative capacity for efficient and effective public-sector performance' (Kapucu 2006: 886) – although the extent of engagement with NPM has differed between countries and settings (Ball 2009). NPM arose out of an ideological critique of traditional forms of bureaucratic governance, which was seen to be insufficiently focused on the needs of citizens and consumers, and from a belief that public sector performance could be enhanced through the adoption of private sector management disciplines (Chubb and Moe 1988). NPM in education often includes an emphasis on increased school autonomy, or school-based management, coupled with school-level accountability and a parallel reduction in the role of traditional 'middle tier' bodies, such as Local Education Authorities. Accountability here positions teachers and schools as those who should 'give account' to education authorities, and to families, primarily through student learning outcomes (Verger and Parcerisa 2020).

The impact of such changes is achieved through a blend of hard and soft governance. Instruments of hard governance – targets, rankings, grades, performance management, benchmarks and indicators – are seen to enhance transparency and hold school teachers and leaders accountable for desired outcomes, while allowing politicians to signal that they are doing their job (Pollitt and Bouckaert 2011). Soft governance, by contrast, is the process whereby, in a neo-Foucauldian manner, 'subjects ... (are) incentivized to regulate themselves voluntarily in accordance with certain directives, priorities or provisos' (Wilkins and Olmedo 2020: 7); or, put otherwise, to engage in 'self-policing' (Greany and Higham 2018; Greany 2020b).

Sahlberg's (2012) critique of the Global Education Reform Movement (GERM) is one widely cited articulation of how NPM approaches have been applied in many education systems around the world. He suggests that there are three symptoms of GERM 'infections': more competition within education systems, increased school choice and stronger accountability including more standardized testing. These symptoms have consequences. First, for schools to compete, they need autonomy; autonomy demands accountability and, at the same time, competition can undermine cooperation. Second, increased school choice introduces market mechanisms, with the assumption that this will drive 'quality' up, although this assumption is not well supported by research (Waslander, Pater and van der Weide 2010). Third, stronger accountability (and teacher effectiveness as a related symptom), as commonly measured through results on standardized tests, has increased 'teaching to the test', narrowed curricula and encouraged 'mechanistic' pedagogy. The pace and scale of these GERM 'infections' worldwide reflect the fact that education has become more important to governments as a means of enhancing 'human capital' and, thereby, national competitiveness in a globalized economy; with international benchmarking surveys, such as PISA, used to compare performance and stimulate policy borrowing between countries despite different administrative traditions as well as inconclusive evidence on the benefits of such policies (Verger and Parcerisa 2020).

Critically, from a governance perspective, policymakers have sought ways to directly influence the technical core of schooling in order to try to increase levels of quality, equity and innovation. The implication of all this for schools and school leaders can be a semblance of autonomy and self-governance, although in practice these changes are commonly experienced as a loss of support coupled with increased pressure to perform against measured targets, for example where student test data are used nationally to hold schools publicly accountable (Ozga 2011). Furthermore, the mixing and overlaying of different governance structures can create tensions that are felt particularly by frontline leaders in local contexts; for example, if they feel a need to prioritize the needs of their school over the needs of particular groups of pupils (Greany and Higham 2018). Thus, for some, democratic forms of education governance, and the contribution this can make to just and equal societies, is 'severely threatened' (Saltman 2020: xviii). For Saltman, there is a contradiction in contemporary educational policy between a constant demand for empirical data and its use and the pursuit of policies that are unsupported by empirical data.

Key concepts in governance theory

The most common framework for considering governance processes centres on the ways in which hierarchy, markets and networks operate separately and in hybrid ways to steer the work of schools (Bevir 2011; Tenbensel 2005). These coordinating mechanisms are positioned as 'ideal types' – or heuristics – that can be harnessed by governmental and non-governmental actors in their attempts to steer policy problems and public service delivery. Most governance arrangements are seen to involve hybrid combinations of these mechanisms, which are adapted to context and change over time. Each coordinating mechanism has its own strengths and limitations. For example, Adler (2001) argues that, in idealized form: hierarchy enables control by using formal authority as a means of co-ordination, but can weaken collaboration and lateral innovation; markets rely on price to co-ordinate supply and demand and promote flexibility, but can corrode trust and undermine relations that support knowledge sharing and equity, while networks co-ordinate on the basis of trust and promote shared knowledge generation, but can become dysfunctional by allowing complacency or exclusivity on the basis of familiarity. Tenbensel (2017: 3) argues against a 'fixed quantum' approach (i.e. assuming that as one mode of governance increases its scope, another must inevitably decrease). Rather, he suggests that the different modes can 'coexist in complementary ways' and that empirical research 'highlights the presence of "positive-sum" rather than "zero-sum" relationships between governance modes' (2017).

Greany and Higham (2018) adopt the following definitions, which we draw on in Chapter 6:

- *Hierarchy* – the formal authority exercised by the state, including through statutory policies and guidance, national, regional and local bureaucracies, and performance management and intervention
- *Markets* – incentives and (de)regulation aimed at encouraging choice, competition, contestability and commercialization
- *Networks* – the (re)creation of interdependencies that support and/or coerce inter-organizational collaboration, partnership and participation

Unpicking the formation and operation of networks and network governance within wider governance processes can be far from straightforward. Network governance frequently involves the state as a participant, working with diverse stakeholders, including schools, in deliberative decision-making and, often, co-designed and collaborative forms of service delivery and oversight. Equally, network governance can refer to the wider ways in which diverse independent groups and individuals come together to co-ordinate action and/or influence policy, for example in new social movements, such as the environmental movement. Networks involving schools and other agencies – that is, the kinds of inter-organizational networks and meta-networks that are the focus of this book – can be positioned in either of these models. In practice, however, it can be hard to differentiate between these types of network governance.

Partly in response to these challenges, Tenbensel (2005) proposes a fourth co-ordinating mechanism – *community* – which is founded on shared identities, for example based on geography, culture, ethnicity, gender, sexual orientation or a common recreational interest. He argues that distinguishing between 'network' and 'community' mechanisms helps differentiate between providers of public services – such as schools – and the communities that engage with them. While both providers and communities can be engaged in 'network governance' (as, indeed, can government), providers are often better placed than communities to participate and benefit, due to both their organizational capacity and the ways in which their shared professional norms, values and trust can be drawn upon to facilitate collaboration. As a result, 'network governance' can be seen positively as a model for professional control or provider autonomy, or less positively in terms of 'provider capture' (Tenbensel 2005: 283). By contrast, 'community governance' is generally associated with populist movements and grass-roots community activism, although it is feasible to argue that organic self-organizing networks of schools which are primarily motivated by shared beliefs and values could also reflect such 'community' governance (Greany 2020a; Frankowski et al. 2018; Nederhand, Bekkers and Voorberg 2016).

Complexity theories

Education is an excellent example of a policy space that has become a far more complex endeavour in the interconnected world we outlined in Chapter 1. The context of the individualized risk society (Beck 1992), a runaway world (Giddens 2002), global complexity (Urry 2003) and the human consequences of a world of winners and losers (Standing 2011) have changed the impulse for, and experience of education, in profound ways. Students remain in formal education for longer yet cannot be confident of the 'return on investment' in the context of spiralling credentialization (Bauman 2012). For teachers, the curricula offering is wider, students and classrooms are more diverse, more stakeholders are involved, and the potential for using new technologies is ever greater (Kamp 2013b). As a consequence, education in the twenty-first century 'must be construed in terms of participation in the creation of possible futures' (Davis and Sumara 2008: 43). This moves us to foundational questions that reach beyond concerns of school effectiveness and governance. For Nowotny

(2005: 15) the current context shows the worth of complexity theories: 'we seek to increase complexity in order to make objects or artifacts perform to the highest degree of complexity. We want to make them do things that less complex systems are unable to do' (Nowotny 2005: 18–9). The ability to do things that less complex systems are unable to do is one driver for policy initiatives that seek to sustain organic networks, or to implement structured networks, in education.

Over recent decades there has been increasing exploration of how education functions as a complex system (Jacobson, Levin and Kapur 2019; Jacobson and Wilensky 2006), and the implications of this for policy actors at different levels (Mason 2008). The complexity of schools is, 'in a colloquial sense … self-evident to those who have direct experience of them' (Hawkins and James 2018: 743). Lemke and Sabelli (2008) suggest that education is one of the most complex and challenging systems for research, while Morrison (2008: 22) argues that schools are:

> dynamical and unpredictable, non-linear organizations operating in unpredictable and changing external environments. Indeed schools both shape and adapt to macro- and micro-societal change, organizing themselves, responding to, and shaping their communities and society.

It is perhaps unsurprising that data to inform ambiguity models in organizational theory have, in large part, been drawn from education settings (Bush 2011). For Hawkins and James (2018: 729) it is 'somewhat ironic' that there is inadequate acknowledgement of complexity 'as a foundational aspect' of schools given the forty years that have passed since Weick (1976) introduced the notion of schools as loosely coupled systems. Working with the 'sensitizing' concepts of Glassman (1973), Weick explored how events in schools are 'coupled' and 'responsive' while also retaining an individuality and separateness. Using the example of a counsellor and a principal, he suggested they were:

> somehow attached, but … each retains some identity and separateness and that their attachment may be circumscribed, infrequent, weak in its mutual affects, unimportant, and/or slow to respond … . Loose coupling also carries connotations of impermanence, dissolvability, and tacitness all of which are potentially crucial properties of the 'glue' that holds organizations together.
> (Weick 1976: 3)

While General Systems Theory had first originated in the physical sciences, its proponents argued such principles were applicable to the social sciences (von Bertalanffy 1972). However, these theories, close cousins to complexity theories, had fallen in and out of favour in social policy over the twentieth century. The critique ranged from

> deficiencies of an "engineering" approach involving models too far removed from reality, to the frustration experienced by many with the early literature that too often had ambitions for a general systems theory that, in trying to explain everything, explained nothing. Systems theory and models have been criticized for their remoteness from empirical data, for an over emphasis on control theory to the exclusion of human agency, for encouraging a centralized grand-planning approach to the challenges of public service provision and for too much reliance on argument by analogy.
>
> (Rhodes et al. 2011: 201)

More recent and 'mature' approaches have renewed interest in these approaches. Complexity theories explore subsystems and how they dynamically interrelate in influential ways. Complex systems approaches shift attention from 'complicated' to 'complex'. A complicated entity can be described and understood in terms of its interconnected component elements. In contrast, a complex entity cannot be understood thus. In a complex entity, component elements which may be simple in themselves are not just connected but, rather, interact and in the process are changed over time (Cilliers 2005).

In this engagement with dialectical processes, complexity theories share similarities with prominent theories of social change in education. Giddens' (1984) structuration theory argued for the symbiotic integration of agency and structure, this duality of structure being integral to an individual's lifeworld. For Bourdieu (1990), the concept of habitus – an embodied 'social understanding' (Taylor 1999: 35) – is a *structuring* structure, while also being a *structured* structure. Structured structures are framed in rules, institutions, roles and behaviours that lean towards the reproduction of the self and the system, while being offset to some extent by agency (Morrison 2005). In his survey of structuration theory, habitus and complexity theory, Morrison (2005: 311) argued that complexity theory offered the 'more complete theory of change'. What differentiates complexity theory is that it is a theory of '*necessary* and *inexorable* change and development for survival' (2005: 320, original emphasis), in a way that structuration and habitus are not. Complexity theory is always of social production, never of social reproduction. The implication of this is that analysis must move away from individual entities – whatever they may be – and towards examining an ecosystem that is focused on, and arising from, a centre of interest: a 'strange attractor' (Morrison 2005: 324).

From a theoretical perspective subsystems, as the component elements of systems, have interrelationships and interdependence that encourage internal equilibrium. The behaviour of each subsystem has an effect on the behaviour of the system but no subsystem has an independent effect on the system (Skyttner 1996). Hawkins and James (2018: 739–45) suggest five subsystems of a whole-school system. First, the teaching staff system, made up of those who have 'formally designated responsibility' to provide curriculum and teach students. Second, the ancillary staff system, made up of those who 'ensure teaching can take place'. Third, the student system, made up of all of those 'for whom the curriculum is provided'. Fourth, the parent system and, fifth, 'significant other systems in the wider system' including inspection and accreditation agencies, policymaking entities and so on. Cross-boundary interactions, particularly between the teaching staff system and the student system, are 'at the heart of the school as an institution'.

Complexity theories focus attention on learning. Senge (1990) positioned systemic thinking as the foundation on which the realization of the concept of the learning organization must be founded. For Byrne (1998: 51) what is 'crucially important about [complexity] is that it is systemic without being conservative ... the dynamics of complex systems are inherently dynamic and transformational'. Through processes of 'feedback, recursion, perturbance, autocatalysis, connectedness and self-organization, higher levels of complexity and new, differentiated forms of life, behaviour and systems arise from lower levels of complexity and existing forms' (Morrison 2008: 20). In this, complex system theories have countered the limitations perceived of 'reductionist discourses of control' (Osberg and Biesta 2010); within a 'structure-determined complex system, external authorities cannot impose, but merely condition or occasion possibilities. The system itself "decides" what is and is not acceptable' (Davis and Sumara 2008: 41). Social scientists often draw on these concepts and ideas 'even where these are not explicitly articulated' (Urry 2005: 235). Complexity perspectives have been imported from the physical sciences, processed, exported, 'sometimes even back from whence they came' (Thrift 2005: 53).

The 'economy of concepts' that underpin complexity theories has allowed the development of general principles for management and leadership that acknowledge the role of structure in institutions while also allowing space for the emergence that happens in lived experience, wherever it occurs. This gets to the heart of the issue of how 'interactions in networks lead to systems that are sufficiently organised to function' (Theisens 2016: 61). Theisen's question of 'how order is created' risks missing the point of this body of theories. For policymakers, complexity theories are of value precisely because they open spaces for thinking about some notion of order *without* stipulating 'how'. We need to move beyond the mechanistic metaphor to completely rethink network governance (Kamp 2013a), eschewing order-creating frameworks that immediately compromise first-order business in the pursuit of second-order rule following (Schwartz and Sharpe 2010). In earlier work, we have drawn on Massumi's (1992) engagement with the concepts of *A Thousand Plateaus* (Deleuze and Guattari 1987) to gain insight into strategies for emergence in the context of hierarchy. Massumi offers five strategies: first, interfere with habitual governance operations; second, seek out what are labelled as poorly functioning spaces for imagination; third, know how to 'pass' in hierarchical spaces by doing 'enough' while maintaining focus on emergent aspirations; fourth, avoid head-on confrontation with hierarchy yet do the work of undermining instruments of hierarchy that are oppositional to the network agenda; and, finally, 'come out' as soon as the network is high-performing and able to survive in the process of system reform (see Kamp 2013b for a detailed review).

Key concepts in complexity theories

Given the evolving nature of the complexity field, it 'refuses tidy description and unambiguous definitions' (Davis and Sumara 2008: 33). However, a number of key concepts and principles can be articulated. In a review of the literature, Amagoh (2016) states complex systems are characterized, first, by non-linearity and feedback, which in turn generate feedback mechanisms. Positive feedback typically generates growth in the system; negative feedback diminishes growth. Second, by dissipative structures: complex systems do not respond to external impulses in a linear manner. If a system is forced away from its usual way of working because of 'flux' in its environment, there can be a process of decline or renewal, or components of both decline and renewal. Third, by self-organization and adaptation: self-organization references the patterns and regularity that result from interaction of system elements following their own rules (Rhodes et al. 2011). Fourth, by connectivity and interdependence: the concept of 'coevolution' is indicative of the mutual influence between elements in the system. Finally, by emergence: new properties emerge from the collective behaviour of system components. Emergence – which in its various forms is commonly regarded as the central construct of a complex system (Jacobson, Levin and Kapur 2019; Hager and Beckett 2019) – is the partner of self-organization and the 'antithesis of external control' (Morrison 2008: 21). Organizations are continually enacting their environments in seeking a 'sustaining' closure that enables them to both maintain their own identity whilst responding to their diverse environments (community, policy, cultural, historical, national and so on). Problems with 'the environment' can be considered as problems about the identity that is being maintained by a given school, or network of schools, at a given point in time. Thus attempts at change must, of necessity, give due attention to the patterns shaping the whole 'organization-environment system'; for schools to understand and thrive in their environment they must understand themselves, their internal images of reality, the nature of their boundaries and the constraints within their environment (Maturana and Varela 1980). For Davis and Sumara (2008: 36) this flags the concept of 'nesting': complex systems are nested within (arising from and giving rise to) other systems. They interpenetrate each other with some relationships cutting across different levels (Cilliers, P. 2001 cited in Hawkins and James 2018: 734).

In recent years, there has been a rapid growth in understanding of the necessary conditions to facilitate emergence. Davis and Sumara (2006), working specifically with complexity, suggest an initial list of four conditions: internal diversity, internal redundancy, neighbour interactions and decentralized control. The first of these, internal diversity, refers to the diversity represented among units/parts/agents which is seen as a source of possible responses to emergent circumstances. In a prescient commentary, Davis and Sumara (2008: 38-9) offer the following example:

> For instance, if a pandemic were to strike humanity, currently unexpressed DNA sequences might bestow immunity upon a few people, and hence ensure the survival of the species – an intelligent response to unforeseeable circumstances. A differently intelligent response to the same circumstances (and a 'more' intelligent response, from the perspective of most members of the species) might arise among the interactions of a network of researchers with expertise in such diverse domains as virology, immunology, sociology, entomology, and meteorology.

They note a 'critical point': the inability to specify in advance the necessary variation for 'appropriately intelligent action'. In this, the case for maintaining diversity within the system is made.

Internal redundancy as the second condition refers to duplications and excesses that are necessary for 'complex coactivity' (Davis and Sumara 2008: 39); examples include common language, similar social status of members, shared responsibilities, constancy of setting. Davis and Sumara note that redundancies 'tend to fade into the backdrop of social action and are only pulled into focus when there is some sort of rupture' yet suggest their 'deep sameness' is vital to maintaining coherence when the system is exposed to stress. There are two roles for internal redundancy: enabling interactions among actors, and compensating for system weaknesses. Redundancy engender overlaps and, thereby, learning (Morgan 2006) yet is often viewed less than favourably in the efficiency drive of NPM. This focus on 'deep sameness' does not diminish the condition of diversity: 'vibrancy … arises in the mix of … redundant and … diverse elements – or, in systemic terms, the sources of its stability and its creativity' (Davis and Sumara 2008: 40).

The third condition, neighbour interactions, engages with the necessity of collective learning. While system actors obviously 'affect' one another's activities, what is less obvious is 'what might constitute a neighbor in the context of a knowledge-producing community' (Davis and Sumara 2008: 40). Here, the authors suggest that these neighbours 'are not physical bodies or social groupings', as important as they may be in their own right. Rather, these neighbours 'that must interact with one another are ideas, hunches, queries, and other manners of representation' (Davis and Sumara 2008). There is an eloquence in Davis and Sumara's argument here, where they note the prominence of 'the conversation' as a metaphor while suggesting more suitable descriptors for this 'ideational interaction' could be 'notions of bumping, colliding, and juxtaposition of ideas' (Davis and Sumara 2008). The 'critical point' becomes that 'mechanisms must be in place to ensure that ideas will stumble across one another, *not* that there must be a particular sort of organizational structure in a social collective' (Davis and Sumara 2008: 40). The question of how to facilitate this stumbling is contingent on contextual dynamics. The authors suggest, however, that this interpretive process demands that leaders 'must relinquish any desire to control the structure and outcomes of the collective' (Davis and Sumara 2008: 41).

Unsurprisingly then, decentralized/dispersed control is the fourth of Davis and Sumara's conditions to facilitate emergence. As in the principles of educational effectiveness and improvement, the focus moves away from the leader and their actions. Here, the term used is 'consensual domains of authority. Within a structure-determined complex system, external authorities cannot impose, but merely condition or occasion possibilities' (Davis and Sumara 2008: 41–2). The acceptability of any given action is decided by the system itself. Thus, 'a person should never strive to position herself or himself … as the final authority on matters of appropriate or correct action' (Davis and Sumara 2008). Here, the point is made that student participation should be facilitated by the structures that enable emergence. Emergent properties and behaviours are unpredictable and a certain critical level of diversity and complexity must be reached to enable 'a sustainable autocatalytic state' (Mason 2008: 37); these theories offer principles that enable researchers to simultaneously examine a phenomenon in its own right while being attentive to the conditions of its emergence (Davis and Sumara 2008: 34).

Actor-Network Theory

Actor-Network Theory (ANT) is a theory about how to study things (Latour 2007: 142). Fenwick and Edwards (2010: 1) suggest ANT is 'a way to intervene, not a theory of what to think'. For them, ANT's 'key contribution is to suggest analytical methods that honour the mess, disorder and ambivalences that order phenomena, including education'. While ANT does not – and does not wish to (Law and Hassard 1999) – comprise a coherent, identifiable, theoretical framework, it offers a distinct sensibility that is of value to education in general, and education policy in particular.

Gorur (2015: 87) suggests that 'researchers of [education] policy who are interested in policy processes, doings and enactments, and who seek to explore the messiness and uncertainty that attends the lives and careers of policies, would be drawn to actor-network theory'. For its 'conceptualisers' (Gorur 2015) – philosopher Bruno Latour, economist Michel Callon, and sociologist John Law – social sciences had moved beyond the capacity of ideas such as 'the social' to offer explanatory adequacy. This different conceptualization of 'the social' as something that is continuously assembled is an important point of departure. Another important point of departure is a broader engagement with the range of actors involved in assembling 'the social'. This is ANT's principle of 'symmetry' between actors. ANT is concerned with ensuring all actors – 'objects, subjects, human beings, machines, animals, "nature", ideas, organizations, inequalities, scale and sizes, and geographical arrangements' (Law 2009) – are considered equally in any exploration of how things come to stabilize in a particular configuration, with particular consequence.

This engagement with a broader range of actors and the granting of symmetry to them is the key contribution that ANT makes to our study of educational networks. They deepen the insights gained through our other lenses. For example, while complexity theories engage with issues of emergence coactivity which may seem similar to ANT, in this they privilege *human* actors: experts, civil servants, principals, politicians, teachers, students, policymakers, parents, managers and so on. Other actors are already stabilized contextual factors such as 'the system', or objects to be used by humans, rather than fully fledged actors in their own right. The symmetrical approach of ANT enables a reading of how a full range of actors assemble in ways that then compel other actors to 'enrol', thereby extending network.

Over recent decades, there has been increasing engagement with ANT in education to explore the formation of associations that produce particular kinds of agency. For Fenwick and Edwards (2010: 3) this approach 'leads us to question common categories and distinctions, such as teacher and learner, curriculum and pedagogy, formal and informal learning'. Thus, Cormack and Comber (1996) traced how policy documents constructed authorized versions of subject, teacher and student. Nespor (2002) explored the effects of standardized tests in assembling materials and people, including the testers themselves. Waltz (2006) illustrated how educators are surrounded by material things that are the source of action; things also pervade preservice teacher training and the daily operation of schools. Pedagogy, too, 'centres around, and is constantly mediated by, material things' (Fenwick and Edwards 2010: 5). Supplementary support services can be seen to be 'a chain of translation, most often forged around accountability and assessment' rather than learning, with policy actors being complicit in this in 'establishing and maintaining a crisis narrative that links failing schools (as measured by standardized assessments) with diminished global economic power' (Koyama 2011: 33). Kamp (2017) used an ANTian sensibility to explore the assemblage of leadership in collaborative endeavours. ANT has been taken up to explore how the PISA not only assesses but also 'translates' the education systems of low-income countries (Addey and Gorur 2020); it has been used to consider the modernist constitution of contemporary discourses of educational governance and leadership (Landri 2021). ANT has demonstrated the process by which neoliberal governance is actioned through translation: the agency of distant global policy actors who not only respond to but 'play an active role in bringing such states of affairs into existence' (Piattoeva 2020: 105).

Key concepts in Actor-Network Theory

Educational change is, from an ANTian perspective, analysed through processes of translation. Translation here refers to 'what happens when entities, human and nonhuman' come together and connect, changing one another to form links (Fenwick and Edwards 2010: 9). The concept of 'translation' was initially proposed by Michel Serres (Brown 2002) to describe the formation of truth claims in science. As a concept, translation aims to uncover the micro-negotiations of actors, illuminating how A 'enrols' B, successfully or otherwise (Callon and Latour 1981). The outcome of this process of translation is unpredictable: actants[4] must 'negotiate' using an array of actions.

Early in ANT's emergence, Callon (1986) suggested four 'moments' of translation. While a 'convenient heuristic' (Gorur 2015: 91) they are not some form of 'method'. For Callon, translations were practiced in four non-linear moments which he referred to as problematization, interessement, enrolment and mobilization. Problematization refers to the moment in which a problem is articulated in such a way that the articulator becomes indispensable to other actors. In this moment, obligatory passage points can be established: a 'single locus' that can exert influence on all transactions between actors. Interessement refers to a moment in which the association between actors is strengthened and actors are precluded from engaging in other actor-networks. The moment of enrolment is when roles and relationships are assigned, thus further stabilizing the network. The fourth moment, mobilization, occurs when issues of representation are resolved and one set of actors can become spokesperson for the collective. Mobilization renders formerly immobile entities, mobile. Translation also signals the distinction between intermediaries and mediators. For Latour (2007: 38–40) an entity that is an intermediary 'transports meaning or force without transformation': whatever is its input will also be its output. Intermediaries are, unsurprisingly, rare. By contrast, there are 'endless' mediators that 'transform, translate, distort, and modify the meaning of the elements they are supposed to carry'. A mediator is always complex, no matter how simple it may look. The distinction between intermediaries and mediators is important in understanding how the social is assembled and, by association, how it might yet be reassembled.

The concept of mediation is necessarily further refined to its four guises. First, mediation can relate to interference whereby each agent interferes with, or translates, the original goal of the other. Second, mediation can relate to 'composition' and the way in which the composite goal becomes the common achievement of each of the agents. The third meaning of mediation references the process of black boxing: the more something succeeds – becomes stabilized – the less it can be understood as attention need focus only on inputs and outputs rather than the complexity that inheres between input and output. Thus, 'like a black box it appears immutable and inevitable, while concealing all the negotiations that brought it into existence' (Fenwick and Edwards 2010: 11). The fourth, and most important meaning, of mediation is delegation: the way both meaning and expression are delegated to non-human objects. Delegation illuminates how a 'prime mover' can be absent, yet present: it acknowledges that a long ago action of an actor can remain active in our day-to-day lives. A form of labour is required to maintain an assemblage. In the context of education, this speaks to sustainability in policy implementation: 'continuous effort is required to hold it together, to bolster the breakages and counter the subterfuges' (Fenwick and Edwards 2010: 11).

While ANT eschews a 'method', its sensitivities and concepts demand an empirical approach, often using case study (Law 2009):

> We need to proceed empirically. … If we are to do philosophy, metaphysics, politics, or explore the character of knowledge, we cannot do this in the abstract. We cannot work 'in general', because there is no 'in general'. All there is are: specific sites and their practices, and then the specificities of those practices. So philosophy becomes empirical.
>
> (Law 2020 cited in Gorur 2015: 93)

Field observation using an ethnographic ethos is the most central data generation technique for the ANT researcher. Back in 1972, Averch et al. argued that effectiveness and improvement researchers found themselves 'in a "flat" area. Movements in various directions from our current position do not seem to affect our altitude. Furthermore, we do not know whether this flat spot is at the bottom of a well, on a broad plain, or atop a tall plateau' (Averch et al. 1972: xi). It is this kind of impasse that lends itself to a productive ANTian reading. In his 'textbook' of ANT, Latour (2007: 21–2) proceeds by way of five sources of uncertainty which we briefly revise here.

Latour's first source – no group, only group formation – speaks to the beginnings of research. While it would seem self-evident for researchers to select a group for study, ANT prefers the process of mapping the 'controversies about group formation' the formation process leaves 'many more traces in their wake than already established connections' (Latour 2007: 31). The second source is that 'action is overtaken'; it engages with the tenet that 'we are never alone in carrying out a course of action' (Latour 2007: 44). In this, however, it is 'crucial *not* to conflate all the agencies overtaking the action into some kind of agency' such as society, or culture or structure and so on (Latour 2007: 45). The third source is that 'objects too have agency'. Here the reference is the symmetry between human and non-human actors that we have surveyed previously. Critical here is that symmetry is not to imply that non-humans fully determine action. Rather, 'there might exist many metaphysical shades between full causality and sheer inexistence' (Latour 2007: 72). Fourth, is the uncertainty 'matters of fact vs matters of concern'. ANT suggests the controversies of science studies offer social scientists a perspective that matters of 'fact' do not describe a 'unified reality'. This source of uncertainty is the 'birthplace' and 'trickiest' point of a sociology of association (Latour 2007: 87). The aim here is to trouble premature notions of indisputability of the 'facts of the matter':

> Until laboratories, machineries, and markets were carefully scrutinized, Objectivity, Efficacy and Profitability – the three Graces of modernism – were simply taken for granted.... Irrationality should be accounted for; rationality was never in need of any additional justification; the straight path of reason did not require any social explanation.
>
> (Latour 2007: 97)

For our purposes, this demands that when networks are implemented, we explore them as 'matters of concern, with their mode of fabrication and their stabilizing mechanisms clearly visible' (Latour 2007: 120). Finally, the fifth uncertainty of 'writing risky accounts' engages directly with our labour in this book. In ANT, good work must be written well, with the criteria being that the social must appear through it. This 'renews' the notion of objectivity. Objectivity in an ANTian account involves narratives of the 'warm, interested, controversial building sites of matters of concern' (Latour 2007: 125).

ANT has the potential to complement theoretical approaches that have remained silent on the machinations that occur between, above and below 'input and output'; it offers potential to offer 're-descriptions' of assemblages of educational administration, management and leadership (Landri 2021: 13). By recognizing that all entities, including educational networks, are performed in, by and through relations, we can then ask 'how it is that things get performed (and perform themselves) into relations that are relatively stable and stay in place' (Law 1999: 4). Further, we can more readily appreciate how things could be performed differently: the immense reserve that is open for change (Latour 1999: 19).

Conclusion

This chapter has set out the four theoretical frameworks and associated concepts and tools that we see as most helpful for our assessment of networks and collaboration in education. Within the lens of educational effectiveness and improvement, we highlight the importance of different forms of capital alongside an appreciation of the integrated ways in which the core technologies of teaching, assessment and curriculum combine to make a difference for learning and wider outcomes, and how inter-school networks can facilitate professional learning and capacity building as part of these processes. In the section on governance theory, we highlight the ways in which hierarchy, markets, networks and community operate in hybrid ways to co-ordinate the work of schools, potentially creating incentives for networking alongside challenges and ethical dilemmas for frontline leaders. Our third lens – complexity theories – foregrounds the idea of schools as open systems that respond to, and interact with, their environment, changing that environment in the process. Complexity theories also highlight how educational institutions, and the people within them, might also be analysed as closed systems that exhibit autonomy, circularity and self-reference, unable to enter into interactions that do not align with their internal images of reality. Our fourth lens of Actor-Network Theory allows the closest focus of all, demonstrating the micro-practices by which leaders and other actors – both local and distant, human and non-human – seek to 'translate' the possibilities for action, including through inter-organizational networks.

Clearly, this chapter is limited to an introductory overview for each theory, but we develop and apply these overviews to the case studies in ways which further develop the conceptual framework. Our approach is unashamedly nimble – these theories, and our orientation to this collection, do not lend themselves to rigid rules of analysis. Rather, we present our four cases and then 'read' them through each of the four lenses in turn, in Chapters 5–8. These chapters provide the basis for the final two chapters, in which we consider the implications of these insights for leadership and its further development.

3

Networks in England

England

England is the largest of the four United Kingdom (UK) nations, with a population of nearly 56 million.[1] The UK is classed as a 'high income' country by the World Bank and has the sixth largest economy in the world by Gross Domestic Product (GDP). England is a key driver of the UK economy, particularly as a result of London's significance as a centre for financial services. Around 80 per cent of UK GDP is now generated through services, although it also has strengths in engineering, pharmaceuticals and other sectors, including the creative industries. However, economic development is widely uneven and the UK is the fifth most unequal country in the OECD.[2] This inequality is also geographic, with median household wealth in London and the South East of England more than twice that in the North West (Raikes et al. 2019). Economic inequality intersects with other forms of inequality, for example in terms of health and life expectancy as well as educational outcomes. Finally, England is culturally diverse, particularly in its urban centres, reflecting a long and continuing history of immigration from different parts of the world. This diversity is reflected in its school population, with 32 per cent of primary aged children and 29 per cent of secondary aged children classed as non-White British in 2017.[3]

Education is compulsory for all children in England from age five to eighteen, although from sixteen to eighteen young people can choose whether to attend school, college or workplace training provision. Most children attend publicly funded (state) schools, although around 7 per cent attend private, fee-paying schools. There are around 22,000 state schools, generally organized into two phases: primary schools (covering ages five to eleven, years R–6, Key Stages 1 and 2) and secondary schools (covering either ages eleven to sixteen or eleven to eighteen, years seven to eleven or seven to thirteen, Key Stages 3–4 or 3–5).

Most children with Special Educational Needs or Disabilities (SEND) attend mainstream primary and secondary schools, but around 1000 special schools serve children with more complex needs.

All primary schools and most secondary schools are comprehensive (with no entrance exam), although a minority of local areas allow grammar schools to select the most able children based on an 'eleven plus' exam. Around a third of state-funded schools are faith schools, usually attached to either the Church of England or the Roman Catholic Church. Most children attend their local primary school, but at secondary level parental choice becomes more significant, particularly in urban areas. Parents can apply to several schools, which do not have to be within their local authority area, with places offered based on the school's published admission criteria in the case of oversubscription. Schools must abide by the national admissions code, although certain types of schools have additional flexibilities within this, for example to select a proportion of children based on specified criteria, such as aptitude, ability or religious faith.[4]

England has a National Curriculum which sets out 'the essential knowledge (pupils) require to be educated citizens' (DfE 2014: 2).[5] The most recent version, introduced in 2014, emphasizes traditional subject disciplines and knowledge – 'the best that has been thought and said' (DfE 2014: 2) – and thus rejects the move apparent in many school systems towards developing 'twenty-first century' skills and competencies (Creese, Gonzalez and Isaacs 2016). The national assessment framework has arguably had more influence on schools than the National Curriculum in recent years, because of the ways in which assessment outcomes are used to hold schools accountable. National tests (known as SATs) in English and Mathematics are taken at the end of primary school, while most children take General Certificate of Secondary Education (GCSE) exams at sixteen.

State-funded schools are held accountable through a combination of mechanisms, which include their performance in national tests and exams and periodic inspection visits undertaken by the Office for Standards in Education, Children's Services and Skills (Ofsted). Ofsted inspections review the school against published criteria encompassing areas such as school leadership capacity, curriculum quality, student behaviour and safety, and student progress and attainment. Following the inspection, Ofsted publishes a report which includes a single grade for the school (Outstanding, Good, Requires Improvement or Inadequate). These reports and grades send important messages to prospective parents and staff, thus influencing school choices, and exerting strong pressure on school leaders.

The education policy context

The focus of educational reforms in England in recent decades has been on raising pupil standards, improving school and teaching quality and enhancing equity. Networking between schools has been encouraged in a range of ways, but schools are also incentivized to compete, creating an 'unusual cocktail of collaboration and competition' (Armstrong and Ainscow 2018: 4).

The 1988 Education Reform Act (ERA) shaped England's current school system, laying the ground for the National Curriculum, national tests, Ofsted inspections and parental choice of school. The Act also introduced Local Management of Schools (LMS – aka School Based Management or school autonomy), giving school governing bodies and head teachers control over budgets, staffing and other operational areas. By 2009 school leaders in England were ranked among the most autonomous in the world in terms of their decision-making powers (OCED 2011). LMS increased the pressure on and importance of school leadership (Gronn 2003): leading to larger leadership teams and more distributed leadership models in most schools over time (Earley 2013). Increased school autonomy involved a parallel reduction in the influence of England's 152 local (education) authorities (LAs), although they have retained a role in overseeing and funding locally maintained schools. Another important aspect of the ERA reforms aimed to increase choice for parents and to strengthen competitive pressures between schools by introducing new schools as well as various new types and categories of school (Courtney 2015). These New Public Management-inspired initiatives were founded on a view that competition between schools (i.e. for students and resources) would enhance quality and make schools more responsive to the needs of parents as consumers (Hood 1991).

The New Labour governments in power from 1997 to 2010 built on the ERA framework, developing what came to be known as a 'high-autonomy-high-accountability' system (Greany and Waterhouse 2016). New Labour invested heavily in education, creating a range of national strategies and programmes that aimed to 'drive up' standards, particularly in key areas such as literacy and numeracy (Barber 2008). Meanwhile, there was a parallel focus on enhancing equity, for example by seeking to integrate schools with wider services for children (Raffo, Dyson and Kerr 2014).

Many New Labour initiatives included a more or less overt focus on encouraging schools to collaborate, both with each other and with wider partners. These initiatives reflected a significant shift from the previous Conservative period, with networks now positioned as important responses to the ICT revolution, globalization and the need to address complex 'joined-up' societal challenges (Jupp 2000; Rhodes 1996). A full list of New Labour's initiatives encouraging collaboration would be very long, but the following examples give a flavour of their scope:

- Education Action Zones – area-based collaborations addressing disadvantage (Ofsted 2003);
- Beacon Schools – high-performing schools sharing practice with partners to raise pupil standards (Rudd et al. 2004);
- Creative Partnerships – schools in challenging circumstances working with arts organizations and creative practitioners to enrich the curriculum (Sharp et al. 2006);
- Fourteen to Nineteen Partnerships – schools and colleges working with local employers in area-based collaboratives to develop academic and vocational curriculum pathways and qualifications (Ofsted 2008);
- Independent State School Partnerships – funding for independent/private and maintained schools to collaborate (Lucas et al. 2017).

One particularly significant initiative was the Networked Learning Communities programme. This ran from 2002 and 2006 and involved around 1,500 schools in 137 voluntary (but funded) networks, all geared towards improving pupil, teacher and organizational learning (Jackson and Temperley 2006). Perhaps the most significant and successful New Labour initiative involving networks was the London Challenge (Ainscow 2015; Baars et al. 2014), which had multiple strands but included a focus on brokering successful schools to support under-performing schools: an initiative that later developed into the National Leaders of Education (NLEs) programme outlined below. New Labour also established a legal framework for inter-school partnerships in 2002, enabling maintained schools to federate together, with a single governing body (and, often, executive head teacher) overseeing two or more schools (Chapman, Muijs and MacAllister 2011). Labour also legislated for and introduced the first academies and academy chains (Hill 2010): in practice, the number of these was small in New Labour's time, but these initiatives laid the ground for the subsequent development of academies and Multi-Academy Trusts by later Conservative governments.

The 'self-improving, school-led system' agenda

The election of Conservative-led governments since 2010 has seen wide-ranging changes in the policy framework for schools. Many of these changes have built on the existing ERA framework, but with a notable change of emphasis compared with New Labour's approach. For example, the National Curriculum was revised to be more 'knowledge-based', with parallel changes in the design and content of national tests and exams. These changes have combined with sharp reductions in the education budget and in cuts to wider services for disadvantaged children, placing considerable pressures on schools (Lupton and Thomson 2015).

A core thrust of the changes introduced since 2010 has been to develop what the government has termed a 'self-improving, school-led system' (DfE 2010), in which partnership and collaborative working between schools would be an essential requirement (House of Commons 2013). The government argued that these reforms would 'dismantle the apparatus of central control and bureaucratic compliance' (DfE 2010: 66) by 'moving control to the frontline' (DfE 2016: 8). In practice, as Greany and Higham (2018) show, the government's approach has been to combine top-down hierarchical pressure and coercion with a mixture of incentives aimed at encouraging lateral school networks that support centrally defined priorities.

The most significant development in this area has been the expansion of academy schools, enabled by the passage of the Academies Act in 2010. A decade later, more than a third of all primary schools (35 per cent) and more than three quarters of all secondary schools (77 per cent) had become academies. Academies are non-profit companies that are wholly funded and overseen by national – rather than local – government, so their expansion has led to a significant reduction in the capacity and role of England's LAs and an increase in the role of the central Department for Education (Greany 2020a). Academies have additional 'freedoms' compared to LA maintained schools, for example they are not required to follow the National Curriculum. The government has encouraged higher performing schools to convert voluntarily to academy status, while schools judged Inadequate by Ofsted can be forced to become a sponsored academy. An academy can operate as a single stand-alone school, but most are part of a Multi-Academy Trust (MAT) (Greany and McGinity 2021).[6] There are now more than 1,200 MATs in England, operating anywhere between two and fifty plus academies within a single organizational structure overseen by a board and Chief Executive.[7]

The second main strand of policy in this area has been the use of 'system leadership' and school-to-school support (Cousin 2019). This has involved high-performing schools and school leaders being designated by the government as Teaching Schools and/or National Leaders of Education (NLEs), with around 750 Teaching Schools and over 1,000 NLEs designed by early 2020.[8] These 'system leader' schools received limited funding and had a remit to support other schools to improve. Teaching Schools also had a remit to develop an alliance of partner schools (the TSA) and to address wider government priorities, such as training new teachers and providing professional development for teachers and school leaders. These 'system leadership' initiatives thus sought to encourage lateral networks and forms of knowledge transfer between schools, partially replacing the support previously provided by LA improvement teams. However, Teaching Schools were always expected to generate their own income, by selling services to other schools (DfE 2010), so the new framework aimed to create a market in improvement services as well as a networked approach, with schools able to select and pay for the services and networks they wanted to access.

How have school networks developed?

Evidence on school partnerships and collaboration over the decades since the passage of the ERA is partial and inconsistent, especially before the turn of the millennium. Several studies from the 1990s identified sharp competition and significant status hierarchies between schools, particularly at secondary level, as the new parental choice reforms became embedded (Glatter, Woods and Bagley 1997; Gewirtz, Ball and Bowe 1995). That said, some schools did develop partnerships at that time, for example as a means of sharing the increased administration burden resulting from LMS (Busher and Hodgkinson 1996; O'Neill 1996).

Following the millennium, as New Labour's various funding incentives and policy initiatives in support of collaboration were established, networks became increasingly common, spanning the full range of partnership areas and types indicated above. However, New Labour did not dismantle the ERA framework, meaning that individual school accountability and parental choice pressures remained strong, so school leaders had to maintain a focus on meeting their own institution's priorities even as they also worked in partnership. Thus, competitive pressures did not stop, leading to an argument that schools were engaged in 'co-opetition' (Muijs and Rumyantseva 2014). Collaboration required new skills as well as values-based commitment from school leaders, leading to calls for the development of 'system leadership' skills and qualities (Fullan 2005).

The partnerships that formed in New Labour's time were not solely driven by policy. For example, Muijs (2015b) shows that many small schools in rural areas entered into voluntary partnerships to bolster their financial sustainability, build capacity and provide mutual support. Nevertheless, there is evidence that some partnerships formed in response to the specific funding pots available, but then largely dissolved once the funding stopped – indeed, according to Glatter (2003), a popular definition of partnership at the time was 'the suppression of mutual loathing in the pursuit of public funding'! Furthermore, the multiplicity of programmes and funding streams under New Labour led to accusations of 'initiativitis' and a 'congested state' (Skelcher 2000), with evidence that some schools felt overwhelmed by the sheer range of opportunities on offer. Despite these concerns, New Labour's investment in partnerships and networks served to shift the culture away from the competitive ethos of the 1990s, making collaboration a core – if still contested – feature of the system. For example, a survey in early 2010 indicated that around three quarters of head teachers were engaged in some form of school-to-school partnership working (Hill 2011).

The Conservative governments' 'self-improving, school-led system' agenda has moved school-to-school collaboration and networks centre stage. Greany and Higham's (2018) mixed methods study analysed the evolution of the network landscape. School leaders reported that formal and informal partnering had become more important for schools since 2010: as one primary head teacher put it, it is 'more and more something we *need* to do' (2018: 78). This perspective reflected a mix of factors, but particularly the loss of support from LAs coupled with the need to respond to significant national policy changes and new accountability requirements. In the national survey, conducted as part of the study, just 2 per cent of head teachers stated that their school did not collaborate with any other school in a meaningful way. Primary schools collaborated with an average of nine or ten other schools, while for secondary schools it was slightly more (ten to thirteen). Collaboration was most common with schools in the same phase and was often long-standing (i.e. five years or more). Most schools had a smaller number of long-term and more intensive ties and a larger number of newer and less intensive ties.

In terms of the nature and focus of collaborative activity between schools, Greany and Higham show that this ranged from the local cluster that does little more than organize an annual inter-school sports day, through to partnerships (such as the Learning Links vignette – Chapter 1) which involved staff at multiple levels and which impacted on virtually every aspect of member schools. Common activities included head teacher meetings, curriculum or subject leader networks, assessment and moderation groups, peer reviews, research projects and joint practice development or shared CPD for staff and providing joint extracurricular provision. Local primary school clusters had usually originated in previous LA-led initiatives, but the ones that had survived and developed had often been overlain with other initiatives and aims over time. These local clusters rarely had formal governance structures, with shared decision-making usually sited informally within a head teachers' group. By contrast, secondary schools tended to collaborate in different ways, often over wider geographic areas, reflecting the fact that they were more likely than primaries to be in competition with neighbouring secondary schools.

The research found that informal networks remained important to schools during this period, but that many were working to formalize their partnership arrangements, for example by developing an existing cluster into a TSA and/or MAT. This decision was generally driven by a desire to access government funding, to increase sustainability and/or to enhance legitimacy and prestige. Inevitably, existing partnerships were changed as a result of adopting the new models. For example, becoming a TSA required one high-performing school to be officially designated, to administer any additional funding and to take responsibility for co-ordinating the work and for reporting the outcomes to the DfE, meaning that this 'system leader' school took on a new position within the partnership as 'first among equals' (Matthews and Berwick 2013).[9]

In summary, schools in England are engaged in a range of partnerships, most often with other schools but also with other partners, including private schools, further and higher education institutions and national and local charities and businesses (Lucas et al. 2017; Greany et al. 2014). These partnerships range in their breadth and depth, but a combination of factors – mostly policy-driven – have served to raise the importance of networks, starting around the time of the millennium but accelerating from 2010 onwards. Today the network landscape in England is complex and highly variable, resulting from historic patterns of competition and collaboration in each locality as well as more recent developments and forms of individual agency.

One emerging issue, which we explore via the case study that follows, is not only how individual schools engage in networks, but whether and how these diverse networks and structures operate together, in meta-networks. The case study focuses on a single LA area, Bampton, which encompasses multiple, overlapping networks as well as a variety of hierarchical structures, including

MATs and the LA. By 2019, key leaders in the area had come to see this level of fragmentation as problematic, because it was preventing co-ordinated action on area-wide challenges and was hindering the flow of knowledge and expertise between schools across the town. These leaders sought to develop a new, place-based meta-network to facilitate collaborative action for and by the town's schools and academies. However, the process of securing consensus and meaningful change was challenging and although a new strategic alliance had been created by the end of the research period, it remained fragile, and local leaders were unsure if it would survive and overcome parallel systemic forces which continued to drive fragmentation.

Case Study: Bampton – shaping a new meta-network in one Local Authority

Bampton[10] is a small Local Authority (LA) with a population of around 250,000. The post-industrial town sits on the edge of a larger conurbation and has high levels of deprivation, with just over a quarter of its 60,000 children and young people living in poverty. Around 45 per cent of school-age children are from a Black, Asian or Minority Ethnic background, mainly from large Pakistani and Bangladeshi populations. The town has just over 100 state-funded primary, secondary and special schools, of which around a third are academies and the remainder (mostly primaries) are LA-maintained. In terms of pupil academic outcomes, schools in the LA perform below national averages at all stages, although the main concerns are at secondary level. However, this picture is mixed, with a small minority of popular schools attracting less deprived intakes and performing much more highly. Twelve MATs operate in the town, including three national chains and nine smaller local and regional trusts. Six of the town's higher-performing schools were also designated as Teaching Schools, while a slightly larger group were designated as NLEs.

Bampton is a government-designated Opportunity Area (OA): these deprived and low-performing areas received additional funding from the national Department for Education (DfE), tied to an improvement plan. The OA funding was time-limited, extending over five years to 2021, and supported work to enhance educational outcomes and address wider issues, such as mental health.

The data for this case study were collected as part of a project commissioned by the OA, which was facilitated by Toby Greany and a colleague (Jane Creasy) in 2019–20. The project brought together a 'strategy group', composed of thirty local leaders, which shaped and supported early implementation of a new vision and approach to school improvement across Bampton. The group's main proposal was to establish a new, school-led membership organization – the Bampton Alliance. Despite considerable challenges caused by the COVID-19 pandemic and associated school closures from March 2020 onwards, the Alliance was launched and began work in autumn 2020.

The case study is structured in three sections: the first sets the context, describing developments in recent years and the main issues for school improvement and collaboration in Bampton, the second briefly describes the main school networks that exist across the LA, while the third outlines the work of the strategy group and the establishment of the new Alliance. The data drawn on includes: interviews with Strategy Group members and wider stakeholders undertaken at the start of the project and in late 2020 after the Alliance had been launched, reports from four strategy group 'away days', and related documentary evidence.

Fragmentation and reformation in the period after 2010

In the years after 2010, the LA was seen to have largely disintegrated in the face of academization, budget cuts and rapid staff turnover. The LA's SEND (Special Educational Needs or Disabilities) provision faced significant budget deficits and was heavily criticized by Ofsted at that time, further distracting LA leaders from a focus on school improvement. The view of head teachers was that, during that period, 'there was no school improvement, you just did your own thing'. There was a lack of trust between schools and the LA, leading to 'a blame culture, heads were fearful of having the finger pointed at them'. This was the period when a third of schools in the LA joined a MAT: some were forced to join a national or regional chain, due to poor performance, while higher-performing schools were likely to form or join one of the local trusts.

Most interviewees agreed, however, that by early 2019 the LA was 'back in the game'. This was largely thanks to the appointment of a new Director of Education two years earlier, who was seen to have improved relationships. The new Director had arrived with a remit to implement the proposals from an earlier review (conducted in 2014–15), which centred on the creation of a 'Bampton Education Partnership'. The Partnership had strong local political support and the LA had invested £1m to get it established. The original vision for the Partnership was broad and ambitious, aiming to encompass all aspects of the education system and to develop a distinctive local curriculum. In practice, it had focused its work more narrowly on monitoring the performance of the LA's remaining maintained schools. A year or so after the Partnership was launched, the government announced that Bampton would become an OA. The OA brought significant additional funding as well as impetus for school improvement and this, combined with the strengthened LA leadership, was seen to have 'lubricated partnerships', demonstrated new ways of working, and begun to improve student exam outcomes and school performance.

However, various structural and cultural issues remained, making sustainable progress challenging. One issue related to school and system governance, which remained complex and fragmented. An LA has no direct authority over the academies in its area, meaning that these schools are not automatically required to adhere to local agreements, for example in relation to school admissions or student exclusions. Furthermore, an academy in a MAT is answerable to its trust CEO and board, which might not be based in the local area. At locality level, the OA had its own separate Board with an independent Chair appointed by the DfE, meaning that the governance of the local system was also fragmented – split between the LA, the Bampton Education Partnership and the OA. Perhaps not surprisingly, school leaders described a lack of trust and factionalism ('us and them') – not only between schools and the LA, but also between different groupings of schools, academies and MATs. MAT leaders were often the most critical of this situation. Although some MAT CEOs had remained engaged with the local system and recognized the improvements made by the LA and OA in recent years, others had not. This latter group were focused on working with their own academies and were sceptical about participating in local discussions or activities, fearing they would waste time and energy. Head teachers talked about how confusing the system was, with no clear lines of accountability, making it 'hard to see how it all fits together'. Although the additional funding from the OA was welcomed, some schools found the range of provision confusing, with 'lots of things being thrown at us'. One outcome was that even when positive things did happen, it was 'difficult to push the work ... out, because the strategic frameworks are weak if they exist at all'.

These issues combined with the high levels of poverty, low levels of academic performance and a view that many local families lacked aspiration, to support a 'narrative of barriers and failures'. Several interviewees seemed to implicitly accept that Bampton could never achieve the kinds of educational performance seen elsewhere and that nothing would really change that. Recognizing this, the LA's Director of Education argued that 'the technical aspects are not the most important – we need to understand the behaviour changes required, and the cultural elements'.

Finally, of course, schools, academies and MATs in Bampton faced competitive pressures, making collaboration and partnership working more difficult. For example, one MAT CEO explained that the trust had been working productively with another MAT in the town, but the second trust had expanded the size of one of its primary schools, impacting negatively on pupil intakes for one of the first trust's schools. As he explained, that 'makes relationships quite difficult, doesn't it?'

School-to-school networks in Bampton

Two factors were seen to have shaped the network landscape in Bampton. Firstly, as one primary head teacher put it, the LA 'has benefited from being quite small, because you can get across it, you know one another well'. Secondly, as the same head noted: 'people are very committed to Bampton', with many of the heads and MAT leaders having worked there for their entire career. This small size and strong civic commitment could, potentially, have enabled the development of dense, high-trust networks. However, in practice, as outlined in the last section, Bampton was characterised by factionalism and an insular culture – 'it's very, very, very parochial in the way it operates' (MAT CEO). The vast majority of schools were engaged in networks, but the depth and breadth of these differed widely and some schools were isolated.

We start by focusing on the six geographic clusters, which included both primary and secondary schools on a voluntary basis. One primary head teacher explained their development as follows:

> They emerged when the LA declined, in 2011–12. The focus in those early years was on (curriculum) enrichment and collaborative support. But then, in 2016, when the LA's capacity declined further, the Heads pushed for a stronger role and the clusters developed further at that time.

The head teachers who chaired these clusters acknowledged that because the approach had emerged bottom-up, there was no template for how they operated. As a result, they were highly diverse: one was 'really about communications between the LA and schools', another was 'just about wellbeing, the heads meet and offload', while a third was more action and outcomes focused. Competition and status hierarchies between schools could prevent meaningful engagement: for example, one former chair explained that 'we were the first to share data, but there were lots of schools that wouldn't share – it's all around competition and league tables'. As a result, chairing the collaboratives could feel challenging – 'you feel like you are the owner of something, but without the power, it's all buy in' – and engagement from schools and academies was variable. One head explained that her collaborative 'got disbanded' when some of the member schools joined a MAT – 'they felt that they were repeating the work, meeting with us, but they were also meeting again on similar sort of things as a trust, and therefore the (collaborative) meetings fell apart'. For these reasons, several interviewees argued that the collaboratives were not fit for purpose and needed reform, but achieving consensus on this proved difficult, not least because some heads valued their collaborative for reasons which did not fit a narrow improvement agenda – 'I would hate not to have the collaborative … . It's valuable to us, for information and intelligence, but the LA don't see a lot of that' (Primary Head).

Meanwhile, a minority of schools had formed stronger local partnerships. For example, the Swan Partnership involved eight primaries and one secondary in one district. Interestingly, these schools were all members of the same cluster, but the cluster also included five other schools that were not part of the Swan network. The Swan Partnership was formally constituted, as a co-operative trust, with a board of trustees and a chair (the head teacher of one member school). The partnership had taken eighteen months to establish and had run for two years at the time of the interviews. According to one head teacher 'the key thing is we employ a facilitator – she keeps us on the straight and narrow'. Network activity was structured through four working groups (school improvement, well-being, transition and curriculum and financial efficiencies). This had enabled significant professional development opportunities for staff, including through subject networks. However, the biggest impact was seen by the heads to have come from undertaking peer reviews between schools, supported by a trained Ofsted inspector. This had 'been really helpful with preparation for Ofsted … the best thing has been getting to see each other's schools'.

In addition to the clusters, Bampton had two area-wide networks – Primary Heads and Secondary Heads, each chaired by a head teacher – which provided the main forum for dialogue on policy, including between head teachers and the LA. Perspectives on these groups varied widely, but there was consensus that neither group had succeeded in developing a shared agenda or ethos across the town and that attendance at meetings had been sporadic.

Finally, as noted above, Bampton had six Teaching Schools and a larger group of NLEs, despite being a relatively small LA area. The result was 'messy', with 'too much competition between TSAs', but the new Director had worked hard to bring these system leaders together to agree areas of specialism and to target their work more effectively onto schools with the greatest needs, based on an analysis of data. The OA funding had helped with this, because it had encouraged groups of TSAs to work together to develop and deliver new strategic programmes and initiatives.

Developing a new place-based 'school-led' network

The strategy group's remit was to develop proposals for a new educational improvement approach which could steer coherent local action across Bampton. The OA Director argued that 'the status quo wasn't tenable' and that the group's 'solution needed to recognize the completely fragmented position in Bampton'. In his view, this fragmentation was setting a 'glass ceiling' on improvement and that, unless it was addressed, any impacts secured through the OA funding would not be sustained in the longer term. In commissioning the project, he was particularly keen to learn the lessons from the previous attempt to create a Bampton-wide approach (i.e. the Bampton Education Partnership), explaining that:

> Rather than rush into something where there's only surface commitment from people, that isn't based on the shared understanding of what the problem is … we need to do a proper piece of work that really unpicks the problems, that people commit to the solutions that need to take place.

In order to support this aim, the strategy group's membership was designed to draw together all the main school constituencies, including faith, primary, secondary and special schools as well as academies/MATs and LA maintained schools. Membership also included key stakeholder groups, such as Bampton's Teaching Schools, NLEs and the LA and OA teams. Achieving commitment and consensus across this diverse group was challenging for several reasons. Firstly, as noted above, relationships were often poor, with multiple factions. Secondly, while the existing Bampton Education Partnership had some vocal supporters within the group, it was seen as 'hazy' and 'unclear' by most maintained school heads and as largely irrelevant by most MAT leaders, so there was a debate around whether to reform the existing approach or to start anew. Thirdly, a key issue was where and how to engage the MATs in any meaningful local arrangements, since these leaders were wary of committing to (and paying for) anything that might duplicate or overlap with their existing internal improvement processes. At the same time, most recognized that many of the challenges they faced (for example with teacher recruitment) were systemic, requiring joined-up action across the locality. The final challenge was how to fund any collaborative work, in particular once the additional OA funding stopped.

Notwithstanding these challenges, the group also had some important advantages. Firstly, the work was commissioned jointly by the OA and LA with support from the DfE's Regional Schools Commissioner (RSC),[11] so it was seen to have legitimacy among the main constituencies. Secondly, it built on the LA and OA's work over the past two years, which had helped rebuild relationships and generate a sense of momentum. Finally, the imminent ending of the OA funding created a degree of urgency around the need for a new approach.

The group participated in four away days, which provided key opportunities to acknowledge and explore issues and to co-design the new approach. Various working groups, consultation activities and visits to existing locality partnerships took place between these sessions. Inputs from respected national figures and leaders involved in developing equivalent locality partnerships elsewhere helped to build understanding of different possibilities and to reassure participants that change was possible. A set of ground rules were agreed at the first meeting and revisited each time, centred on core commitments such as 'We are here for the children' and 'Trust, honesty and constructive challenge are essential'. Nevertheless, building trust and honesty within the group was challenging and discussions sometimes moved backwards as well as forwards. Despite these issues, attendance at the meetings remained high and interviewees argued that relationships and levels of trust became stronger as the work progressed.

During the first away day, the group agreed two statements – one setting out the 'case for change' and the other 'what we are trying to achieve?' These statements were consulted on with all schools across Bampton and became the touchstone for assessing the proposals. The 'case for change' acknowledged 'stubborn inequalities in opportunities and outcomes' for children and young people in Bampton and that the current school improvement model 'is not yet fully addressing these issues successfully or sustainably'. The vision statement included a commitment to a 'cohesive, self-aware and empowering professional culture characterized by proactive collaboration, rigorous peer challenge and accountability, and, where necessary, credible peer support that leads to focussed action and measurable impact' and to 'a learning system that helps us achieve our collective aims'.

By March 2020 the group had developed and agreed a set of priorities and proposals for a new approach. These proposals sought to balance the tensions inherent in the system: for example, between a desire for a unified vision and approach versus a more flexible model which recognized the diversity of structures and accountabilities in operation across different MATs and maintained schools. The core proposal was to establish a new Bampton Alliance, which replaced the previous Bampton Education Partnership and was launched in September 2020, with an independent chair and a Foundation Board. The Alliance was launched in the midst of the COVID-19 pandemic, a time when school leaders were overwhelmed with multiple pressures (Greany et al. 2021), so the fact that the work continued to develop in that period indicates the degree of commitment that had been generated. The OA and LA funded the first year of the Alliance's work jointly, but the aim was to develop the Alliance as a separate membership organization over time, with schools and academies paying a per pupil fee to sustain the work.

The final interviews were conducted in late 2020, as the newly formed Alliance was commencing its work. Interviewees were positive about the impact of the strategy group's work, arguing that it had helped to improve relationships, including with MATs that had previously disassociated themselves from town-wide developments. This was already leading to more joined-up action across the town, in particular in response to the significant challenges presented by the COVID-19 lockdown. For example, one MAT CEO explained:

> I think that the (strategy) group has had a really positive impact in getting us to where we are now and being in the position we are with the Secondary Heads group. For example, we are now having regular 'research breakfasts', looking at evidence. We're talking about those as being the best thing that that group has ever done, and we've got a framework for CPD now that we are all signing up to that will be available across Bampton.

Interviewees were also optimistic about the potential of the new Alliance to develop a more coherent and strategic approach to improvement across the town, although they acknowledged that it was too early to really assess progress. They all agreed that it would be essential to recruit a credible school leader as CEO.[12]

Conclusion

England's school system has experienced multiple – sometimes frenetic – reforms over several decades. The broad trajectory of these changes has been to shift from a system characterized by strong, independent and relatively cohesive local authorities (in place until the 1980s), to a system of autonomous and highly accountable schools overseen by national and local government in – sometimes uneasy – combination (until 2010), to the current fragmented landscape that combines strong national steering with weak local authorities and a rapidly mutating landscape of MATs, stand-alone schools, networks and alliances. The early stages of the second of these periods – that is, late 1980s to early 2000s – saw sharp competition between schools, and the pressures to compete for students, resources and prestige have by no means disappeared. However, since the early 2000s, there have been significant top-down incentives, pressures and, sometimes, direct requirements for lateral collaboration between schools. Today, the vast majority of schools do collaborate, often in multiple networks simultaneously, most often with a focus on school improvement but frequently providing varied combinations of wider benefits, including legitimacy, solidarity, emotional support, the sharing of resources and so on. The strength and depth of these networks vary widely, reflecting historic and socio-cultural factors as well as the agency of individual leaders. Many of these networks receive funding and other forms of recognition or support from central or local government, but many – perhaps most – are 'school-led'.

The swirling mix of structural and network changes underway since 2010 has created fragmented and often balkanized local landscapes, as is evident in Bampton. Creating and maintaining a degree of local coherence or shared endeavour in such landscapes is challenging. We finish with insights from two leaders from Bampton, which illustrate these issues.

The first is from the OA leader who commissioned the strategy group work. He observed how England's fragmented system can lead to stasis if nobody steps forward to initiate change:

> I think the lesson was that leadership was really important. In the fragmented system where people have ... lots of diverse responsibilities ... at some point someone has got to step forward and say 'right, I'm going to do something'. And what was fascinating to me, is that people are not lining up to do that ... people in the system either can't or don't want to. And that's really interesting, isn't it? If the whole basis of the school improvement policy is based upon, you know, locally led 'system leadership', it does actually involve at some point a person, a man or a woman, saying 'right, well I'm going to lead it'. If no one makes that decision then you've got nothing to work with.

The second is from the CEO of an established locality partnership, who had been commissioned to help set up the Alliance in Bampton. He reflected on the skillsets required for leading a locality partnership, arguing that 'being the glue in the system does require quite a lot of nuance'. He identified two keys to success. Firstly, it is essential to sustain meaningful engagement with all schools, but this can be challenging if the partnership is given formal responsibility (by the LA) to challenge maintained schools that are seen as underperforming. In these cases there is a temptation to draw on bureaucratic and hierarchical levers, such as writing official warnings or forcing the head teacher to leave, but in this CEO's view such approaches can actually make things worse, because school leaders lose trust and stop engaging. Secondly, leaders in a 'school-led' partnership need a flexible, affordable but high-quality improvement offer: otherwise, schools will not buy in, particularly the MATs that have an understandable concern that the partnership's offer might duplicate their own internal systems and processes.

In the next chapter we outline the equivalent landscape in New Zealand, before analysing all four cases through the four lenses in Chapters 5–8.

4

Networks in Aotearoa New Zealand

Aotearoa New Zealand

Aotearoa New Zealand (Aotearoa or New Zealand) is a bicultural, culturally diverse, South Pacific nation with, in 2020, a population of some 5 million people living for the most part on two main islands – the North Island and the South Island.[1] It is a former British colony with, over recent decades, increasing weight being given to a founding document signed by some 500 Māori chiefs and representatives of the British Crown – te Tiriti o Waitangi [the Treaty of Waitangi]. Te Tiriti provides a foundation for partnership and equality for indigenous Māori and those who came to New Zealand shores. In social policy arenas such as education, commitments under te Tiriti have become central to the way that policy is conceptualized and implemented; te Tiriti also offers a resource for collaborative endeavours given the priority afforded to the collective within Māori society (Rameka 2018).

Queen Elizabeth II is Head of State of this unitary parliamentary representative democracy. The defining characteristics of Aotearoa ranked highest by New Zealanders in 2016 were 'freedom, rights and peace' and 'environment' (mean rating 9.1), followed by 'the people in New Zealand' (mean rating 8.5) (StatsNZ 2016). A World Bank 'high income' country, with an open economy based on free market principles; it has sizeable manufacturing and service sectors which complement an agricultural sector recognized for its efficiency. Aotearoa is often perceived as a land of economic and political stability: in 2020, the global anti-corruption organization Transparency International maintained New Zealand's first equal status with Denmark (https://www.transparency.org). Over the past two years, New Zealand has gained increasing international profile for the leadership of Prime Minister Jacinda Ardern subsequent to the 2019 mass shootings at two Christchurch mosques, and during the COVID-19 global pandemic. However, Aotearoa presents some weak well-being statistics.

On comparative child well-being measures published by OECD in 2009, New Zealand ranked twenty-first on material well-being, fourteenth on housing and environment, thirteenth on educational well-being, twenty-ninth on health and safety and twenty-fourth on risk behaviours. A quarter of children and young people lived in homes with low incomes (Tomorrow's Schools Independent Taskforce 2018). The 2021 'snapshot' of New Zealand's well-being indicators (stats.govt.nz/topics/well-being) suggests that while most New Zealanders are satisfied with their lives and believe their family is 'doing well', a notable percentage are not. Thus, for example, 19 per cent rated life satisfaction as lower than seven out of ten; 11 per cent of fifteen- to twenty-four-year-olds reported high levels of psychological distress in the preceding four-week period; 17 per cent rated family well-being as lower than seven out of ten; one-third of households did not have enough income and 17 per cent of people reported experiencing discrimination in the past twelve months.

Formal education in Aotearoa is currently compulsory from six to sixteen years of age, with most children starting school after their fifth birthday. In 2020, there were 2,536 schools, including twenty-five teen parent units hosted by secondary schools, and thirty-seven specialist schools which teach students from Years 1–13 who have high levels of need. The majority of schools in Aotearoa are English-medium state schools although some 15 per cent of students attend private (5 per cent) or state-integrated (10 per cent) schools. State-integrated schools are schools with special character that are, however, funded by the government and follow *The New Zealand Curriculum*. Schools are at primary (Years 0–8 for 'full' primary schools or Years 0–6 for 'contributing' primary schools), intermediate (Years 7–8), and secondary level (Years 9–13) (sometimes in combination as 'composite schools'). New Zealand is unique in maintaining intermediate schools for students at Years 7 and 8. Te Aho o Te Kura Pounamu [the Correspondence School] is based in the capital city, Wellington. Māori medium education is provided in kura kaupapa Māori, state schools which deliver *Te Marautanga o Aotearoa*, the curriculum for Māori-medium teaching, learning and assessment. Schools that offer Māori-medium programmes can also use *Te Marautanga o Aotearoa* for such programmes, alongside their use of the *The New Zealand Curriculum*[2] (Ministry of Education 2015b). The curriculum is not prescriptive, offering room for adaptation to local needs; its 'principal function is to set the direction for student learning and to provide guidance for schools as they design and review their curriculum' (Ministry of Education 2015b: 6).

The senior school qualification is the National Certificate of Educational Achievement (NCEA), which provides three qualification levels through a structure of both 'achievement' and 'unit' standards, developed consequent to the introduction of New Zealand's reformist National Qualifications Framework in the 1990s (see Kamp 2019a for a detailed review). State schools and state-integrated schools are funded annually on the basis of their roll, with additional funding – targeted funding for educational achievement, special education and careers information – based on their decile ranking. School deciles rank schools from decile one to decile ten, based on socio-economic indicators. Some 10 per cent of schools are classified as either decile one or decile ten. Deciles were intended to target funding for state and state-integrated schools to mediate barriers to learning faced by students from lower socio-economic communities: the lower the school's decile, the higher the funding. Decile funding will be replaced with Equity Funding from 2022; this is argued to more accurately identify student need and provide more funding for those schools serving disadvantaged students. In accepting state funding, school boards must: i) set priorities and manage the school's total funding, ii) follow the National Administration Guidelines,[3] iii) meet their obligations as good employers and iv) comply with legislative and contractual requirements.

Schools reflect the increasing cultural diversity in New Zealand society, particularly in the North Island with Auckland being described as a 'superdiverse' city where many schools have students from more than twenty cultures (Tomorrow's Schools Independent Taskforce 2018: 24). This evolution of the cultural landscape is expected to continue.

State education is free, although some schools seek a donation to top up government funding.[4] Just over a third of schools, mainly in cities, have enrolment schemes giving priority to local students; from 1 January 2021 enrolment schemes are designed by the Ministry rather than school boards of

Table 4.1 Ethnic identity of school-aged children as per cent of total school-aged population (Tomorrow's Schools Independent Taskforce 2018: 24). Reproduced with permission

	1996	2001	2006	2013	2017	2030
European or Other ethnicity (including New Zealander)	77%	74%	72%	71%	71%	68%
Maori	23%	23%	23%	24%	25%	27%
Asian	7%	8%	10%	12%	13%	20%
Pacific people	9%	10%	11%	13%	13%	15%
Middle Eastern/Latin American/African	1%	1%	1%	1%	2%	3%

trustees. The Education & Training Act now requires any enrolment scheme to 'make the best use of existing networks of State schools' (Parliament of New Zealand 2020). However, over 500 New Zealand schools do not have local networks, being classified as 'isolated' by the Ministry of Education.

The education policy context

In his discussion of the scale of New Zealand's schooling reform in the latter decades of the twentieth century, Howard Fancy (2007: 325) cites Fiske and Ladd's book *When Schools Compete – A Cautionary Tale*: 'Rarely has any country engaged in such a sustained and far-reaching overhaul of its education system'. State provision of free, secular and compulsory education in Aotearoa began with the *Education Act 1877*. Under the Act, all children aged seven to thirteen had to attend school while being entitled to attend school from age five to fifteen. Through the first half of the twentieth century, state provision would grow in scale and expand into various forms of secondary provision. From the 1940s to the 1980s these developments were largely controlled by a national Department of Education with regional offices, and ten Education Boards (Thrupp et al. 2021). The 'far-reaching overhaul' that occurred from the mid-1980s had its genesis in global economic conditions and local drivers including significant fiscal deficits, rising unemployment and an impetus for political change. From 1984 to the early 1990s a radical reform of mechanisms of government – the New Zealand Experiment – was undertaken by New Zealand's fourth Labour government, and continued by successive National governments (Kelsey 1995).[5] The reforms were suggested to be 'closest in the world to the application of "economic rationalism"' (Easton 1994: 78). A combination of 'orthodox economics' and New Right orientations towards small government resulted in an 'unusually thorough-going' reform process (Easton 1994). The restructuring of the public sector was largely generic and informed by analyses undertaken by the Treasury.

> Fundamental to this analysis was the premise that human behaviour is primarily self-interested. Government institutions and the relations between them therefore had to be designed to appeal to self-interest, offering decision-making freedom, but also to guard against it, through the separation of roles and the casting of relations as contracts with specified measures of performance.
> (Wylie 2012b: 77)

Within this broader context, wide-ranging reviews of education were implemented, including the Picot taskforce on educational administration which resulted in the report *Administering for Excellence*[6] (Department of Education 1988). The adoption of the Picot taskforce recommendations initiated the *Tomorrow's Schools* (Lange 1988) reforms which set the stage for education in Aotearoa for the past thirty years.

Under *Tomorrow's Schools* schools became fully self-managing, run by parent-elected Boards of Trustees. Aotearoa was unique in this regard: 'the only country that ... built its national school system on schools operating on their own' (Wylie 2012b: 4) thereby bypassing what was described as 'inefficient bureaucracy at the intermediate level' (Lubienski 2014: 428). Boards would appoint principals, would be the legal employers of teachers and would be responsible for the overall management and performance of a school, allocating the funding they received in ways that would best meet the needs of their school. The services they may wish to acquire to meet those needs would also become self-managing: purchased by schools rather than being centrally provided. The broader context made it unsurprising that schools under this regime would be run like businesses (Thrupp et al. 2021). All departmental administration at the regional level was removed and the ten Education Boards abolished, leaving schools isolated and disconnected from any consolidated framework of informed support and capacity-building (Wylie 2012b). The model was one of 'local autonomy within central guidelines', wording that was 'carefully chosen', shifting the balance – and much responsibility – to the local, whilst not dispensing with central control (Fancy 2007: 327).

While 'self-management' of schools was initially positioned as a mechanism for partnership between parents and schools through parental elected boards of trustees having input to the governance of schools (Lange 1988), an array of at times conflicting self-management discourses evolved (Gordon, Boyask and Pearce 1994: 18).

- 'self-management as being wholly responsible for decisions over staffing and industrial relations ...;
- self-management as the basis of competition between schools;
- self-management as compliance with national legislative requirements;
- self-management as parents taking responsibility for (as opposed to developing partnerships to promote) their children's education;
- self-management as making schools into good businesses.'

Gordon suggests the new discourse emphasized business and competitive elements of governance over cultural and democratic aspects, as well as leading to a substantial increase in administrative work for principals (Gordon 2015). Other major levers of influence in schools – curriculum and qualifications reform – were implemented 'on the heels' of *Tomorrow's Schools* (Fancy 2007). This collective pace of reform was demanding but was facilitated by the prevailing 'latitude' in the system prior to *Tomorrow's Schools*: although the system had been highly centralized, government largely worked through guidelines rather than prescription. In this, principals and teachers were accustomed to developing and implementing policy at the local level (Wylie 2012a, 2012b).

Tomorrow's Schools generated atomization and increasing inequality in Aotearoa's education system, although marketization and habit tended to standardize modes of accountability (Boyask 2020). The intent of Tomorrow's Schools was for improved schooling outcomes and, over the intervening period, NCEA achievement has lifted: by 2018 85 per cent of eighteen-year olds had achieved NCEA Level 2 or equivalent. However, commentators suggest this was achieved through the shift to a standards-based examination system (Gordon 2015), as well as the introduction of government targets. Progress to address persistent inequality in engagement and achievement by Māori was not evident (Clark 2017; Gordon 2015). Over the years, the relative position of the New Zealand system in OECD/PISA rankings has declined and New Zealand's own cross-cycle performance in PISA has declined (Tomorrow's Schools Independent Taskforce 2018). In national monitoring, concerns have emerged about the proportion of students not meeting curriculum levels at Years 4 and 8 (Darr 2017).

While there had always been competition in the system, previously 'it was not relied upon to improve the system' (Wylie 2012b: 195). The majority of parents in New Zealand had choice of schools in their local area (Musset 2012). Some schools and particularly those in affluent areas thrived, acting at times in a predatory manner to enhance their position in competitive local hierarchies (Lubienski, Lee and Gordon 2013) regardless of the consequences for other local schools (Gordon 2015). Other schools, often in poorer areas, lacked the professional skills to manage the demands. Boards of trustees in 'failure schools' found the trustee role difficult while those in affluent schools generally found the role relatively straightforward given the security of stable or increasing funding, a high level of autonomy and the absence of close scrutiny to which vulnerable schools were subjected (Gordon, Boyask and Pearce 1994). This, combined with the actions of 'aspirational families', saw increased funding in oversubscribed schools who, through selection policies and enrolment zones, could also mediate beyond-school factors by excluding the most disadvantaged students. Undersubscribed schools were, however, required to take all students who wished to attend (Thrupp 2010). This combination of factors led to an array of negative impacts that had long-term consequences for undersubscribed schools and their communities (Tomorrow's Schools Independent Taskforce 2018: 70). Lubienski (2014: 432) argues

> there is little doubt that the *Tomorrow's Schools* reforms have positioned articulate, active parents in the more affluent classes to assert their influence in repositioning public schools to act as private goods serving their own interests .... In the absence of an intermediary authority responsible for equity concerns and accountable to the wider community, state schools are reconfigured to serve the interests of such parents, as well as the interests of the schools in a competitive environment, in excluding students who might drag down the schools' reputation.

The Education Review Office (ERO) was formed under the Education Act 1989 to provide and manage an accountability framework for self-managing schools, including through periodic low-stakes review visits. While many schools welcomed discussions with ERO reviewers, a 'significant number' have had concerns about the focus, process and variability of reviews (Tomorrow's Schools Taskforce 2018). Soon after its implementation, ERO highlighted disparities in school performance, including influential reviews of widespread failure in three of the poorest communities in the country: Mangere Otara, East Coast and Northland (Fancy 2007). Commencing in 1997, the *Strengthening Education In Mangere and Otara* project, involving forty-five schools, was one of the first policy initiatives that involved a commitment to partnership between schools, community and the Ministry of Education (Robinson and Timperley 2004). The project report accepted Fiske and Ladd's (2000) assessment that the 15,000 volunteers who governed New Zealand schools at any time were doing at least as well as the public servants who had preceded them. However, there was emerging evidence about variable board performance, with those in small and low decile communities being most at risk (Robinson and Timperley 2004: iv). For Wylie (2012b: 126), the *Strengthening Education in Mangere and Otara* project showed 'how vital for school development are interconnections focused on joint work and knowledge building, and how limited is any national policy that relies on self-managed schools left to themselves'.

By the second half of the 1990s, school improvement clusters were the 'prime response ... to the inequalities of educational opportunities that had fuelled the impetus for the *Tomorrow's Schools* reforms, and which continued – and, indeed, often appeared to worsen – when schools had been "freed" to self-manage' (Wylie 2012b: 120). By 2001 approximately 10 per cent of schools were in voluntary schooling improvement clusters, usually governed by school principals, and supported by Ministry of Education staff around Aotearoa (Wylie 2012a, 2012b). Not every school in a cluster was in need of support; some were involved because of their shared locale, the attraction of potential resourcing and the opportunity to network. None of the clusters were in middle-class or wealthy communities. Early clusters focused primarily on the improvement of board governance, school leadership and school-community relationships (Robinson, McNaughton and Timperley 2011). Later clusters were required to focus directly on lifting student achievement. By 2009, thirteen of nineteen clusters working with over 15,000 students across ninety-nine schools demonstrated some effect size gains in reading comprehension and writing (Timperley et al. 2010).

In 2008, networks were given further impetus with the establishment of Network Learning Communities (NLC) as part of Ministry of Education support to assist schools in engaging with and implementing the revised *New Zealand Curriculum* (Ward and Henderson 2011). Regional school support providers[7] were funded to establish and maintain NLC. From 2008, 100 leaders were appointed to lead NLC, 70 per cent of whom were principals. Other leaders included middle management, classroom teachers and senior management. The majority of the NLC (84 per cent) were composed of one type of school only. While over 600 schools were engaged, only twelve (16 per cent) involved cross-sector clusters. A NLC evaluation indicated a positive orientation to the initiative including enjoyment of the opportunity to network, to learn about other schools and to support one another in implementing the revised curriculum. The most common reason for leaders to invite others to join their community was because of prior collaborations – existing bonded networks – suggesting an absence of weak ties (Granovetter 1983) that would broaden learning across communities. NLC did not appear to act as professional learning communities (Watson 2014); in other words, challenge and critique were not evident.

Learning and Change Networks (LCN) were the next policy network initiative. In 2010, NZ$7 million was set aside by the Ministry for facilitation services to enable nationwide LCN, initially to support primary and intermediate schools with the implementation of National Standards in reading, writing and mathematics (Annan and Carpenter 2015). National Standards had been introduced by the National government in 2008 and were vehemently opposed by the NZEI, New Zealand's largest education union.[8] Around 10 per cent of schools were involved in LCN, with each LCN being granted twenty-four days of facilitation services over a two-year period (Patterson 2014). The LCN strategy was 'unique in that it aims to intimately involve students, families, and whānau/ extended family in the work of the network, and that it expects schools and communities to take ownership and define the plan for change' (McKibben 2014: 5).

The theory of improvement for LCN was to use expert facilitators contracted from the University of Auckland to challenge and critique limiting school beliefs and practices. This would result in: the potential for enhanced achievement, new insights into student learning, enhanced confidence and enthusiasm for learning by students, the development of new pedagogical relationships across diverse learning spaces, enhanced use of data – both qualitative and quantitative – in decision-making and the broadening of leadership expertise that enables the transfer of skills to other initiatives. In 2014, there were fifty-three LCN networks of schools involving seven early childhood centres, nineteen kura, 285 primary schools, twenty-five intermediate schools, thirty secondary schools and fourteen special education schools. In a sample of fifty-three LCN schools (out of 389) that provided National Standards data in 2012 and 2013, the Ministry found a 17.2 percentage point increase in the proportion of students achieving 'at' or 'above' the expected standard, compared to a 9.4 percentage point increase for a matched control sample. However, the authors noted that not much could be read into this gain, indicating that further time was needed before progress could be accurately assessed (Patterson 2014). Patterson's report noted the overlap of LCN with the incumbent National government's 'hallmark education policy' *Investing in Educational Success* (Ministry of Education 2014) and suggested successful LCN could lead the way. It is to this 'hallmark policy' that we now turn.

Kāhui Ako | Communities of Learning

Since 2013 the major policy initiative to network schools has been the implementation of Kāhui Ako | Communities of Learning as one dimension of the government policy *Investing in Educational Success* (IES). IES was designed to provide 'targeted tools and resources to build teaching capability and improve learning … and achievement for all students' (Ministry of Education 2016a: 2) through three instruments: first and most substantially, Kāhui Ako | Communities of Learning; second, a teacher-led innovation fund; third, a principal recruitment allowance that would enable struggling schools that met particular criteria 'to attract highly effective tumuaki/principals who can provide the leadership impact needed to lift ākonga/student achievement'.

Kāhui Ako are voluntary collaborations of early childhood, school, kura and post-compulsory education providers who work together to address the number one challenge for the compulsory school system in Aotearoa: achieving equity and excellence for students (www.ero.govt.nz). The policy for Kāhui Ako attracted substantial funding: an initial investment of NZ$359 million over four years, with NZ$155 million for subsequent years. The intervention logic for Kāhui Ako is that equity for students will be evident in: first, shared accountability and collective responsibility for students; second, 'deliberate' collaboration; third, building and sharing teaching and leadership expertise; fourth, new career pathways for 'good' teachers and 'outstanding' principals; fifth, evidence-driven action; and sixth, productive partnerships with families, iwi,[9] employers and the community (Ministry of Education 2018a: 5). While Kāhui Ako are voluntary, schools and their staff are effectively incentivized to engage through the provision of additional and generous resourcing for staff release of positional roles and through the enticement of new career opportunities (Charteris and Smardon 2018). Despite this incentivization, tensions in the policy were evident to stakeholders early in the implementation process (Wylie 2016). These tensions will be surveyed in Chapters 5–8 of this collection.

Kāhui Ako function through a system of collaborative roles: a community of learning leader (usually a principal), across-school teacher roles and within-school teacher roles.[10] Appointments are for two years, with appointed teachers granted staff release time of up to two days per week (.40 for leaders and across-school teachers; .08 for within-school teachers), along with travel grants and networking allowances. At the time of writing there are over two-thirds of New Zealand schools – some 610,000 children and young people – learning within 221 Kāhui Ako (Tomorrow's Schools Independent Taskforce 2018). However, since 2019 there has been a moratorium on the approval of new Kāhui Ako. Education providers can still join, or leave, existing Kāhui Ako. This moratorium likely reflected a number of contextual drivers. The official position was 'an ongoing community of learning | Kāhui Ako budget underspend' which was to be used to fund settlement of teacher and principal collective agreements.[11] However, the sustained moratorium possibly also reflects the ongoing work resulting from the Labour government's ambitious system-wide process of reform, Kōrero Mātauranga [Education Conversation] of 2018–19.[12]

Comprising a comprehensive consultation process involving stakeholders across Aotearoa, the Education Conversation was to form the platform for 'significant changes being proposed to almost our entire New Zealand education system', and to develop a vision for 'the future of education in Aotearoa for the next 30 years' (https://conversation.education.govt.nz/). This programme of work included an independent review of *Tomorrow's Schools*. The resulting report *Supporting All Schools to Succeed. Reform of the Tomorrow's Schools System* (Ministry of Education 2019: 5–6)[13] put the position that

> Our system is currently designed so that schools largely operate as autonomous, self-managing entities. In practice, this means that they frequently operate largely on their own, under increasing pressure, and often with slow and uneven transfers of professional knowledge, skills, and best practice. The result is wide variability in learner/ākonga outcomes across and within schools/kura. The nature of the relationship between schools and central government is also highly variable, and trust needs to be rebuilt throughout the system. This document outlines the Government's approach for the reform of the governance, management, and administration of the schooling system. This involves a reset from a highly devolved, largely disconnected, and autonomous set of institutions, to a much more deliberately networked and supported system that is more responsive to the needs of learners/ākonga and their whānau.

Three domains of work were proposed to achieve this 'reset'. First, ensuring sufficient system support functions that are 'appropriate' in scale, principles of decision-making and local presence. Second, building principal leadership of the schooling system. Third, 'a better balance' between local and national responsibilities for school property and network provision, including the centralization of planned and preventative facility maintenance. A further key component of some degree of re-centralization is the proposal for a 'network-based approach' to enrolment zones that will mediate predatory behaviour by some schools. A range of other features of the reset of the governance, management and administration of the schooling system are detailed in *Supporting All Schools to Succeed.* These are assembled around the Labour government's five objectives for education (Ministry of Education 2019: 23): learners at the centre, barrier-free access, quality teaching and leadership, future learning and work, and world-class inclusive public education: 'New Zealand education is trusted and sustainable'.

In summary, schools in Aotearoa New Zealand have over recent decades experienced an array of policy-driven networking initiatives, as well as engaging in organic networks, in their efforts to achieve the moral purpose of schooling. Network initiatives were taken up by policymakers to mediate the competitive ethos accelerated by the introduction of *Tomorrow's Schools*. Yet even before

Tomorrow's Schools, there was 'no national, systemic way to support schools in the work of development and real change; no way to keep building networks or share experiences of what schools were doing and develop the work further' (Wylie 2012b: 31).

The re-election of the sixth Labour government in 2020 gave a strong mandate for the Education Work Programme[14] developed through the Education Conversation to proceed. In that body of work, there is support for Kāhui Ako moving forward with references to less prescription, enhanced trust and developing an interdependent education system (Ministry of Education 2019; Tomorrow's Schools Independent Taskforce 2018). However, the government – to the disappointment of some – stepped back from the 'scale of structural change proposed by the Taskforce', suggesting it would be 'too disruptive and distracting' for students, teachers and school leaders (Hipkins 2019). Progress on the Work Programme has undoubtedly been affected by disruption associated with the COVID-19 pandemic. Yet such disruption is precisely the sort of event when the collective can potentially support its component parts in finding innovative solutions that sustain students in their academic endeavours and that build collaborative capacity in a previously fractured system. In what remains of the chapter, we explore what is known of the potential of Kāhui Ako at this point in time.

How have Kāhui Ako developed?

While collaborative initiatives were already in place in jurisdictions other than Aotearoa, Kāhui Ako occupy the leading edge of global network policy given they potentially form a 'country-wide system of communities' (Education Review Office 2017a). To date, New Zealand reinforces the complex and contested dimension of collaboration. Thrupp's (2018: 141) overview of the implementation of *Investing in Educational Success* argued that critique has been essential to policy: 'It was those who opposed the policy on principled grounds and those who "entered the tent" on principled grounds who contributed to the improvement of the IES policy'. The National government's original proposal had advocated for four new leadership positions with additional remuneration: expert and lead teachers, and executive and change principals (Clark 2017). After substantial revision to lift the focus on collaboration, the policy as launched was greeted with scepticism by many education stakeholders, not least for its high level of prescription around the foci of collaboration (Thrupp 2018).

Kāhui Ako structures are experienced by some as stifling. At implementation, there were a number of 'mandates and conditions' (Charteris and Smardon 2018: 33–4), including a requirement to focus only on achievement challenges and related reporting requirements approved by the Ministry of Education. In the process of formalizing what were at times existing collaborations, and subjecting them to the accountability requirements that come with the provision of financial support, first-order business – the moral purpose of schools – seemed hostage to second-order business of accountability, an effect that had been witnessed elsewhere in the region (Kamp 2013b). This prescription had led to opposition by some influential and 'politically-minded' principals, even where they were involving their schools in unfunded collaborative opportunities, leading to one of our interviewees to comment:

> It's mind-blowing to think that [some principals] were so staunchly against a policy and its implementation of something that actually they're already doing but it's actually costing them to do. ... They didn't want to hear it. They didn't want to understand it. They perceived it to be something that it actually wasn't.

Kāhui Ako leadership occurs through the roles of community of learning leader, across-school teacher and the within-school teacher. From 2017 to 2019 the Ministry also funded external expert partners and change managers to support leaders in developing theories of practice aligned with achievement challenges. A 'correlation between a clear, shared, theory of improvement and the performance of the across-school teachers, and to some extent of all Kāhui Ako staff' was noted by some evaluation partners (Absolum nd). Kāhui Ako leaders are responsible for leadership in building productive collaboration, facilitation of the ongoing development and implementation of the approved achievement plan, professional growth of the Kāhui Ako principals and teachers and providing leadership in the use of professional expertise across schools to meet the achievement challenges (Ministry of Education nd). Recruitment and selection of staff for the formal leadership roles in education networks are critical. The Community of Learning Role Selection and Appointment Information provided by the Ministry is unsurprisingly detailed, running to sixteen pages of directions and requirements.

In their reviews of the evidence, the Education Review Office (2016, 2017a, 2017b) underscored the critical role of, particularly, Kāhui Ako leaders: 'effective leadership is a defining characteristic' of those communities that have proved effective in making a difference for students (Education Review Office 2017b: 10). Leaders have 'a crucial role to play' (Education Review Office

2016: 10) in developing vision, negotiating achievement challenges that are meaningful to all stakeholders and ensuring needed resources are in the right place at the right time. Kāhui Ako leadership roles are argued to be 'complex and dynamic' and 'require more than a replication of the knowledge and skill-sets required to lead a school' (Education Review Office 2017a: 17). The Ministry of Education provides extensive guidelines to support leaders, principals and boards in their simultaneous roles as both 'top' and a 'middle' in leading collaborative educational endeavours (Ramsey and Poskitt 2019).

Thrupp (2018) argues that networks in Aotearoa are mediated by often 'unremarked' power tensions. Education policy development and implementation continue to be shaped by the neoliberal and new public management frameworks that we outlined in Chapter 2, all of which has the potential to erode trust (O'Neill and Snook 2015). There is a need for political leadership in forging a context aligned with a collaborative ethos (Kamp 2019b), some of the opportunity provided by the Education Conversation for structural change was not, at the end of the day, taken by the Ardern government. In his review of the enduring problem of inequality of school achievement in Aotearoa, John Clark (2017) noted that education policy actors from Beeby[15] onwards have continued to first look to within-school solutions in addressing inequalities, despite awareness of the evidence of the weight of extensive beyond-school issues (Coleman 1966). In government, Labour gives greater weight to beyond-school factors such as home life, social and economic factors (Clark 2017). Within the government's Education Work Programme, Kāhui Ako are positioned as having a role to play in 'the strengthening of collaborative networks across the system … a key element for creating trust, and building an interdependent education system' (Ministry of Education 2019: 34).

Case study: Aupaki Kāhui Ako | Community of Learning

The case study is of one of sixteen Kāhui Ako located around Christchurch City. In 2020, 215 education providers were involved in Kāhui Ako around the Christchurch City area. While two Christchurch Kāhui Ako are networks of schools, the majority also involve early childhood education and/or tertiary providers. The largest Kāhui Ako in Christchurch City has thirty-three separate organizations involved, the smallest has eight (all of which are schools). The case study – Aupaki Kāhui Ako – is a collaboration of eight schools (six primary, one teen parent unit and one secondary) and eleven early childhood education providers. Geographically, seven of the eight schools of Aupaki are peppered around the beautiful bays and valleys on the edge of Banks Peninsula. Linwood College, the one secondary school in the community, is located closer to the inner city.

Contextually, Christchurch City is the second largest city in Aotearoa, with a population of around 370,000. Christchurch as a whole offers a unique case of collaboration given the profound impact of the sequence of earthquakes that devastated the city and left 185 dead on 4 September 2010 and 22 February 2011 (see Jansen and Wall: nd for an overview). There was extensive damage to the built environment, with 163 primary and secondary schools affected. In the aftermath, an estimated 70,000 people moved away from Christchurch, including 7,581 students who left to enrol in schools away from the city (Freeman, Nairn, and Gollop 2015).

A number of schools in the central city and the eastern suburbs were so damaged they were unable to reopen without either significant repair, or in some cases, a total rebuild. A priority in 2011 was to get students back at school as soon as possible; to achieve this nine schools – primary, intermediate and secondary – became 'guest' schools sharing the site and facilities of a 'host' school (Ham et al. 2012). Teachers in all schools were faced with providing elevated levels of emotional support for students and families in distress, a situation that continued for a number of years in the post-earthquake context (O'Toole 2018). Ten years later, rebuilding is still in process. Within the NZ$1 billion rebuild of 153 schools (Kenny 2020), modern learning environments and multi-school campuses have been introduced (Fickel, Mackey and Fletcher 2019).

The Aupaki Kāhui Ako was an evolution of an existing collaboration, the Bays Cluster, an independently formed collection of full primary schools in the south east of Christchurch established in 2007 (Aupaki Kāhui Ako 2017: np). With the introduction of Kāhui Ako as a policy initiative, discussions took place between the Bays Cluster boards and principals, and the board and new principal of Linwood College. One of the drivers here was to streamline transition from early childhood education to secondary school 'and beyond', with recognition of the 'role wellbeing plays in the successful transition' of students (Aupaki Kāhui Ako 2017: np). In 2021, Aupaki Kāhui Ako leader is the principal of Lyttelton Primary School. The achievement challenge documentation for Aupaki notes that while there had historically been a 'well-established' relationship with Linwood as the closest secondary school to the Aupaki primary schools, that had 'wavered' in recent years.

This was a complex scenario. Linwood College had suffered a damaging decline in enrolments in the context of *Tomorrow's Schools*. To enable parental choice, state enrolment schemes had been abolished in 1991 by the fourth National Government. As a low-socio-economic decile three school, Linwood enrolments dropped by around 25 per cent as aspirational parents accessed higher-decile education opportunities for their children. The school sustained itself by enrolling high numbers of international students, and through 'successful leadership'.[16] After the 2011 earthquake, and in a context of internal discord, the roll dropped further from over 1,000 students to 716 students (O'Callaghan 2015) and, at the time of the establishment of Aupaki, just 631 students (Aupaki Kāhui Ako 2017).[17]

Linwood College was an 'associate member' in the establishment of Aupaki: it is the only secondary school in Aupaki and, at the time of writing, students from Aupaki schools are zoned for Linwood College. While Linwood College is a decile three school, all other Aupaki schools are decile nine and ten. Currently only a small percentage of Aupaki students enrol at Linwood however that percentage is increasing, and will likely further accelerate when Linwood returns to its rebuilt campus and is relaunched as Te Aratai College. Linwood is one of only two schools in Aotearoa that are members of two Kāhui Ako. Linwood's primary community is with Tamai Kāhui Ako, comprised of sixteen early childhood education providers and eight schools (three at decile two, two at decile three and one at decile four), all of which are currently in zone for Linwood. As such, funding and time allocations that Linwood receives for its involvement in Kāhui Ako do not come to Aupaki. Given the demands on time and energy faced by lower-decile schools in their daily operations, this aligning of the funding to Tamai rather than Aupaki seems appropriate and, by aligning Tamia and Aupaki's achievement challenges, it is expected that students within both Kāhui Ako will benefit.

The achievement challenge that was established, and approved, for Aupaki Kāhui Ako in 2017 was based on an analysis of achievement data. As a whole, the Kāhui Ako was achieving favourably compared to national data on National Standards. Yet, inequities for Māori and Pasifika students in Years 1 to 8 were evident; while Māori and Pasifika students at Aupaki were at times achieving above the national achievement levels for Māori and Pasifika in reading, writing and mathematics, at the same they were achieving at far lower levels than Aupaki students as a group. At secondary level, students at Linwood were, as a group, 15 per cent below national percentages for achievement at NCEA Level 2.

Aupaki focused on achievement challenges that were in alignment with the focus of the policy guidelines. These were to i) lift the achievement of boys in writing (a target that some research respondents questioned given boys' achievement was well in excess of national achievement levels in reading, writing and mathematics); ii) lift the achievement of Years 1–8 Māori learners in reading, writing and mathematics; and iii) increase the percentage of secondary learners leaving Linwood College having achieved NCEA at Level 2 or higher. In the pursuit of these achievement challenges, they had consistently submitted applications for centrally funded professional learning and development. That has proved to be an arduous and unsuccessful process. In part this was due to changing priorities and timelines at the centre. In part, applications were compromised by member schools already having been awarded central funding which compromised the collective application. This is illustrative of processes yet to be smoothed: if the government made an overt commitment to Kāhui Ako then they could channel funding for professional learning and development to collectives that were geographically close. Similarly, if Aupaki had reached the idealized highly functioning state, all resources – both human and other – would be seen as belonging to the collective, regardless of who had secured the resource.

In the interviews we undertook with Kāhui Ako leaders in Christchurch, principals and Ministry staff to inform this chapter, only one respondent was ambivalent as to the potential of the policy. Yet, this is political territory. In an article by Radio New Zealand, the President of the Principal's Federation, Perry Rush, had been reported as indicating they had 'spoken with 800 principals, over 98 per cent of those principals are calling for the dissolution of Kāhui Ako' (Gerritson 2020). In a context where educational resources are limited, investment in networks is at the cost of funding being unavailable for other pressing demands. In reflecting on this development in the context, a principal in our research noted the problem in such a political point being made:

> [Perry] was very vehemently against National Standards when they came out, as most of us were. ... National Standards were about raising achievement. It was all data-centric. His statement on National Radio ... he wrapped it up around the Kāhui Ako and that there was no evidence to show that they raised student achievement. He used that language. I thought, 'What are you doing?' He knows that to raise student achievement we look at the underpinning things that influence learning. It's around good quality teaching practice, and how are we lifting the practice of our teachers, so they do a better job that supports really strong relationships with our kids, for example. Or, the engagement and the partnership that we have with our families and all those types of things. The

culture of sustaining practices. All that stuff underpins achievement … . It's not going to happen straight away. But, then for him to say, 'There's no evidence of improved student achievement', I'm thinking, 'What do you mean by student achievement?'

The Aupaki principals we spoke with emphasized the critical task of establishing new, and deeper, relationships as 'the very first starting point … to make a difference to the kids'. There is both a practical and symbolic value to the endorsement given to networking by the presence of a national policy. At a practical level, the time release for the Kāhui Ako roles had an enabling role:

> What does a highly functioning Kāhui Ako look like? If you really, really want that, somehow something's got to be put in place to enable that to happen; otherwise you will always get … a level of cooperation and a level of collaboration between school leaders and between schools … but will it get to that high functioning stage?

The capacity for staff to be out of their schools, learning about other contexts, and other ways to understand a challenge and its range of potential responses, was a necessary preliminary to getting to 'that high-functioning stage' that could not occur at scale without the funding for dedicated roles and leadership responsibility at the beyond-school level. Ministry staff noted that each Kāhui Ako differed in terms of their stage of development and how deeply the notion of collaborations had permeated through the collective and whether classroom teachers were actively involved in, or even aware of, the Kāhui Ako's work. In Aupaki, respondents suggested teachers would be conceptually aware of the kāhui and were increasingly involved in collaborative projects. However, one respondent noted

> many would not understand what positive benefit it has had. By many, I mean really most and a good number wouldn't know what our priorities are. Ask again in a years' time with this new structure and absolutely they will.

Kāhui Ako challenge hierarchical leadership. Aupaki's lead is a principal with ten years' experience, who had prior experience in another Kāhui Ako. Having moved into the area, he brought his primary school into Aupaki, and was then appointed to the leadership a year later. He commented on the necessity of being comfortable with the ambiguity that an emergent policy context demands:

> I remember the interview and the process of going through that, one of the questions was something around 'comfortable with dealing with ambiguity and uncertainty'. It's like, 'What do you mean by that?' I've realised what it means. It's that actually there's no definitive answers around how you do this.

Conclusion

In the Tips and Starters document for Kāhui Ako (Ministry of Education 2015a: 2–3), leaders are advised that they are collaborating when five elements are present. First, when they come together for an agreed purpose that they believe in, and recognize will benefit from collaboration. Second, they work to common goals that have been developed on the basis of wide evidence and that are achievable; in the process they are open to honest dialogue and critique. Third, they adopt a respectful dialogic approach in developing their approach to working collaboratively. Fourth, they build relationships that foster a sense of belonging for all while engaging productively with diversity. Fifth, they share leadership so that participants' strengths are recognized and used.

All of these elements are present in the Aupaki Kāhui Ako, even if only in a fledgling way. While leadership is shared, the Kāhui Ako leader needs to create the conditions where others can and will step into that leadership space.

> I've got the leadership hat on, in terms of I'm the Lead Principal. I do lead, but the way that is done, we've really worked on our … we defined how we wanted to communicate and how we wanted to operate as a group; how we felt it was best that we would make decisions as a group. I think the best thing I could have done is just been consistent with that.
>
> But, then it all comes back to the strategic stuff that we set up as a group right from the start. It's like in your own school: if you can connect everything you do to the purpose that's been set, that you've worked on to set as a school, and for us it's through our community and our boards, and that's the direction that we're mandated to work towards. If you can connect all your actions to those specific things you've been mandated to do, and you can be clear in how you communicate that, I think you will develop trust.

Canterbury as a region is likely to be positioned in ways that other regions are not. The experiences gained in the aftermath of the earthquakes of 2010 and 2011 had thrown 'business as usual' aside. Interviewees noted, and acknowledged, that the Canterbury Ministry was different: they 'were looking for change. They wanted to operate in a way that was more supportive of schools in Kāhui Ako and they wanted to do it internally and they wanted to do it externally facing as well'. Across the Christchurch City Kāhui Ako, there was recognition in the Ministry and participating schools of the pivotal role of the across-school teacher. Some across-school teachers have developed collaborative professional learning opportunities, have used social media to build community and share evidence, have ensured Kāhui Ako is part of all-school inductions of new staff and have attended Ministry-facilitated symposia that focus equally on content and collaborative process. In other Kāhui Ako, principals have recognized that a reset was required to better leverage the roles through clearer expectations, support and configuring school-level leadership in ways that gave authority to these middle leaders, thereby giving a stronger endorsement to progress the agreed achievement challenges.

5

Analysing Networks through the Lens of School Effectiveness and School Improvement

Introduction

As we outlined in Chapter 2, school effectiveness research focuses on the internal factors that make schools more or less successful in improving outcomes for children, while school improvement research considers the learning conditions, cultures, practices and processes which enable such change. School effectiveness and improvement research has been hugely influential, driving a focus on school-level structures, processes and quality indicators in countries around the world, including our case study countries. However, as we note, the research has also been critiqued for its normative and technocratic focus on within-school factors, an overly narrow conceptualization of schooling and school outcomes, and an under-theorized assessment of how and why educational outcomes differ across different contexts. Despite recent efforts by scholars to examine the ways in which students, classrooms and schools are nested within wider systems (Creemers and Kyriakides 2008), research in this field has rarely considered the role of inter-organizational networks in influencing processes of change or educational outcomes.

In this chapter we draw on David Hargreaves's model of school effectiveness and improvement (2001, 2010, 2012a, 2012b) as a framework for our assessment of networks in England, New Zealand, Chile and Singapore. As noted in Chapter 2, we selected this model because it is both informed by wider social theory and positions inter-organizational networks as a core mechanism for enhancing school improvement and effectiveness. Hargreaves's original model (2001) focused on schools' capacity to improve and set out four key concepts: intellectual capital, social capital, leverage and institutional outputs. His later work built on this model, arguing that schools must form 'deep' partnerships with joint practice development between teachers at their heart, since this will build social capital and ensure continuous individual and collective learning and improvement. According to Hargreaves, developing 'deep' partnerships requires sophisticated skills and qualities from school and system leaders, including a commitment to co-creation as a means of developing trust, reciprocity, collective moral purpose and robust peer evaluation and challenge between schools.

The case studies of networks in England, New Zealand, Chile and Singapore show how school and system leaders in each country have been encouraged and/or required to focus on effectiveness and improvement at the level of individual schools. Many reforms aim to enhance the quality of teaching and learning in classrooms, for example through changes to the curriculum or the assessment of learning, or by investing in the skills and capacity of school leaders and teachers. In addition, all four systems see a role for inter-school networks and partnerships in supporting schools to improve – both individually and collectively. We explore commonalities and differences in these network approaches, arguing that these differences relate – at least in part – to wider differences in how school effectiveness and improvement are conceptualized, assessed and incentivized in each country.

The chapter is structured in four sections, followed by a conclusion in which we reflect, briefly, on the implications for leadership in networks. The section headings reflect Hargreaves's original (2001) framework, but we draw on concepts from his later work where appropriate. We focus mainly on the detailed case studies of networks in England and New Zealand (Chapters 3 and 4), but also consider the cases of Chile and Singapore (Chapter 1) where appropriate.

Capacity to improve

Hargreaves (2001: 488) argues that the focus of all school effectiveness and improvement efforts should be on schools' 'capacity for improvement', which he characterizes as an ability to manage change in the context of instability and reform. Clearly, a school's 'capacity to improve' will depend on a range of factors, such as the skills and expertise of its staff, its level of resources in relation to the challenges it faces and so on. Schools serving more deprived communities generally face more intense challenges and require additional capacity in order to overcome these successfully (Klar and Brewer 2013), so how a system or network works to build and spread capacity has important implications for equity. In Chapter 2 we suggested that one way to understand 'capacity to improve' is to ask how well schools self-evaluate themselves and then work to identify and address improvement priorities, reflected in the phrase 'the best schools are the best at getting better'. Networks have the potential to support these processes, for example by enabling schools to engage in self and peer-evaluations and/or by helping to address capacity deficits through schools agreeing to share resources. In this section we start by assessing how policy and practice in our case study countries shape and support capacity assessments and development in individual schools. We then explore how our case study networks support these efforts and conclude with a discussion of how to assess the capacity of networks themselves.

All four systems focus to some extent on assessing school quality. These assessments are then used to decide whether and how capacity needs to be enhanced, for example through focused school improvement efforts. However, the approach to these assessments differs widely across the four contexts: some are largely summative and 'done to', while others are more formative and 'owned' by schools themselves. Some rely more heavily on output measures (for example performance in standardized tests), whereas others include an assessment of key process measures, such as the quality of leadership or the extent to which teachers receive high-quality professional development. For example, in England and Chile all schools are inspected and given a public grade which is essentially summative and relies heavily on test performance, whereas in New Zealand the Education Reform Office's inspection reports are made publicly available but do not provide a single performance grade,[1] while in Singapore inspections and school rankings were abolished in 2000 and replaced with a formative school self-evaluation model, backed by external validation every five years. Lee, Ho and Yong (2021: 170–1) show how these developments in Singapore formed part of a wider set of reforms aimed at building the capacity of schools, including through the development of networks (see Chapter 1). They describe the development of school self-evaluation as follows, showing how it has evolved over time and its aim to assess wider outcomes beyond performance in standardized tests:

> MOE introduced the School Excellence Model (SEM) in 2000 to task schools with their own quality assurance while removing centralised control … . School management teams were trained to self-evaluate the quality of their school using a common framework … . The SEM provides broad standards and performance indicators that go beyond academic outcomes to emphasise students' holistic development … . SEM does not dictate a prescribed approach for school evaluation but allows for variations in how schools develop capacities for innovations and achieve excellence … . School leaders are trained to understand that there are various approaches to achieving outcomes … . SEM has been modified over time to be less onerous and to help schools focus on the substance and not the form of SEM.

These differences in how school quality and capacity are assessed are reflected in how schools are held accountable and how school improvement efforts and interventions are structured. In England and Chile, the consequences of 'failing' an inspection are significant and school principals risk losing their jobs if their school is taken over by a MAT (England) or is closed (Chile). In contrast, the emphasis on formative assessment and the absence of public rankings and gradings in New Zealand and Singapore means that the process is less high stakes.

All four countries have developed a range of school improvement and capacity-building programmes that are not specifically network-based, although in practice these interventions almost always interact with networks to some extent. Examples include the Opportunity Area programme in England (Chapter 3) and the two non-Kāhui Ako strands of the *Investing in Educational Success* (IES) in New Zealand (i.e. teacher-led innovation fund and principal recruitment allowances for struggling schools – Chapter 4). However, we focus here on our case study networks, asking two questions: i) how do these networks assess the capacity and needs of member schools? and ii) how can we assess the capacity of these networks to undertake school improvement? The following chapter sections focus on how networks operate to develop school and network-level capacity, for example by enhancing social and intellectual capital.

Starting with the question of how networks assess the capacity of member schools, we see how the nature of the national framework influences network activity in each case. For example, the summative and high-stakes nature of Ofsted inspections in England means that most networks include a strong focus on assessing school quality and capacity. These assessments can certainly help the school to prepare for its next Ofsted visit, in a performative sense (Courtney 2016), but they can also support genuine improvement – for example, if they help ensure that subsequent capacity building efforts are well targeted. We see this emphasis in both the smaller Swan Partnership and the area-wide Bampton Education Partnership. In the Swan Partnership, head teachers reported that the peer reviews between schools, supported by a trained Ofsted inspector, had 'been really helpful with preparation for Ofsted'. Similarly, the Bampton Education Partnership had started with a broad set of aims, but in practice had focused its work on monitoring Local Authority maintained schools. Termly visits, undertaken by accredited peer head teachers, informed a rating for each school. Schools judged 'amber' or 'red' were then prioritized to receive additional support, for example from a designated 'system leader' school (for example National Leader of Education or Teaching School). The Partnership's approach was seen to have some benefits, but was also criticized by many interviewees for being too bureaucratic and because it prevented schools from engaging in more developmental work.[2] In contrast, New Zealand's more formative and less punitive national approach to school evaluation means that school networks do not feel the same pressure to prioritize such evaluations in their own work. We see this in the Aupaki Kāhui Ako in Christchurch, which did start its work by undertaking two surveys of teachers across member schools aimed at assessing the issues they faced and areas of expertise they could share, but did not use these data to rank or rate individual teachers or schools.

England and New Zealand's approaches to assessing school quality and holding leaders accountable can each be seen to have pros and cons when considering the implications for networks. England's summative and high-stakes model means that school principals feel intensely accountable for their school's performance, perhaps encouraging a more instrumental mindset in which partnership working is only prioritized if it will have a direct benefit for the school. As we saw above, both the Swan Partnership and Bampton Education Partnership focus on assessing school quality in line with the Ofsted framework, but there are significant differences between Swan's peer review approach, which the school leaders have collectively agreed and value highly, and the larger Bampton Education Partnership's termly assessments, which many find formulaic. England's model carries risks because it can narrow the focus of partnership work, but it also has a positive side: the framework gives school leaders a shared language and set of tools for assessing their work, potentially enabling more focused dialogue and targeted action than would otherwise be possible. The absence of school reviews in New Zealand's Aupaki Kāhui Ako does not necessarily mean that the collectively agreed 'achievement challenges' are not well-evidenced or appropriate, and there seems little doubt that the partnership is more able to focus on developmental activity because it is not distracted by such assessments. However, there is a balance to be struck: as we explore below, improvement partnerships can benefit by operating as an 'epistemic community' (Glazer and Peurach 2015), characterized by shared language, tools and theories of action for teaching and learning. In the absence of a clear national framework and in the face of local resistance to 'data-centric' approaches, the challenge for Aupaki Kāhui Ako's leaders is to gain meaningful buy-in to shared approaches that allow for meaningful collaboration at classroom level.

We turn now to the question of how to assess the capacity of networks – that is, how well can they support member schools. One approach would be to consider resourcing, where an economist might assume that the greater the resources available, the greater the capacity and impact of the network, but it is not clear that better-funded networks inevitably achieve more. In self-funded partnerships, such as Swan Partnership in Bampton where each school contributes £3,000 each year, the funding covers minimal core costs, but member schools recognize that they must also contribute far more than this in kind, for example through their own time. In externally funded partnerships we have observed schools spending vast amounts of time arguing over how these extra resources will be distributed, rather than getting on and using them, or augmenting them through in-kind contributions. In truth, even in the most generously funded networks, the level of funding is small when compared with the combined budgets of the participating organizations – usually less than 1 per cent of the total. This suggests that while networks can benefit from having some core capacity, such as the various facilitators, convenors and cross-school roles described in the case studies, this central capacity is most powerful when it unlocks the capacity of other people, expertise and resources distributed across the network. This is where the eight features of successful networks set out in Chapter 1 become important: does the network have shared goals, how does it facilitate collective commitment and contributions, to what extent does it reflect shared values, practices and attributes, and so on? Alignment in these areas can unlock this distributed capacity and direct it towards the achievement of shared priorities. By the same token, generous external funding will achieve little if these features are absent.

In practice, the eight features of successful networks set out in Chapter 1 interact in complex ways, both with each other and in relation to the context of the network and its schools, so the task of leaders is to understand and assess these interactions and to work through the tensions and issues that will, inevitably, arise. We conclude, therefore, by highlighting three questions which indicate the kinds of challenges and dilemmas that leaders face as they undertake this work:

i.   How best to engage with hierarchical and funding incentives, which can augment core capacity but can also introduce bureaucracy and create dependency? In New Zealand, the government's Kāhui Ako framework has been, and continues to be, seen by some as too prescriptive and some existing networks have chosen not to apply for the additional funding. There are also tensions in how Kāhui Ako connects with other improvement resources. For example, leaders in the Aupaki Kāhui Ako were frustrated that, despite several time-consuming applications, they were unable to secure central funding for the professional learning and development they (think they) need. The formal requirements associated with Kāhui Ako funding can also create unhelpful dynamics; for example, if they create a sense that network leadership resides 'only' in the formally appointed leaders – perhaps allowing other leaders to sit back and observe rather than creating the shared commitment and investment required across the network.

ii. How to develop capacity across non-homogenous partnerships? In both England and New Zealand we see partnerships involving multiple primary schools and a single secondary school. In New Zealand, most Kāhui Ako involve early childhood education and some also involve tertiary-level providers. How do leaders in these networks avoid power imbalances in such pyramid models, and how do they ensure that (mostly subject specialist) secondary teachers can benefit from working with (mostly generalist) primary teachers?

iii. How to assess capacity limitations, for example to know when a partnership arrangement is not the optimal solution? Partnerships work well where all can contribute and all can benefit, even if there are ebbs and flows in the balance of these exchanges over time. But are there some situations that partnerships cannot cope with: for example, if a member school fails and requires intensive 'turn-around' support aimed at changing systems, processes and possibly even personnel? Evidence from England indicates that voluntary networks often struggle to provide this level of support, which is why the more formal MAT sponsorship model has been adopted in these contexts (Greany 2018a).

Building on this brief exploration of capacity at school and network level, we turn next to the issue of intellectual and social capital between schools.

Intellectual and social capital

In Hargreaves's model, intellectual capital refers to the overall knowledge and experience of a school's stakeholders, which is developed through creating new knowledge (exploration) and transferring proven knowledge between contexts and people (exploitation). The key focus here is on teachers and teaching, and working to strengthen the knowledge, skills and practices required, given the strong evidence from school effectiveness research that this is how schools can make the greatest difference to student outcomes (Higgins et al. 2015). Social capital underpins the development of intellectual capital, enabling the sharing of knowledge and expertise: it develops through trust, norms of reciprocity and networks. For social capital to evolve, there must be a commitment to take action – to invest – for shared and individual benefit. Hargreaves argues that joint practice development combined with robust peer evaluation and challenge can build social and intellectual capital as well as shared commitment (collective moral purpose) across schools, thereby supporting continuous improvement.

In Chapter 1 we noted that knowledge and expertise cannot be simply transferred from one context to another; rather, it must be continuously reviewed and transformed as it is taken into different settings. This supports Hargreaves's emphasis on joint practice development and explains why many partnerships adopt enquiry models, such as action research or communities of practice, as a means of structuring such efforts. However, more recent work on epistemic communities in education (Glazer and Peurach 2015; Malone, Groth and Glazer, 2021) indicates that the development and movement of intellectual capital across dispersed networks require a more concerted effort to develop shared theories ('mental maps'), codes (including technical language to describe aspects of teaching and learning) and tools (such as text books or lesson plans) which provide the platforms necessary for teachers to work together to articulate and share practice. Glazer and Peurach (2015: 180) do not deny that social capital is important for the sharing of practice, but suggest that it is not sufficient in and of itself, and that shared intellectual capital must be built on the foundation of an epistemic community:

> Whereas theories of social capital typically assume that individuals share the cognitive frames and prior knowledge needed to support meaningful interaction, the epistemic community model centers on the *development* of shared cognitive frames, knowledge, and vocabulary that social capital models typically assume.

This suggests that joint practice development may be necessary but not sufficient for the development of shared intellectual capital across schools. Or that joint practice development needs to be actively geared towards facilitating the development and embedding of shared theories, codes and tools across the network, thereby enabling teachers to collaborate without needing to endlessly reinvent the pedagogical wheel. Greany (2018a) studied improvement approaches in four different group arrangements in England (MATs, federations, Teaching School Alliances and local authorities), showing how leaders work in different ways to develop aligned and/or standardized approaches to pedagogy, curriculum and pupil assessment, which could be seen as foundations for an epistemic community. One way in which they did this was to draw together subject leaders from each school to co-design a preferred approach, which was then codified and embedded across member schools. Glazer et al. (2022) bring these concepts together with work on organizational learning (Lipshitz, Friedman and Popper 2007; Holmqvist 2003; Argyris and Schön 1978) to show how educational groups in England and the United States are working to develop:

- a shared theory and language for teaching and learning
- alignment around defined tools and processes (for example curriculum)
- enabling routines which structure the collaborative work of teachers
- boundary spanners – people who help build the collective knowledge base and who move knowledge around the system
- shared measurement tools
- sense-making structures and a culture of improvement-oriented peer evaluation and challenge

If we consider the networks in Aotearoa New Zealand, England, Chile and Singapore, we see that all are working to foster intellectual and social capital, but that levels of sophistication vary and that forging the kind of epistemic learning system outlined above is challenging for partnerships of autonomous schools. The networks developed by nodal schools in Singapore, selected and supported by the Ministry of Education to develop, codify and disseminate new practices in relation to the use of ICT, provide some of the most sophisticated examples. Toh et al. (2016) focus on the extent to which these networks support epistemic carryovers, where networking leads to changes in teachers' values and beliefs about learning and the nature of knowledge. They argue that such epistemic impact occurs within a wider ecosystem approach to innovation, which relies on parallel structural, social-cultural and economic changes, enabled through active support from the Ministry within a small and cohesive system. This approach appears to have been successful in overcoming the risks, highlighted in Chapter 1, of attempting to transfer knowledge from 'expert' to 'less expert' schools or teachers, which can excite resistance and can fail to adapt the practice to the needs of different contexts.

Singapore's nodal schools were selected precisely because of their intellectual capital, as ICT pioneers they could focus on developing and codifying their innovation before considering how best to diffuse it. In contrast, networks in England and New Zealand bring together autonomous schools in the pursuit of more incremental forms of improvement.[3] This might explain why these networks focus on building social as much as intellectual capital, building trust by valuing the contributions of all schools equally. A focus on joint practice development might be ideal for this purpose, but the risk is that it recycles low-level practice – meaning that all forms of practice are acknowledged as equal, due to a fear that prioritizing one approach above another might crush social capital (Robinson 2019). This is precisely why Hargreaves argues that partnerships must work to develop peer evaluation and challenge, to allow for robust critique and refinement, but he acknowledges that this is the most difficult aspect of partnership working. Failure to get the balance right between developing social and intellectual capital can lead to frustration if the pace of development is too slow ('co-blabberation' as one school leader in England describes it) or, equally, to fragmentation if one partner is seen to impose their intellectual capital in the absence of sufficient social capital.

We see these issues at play in Bampton, in England. The Swan Partnership had succeeded in establishing a set of routines which served to build intellectual as well as social capital, for example through its subject networks and professional development programmes. Its model of peer reviews between schools, supported by an external facilitator, suggested a commitment to Hargreaves's peer evaluation and challenge. The research did not allow for a detailed exploration of whether and how these processes had enabled the development of an epistemic community, but studies of similar partnerships across England (Greany and Higham 2018; Greany 2018a) suggest that such developments are likely to be nascent, with alignment in some areas negotiated on a voluntary and pragmatic basis, but with continuing challenges in relation to sharing practice. For example, the Learning Links partnership, described in Chapter 1, has gone further than the Swan Partnership in some respects, with shared models for moderating student work, for sharing data on student progress and for 'sense-making' through shared governor meetings. The Learning Links partners had trialled several different approaches to sharing practices between schools – including a good practice brochure and a co-ordinated brokerage system for school-to-school visits – but these had proved unwieldy or ineffective and so had been abandoned. At the time of the research, the schools were trialling an informal but structured approach to visits, in which each school organized its own visits but using a common format for preparation (including a training session on the theory of a specific practice), observation in pairs (with time for post-observation discussion), action planning and feedback.

Similar issues are apparent in Aotearoa, although the formalized nature of Kāhui Ako, with defined achievement challenges and reporting timescales, might perhaps encourage a stronger focus on developing shared intellectual capital. Like the Swan Partnership, Aupaki is small, comprising eight schools and eleven early childhood education providers, and locally focused. It evolved from the former Bays Cluster of primary schools, providing a basis for social capital, although this did not initially involve Linwood College that is now an associate member of the Kāhui Ako. Intellectual capital and joint practice development processes are evident in Aupaki, partly thanks to the experience of the current Kāhui Ako Lead Principal who came into the role with previous experience of working in another Kāhui Ako, along with ten years' experience as a principal. He has focused on developing collaborative practices, but has started with relationships and listening: 'you have to know each other and get in each other's shoes'. As noted above, the network started by surveying all its teachers to establish their practice priorities and to identify sources of expertise within the member schools. The school principals have all agreed to adopt shared indicators of success, including the indicators established for education by the local iwi [tribe], Ngāi Tahu, as well as the Kāhui Ako's endorsed achievement challenges.

Leverage and outcomes

For Hargreaves, leverage and outcomes are intimately linked: indeed, leverage 'is about the relation between teacher input and educational output' (2001: 489). He argues that 'understanding school improvement means discovering how schools can learn to implement, that is, combine and sequence, the high leverage strategies of effective schools' (2001: 490). In his view this requires teachers to draw on external evidence and, where necessary, to innovate, but also, critically, it requires schools to create the systems, processes and collaborative professional learning cultures required to leverage – that is, scale up and systematize – these successful practices to achieve impact.

Achieving all this within a single school is challenging, particularly in the context of ever more demanding aspirations for excellence and equity in most contemporary school systems. Achieving this across a partnership requires even greater levels of sophistication, requiring network-level strategies for securing leverage together with school-level leaders and teachers who can meta-cognitively analyse and articulate their own practice in ways that can be shared across the group. As we explored in the previous section, shared theory, codes and tools can help, not least because they support shared 'sense-making' and enable boundary spanners to communicate and embed new practices more effectively. However, the challenges cannot be underestimated, as the following quote from the Chief Executive of a MAT in England captured in an earlier study indicates (Greany 2018a). The MAT does have some shared tools, including a standardized approach to assessing student learning across the trust, but it is still working to really understand why it is that some practices are more or less successful, and how this learning can best be leveraged to impact across the group:

> We (can) now more actively compare schools … with a clearer focus on the data, but also the analysis and understanding what we're comparing. For example, one of our academies, last year, had the third highest value added scores in the country (i.e. demonstrating that disadvantaged students have made accelerated progress in their learning), and that, of course, was a cause much celebration. Some of our other academies were nowhere near as successful. The interesting thing was neither the successful ones nor the other ones really understood how that had happened! As a result, we now have, as a trust, a really clear idea of the impact of our decisions on value added scores, and we're tracking that more closely. Because we're doing that together, we're comparing more closely, and it's allowed us to drill down far more effectively into those things that make that kind of difference.

Singapore's approach challenges any simplistic notion that epistemic communities can only work successfully where assessment systems and other such tools are standardized. For example, although the School Excellence Model (SEM) is a shared tool, it allows for considerable flexibility in relation to how leverage and outcomes are defined. The quote above from Lee, Ho and Yong (2021: 170–1) explains how school management teams are trained to self-evaluate, using the SEM's broad standards and performance indicators, but it is made clear that these indicators must be adapted to the school's context and that 'there are various approaches to achieving outcomes'. The role of the cluster superintendents and the various network learning communities is then to ensure that learning about how different schools approach their improvement priorities is shared to support systemic learning and progress.

Several partnerships in Bampton, England, offered scope for leverage and improved outcomes across schools, although the fragmentation of the system into various MATs and Local Authority structures meant that it lacked the sophistication of Singapore's approach. The clearest examples came where designated 'system leaders' – that is, National Leaders of Education (NLEs) and their home school teams – were allocated to support struggling schools.[4] The

Opportunity Area funded more than twenty of these partnerships, most lasting between two terms to a year, as a way of securing improvement in the town's lower-performing schools. Many of these NLEs were based in schools in Bampton but some came from schools across the wider region, helping to introduce new ways of working and additional capacity. These interventions were commissioned and formalized through a contract, setting out specific targets for how the supported school should be improved and over what timescale. Research across various localities has shown that such school-to-school support partnerships can have a measurable impact on pupil outcomes and school quality, and that the providing system leader school often benefits as well, for example because its teachers and leaders are given a chance to reflect on and apply their expertise in new contexts (Armstrong Brown and Chapman 2020). Muijs (2015a: 582) studied such partnerships in depth and found that:

> Effective partnership working entailed intensive intervention by the supporting school. Headteachers and other members of senior management were typically involved in the partnership work, and often spent a significant amount of time in the supported school. A lot of the successful models revolved around doing very concrete delineated activities, based on clear and limited goals ... in three main areas: leadership development, development of teaching and learning approaches, and generating quick wins.

This focus on 'concrete delineated activities' was also evident in the school-to-school partnerships in Bampton and these efforts were often successful in improving outcomes. However, the pressure to generate quick wins and to demonstrate rapid improvements in pupil outcomes coupled with the power differentials inherent in the system leadership model could sometimes compromise the development of more equal partnerships characterized by shared social and intellectual capital. Some NLEs appeared more successful than others at managing these tensions, by working in ways which: a) fostered social capital, by emphasizing the need for mutual respect and trust between the staff of both schools (i.e. 'doing with, not doing to'); b) developed shared intellectual capital, by engaging in co-design and avoiding imposing predefined models from the high performing school; and c) built the capacity of staff in the receiving school, through a coaching and mentoring approach, making it more likely that when the support school team withdrew the improvements would be sustained.

In a similar vein, peer reviews between schools, such as those being undertaken by the Swan Partnership in Bampton, can provide an enabling routine which allows school staff to observe and learn from each other, thereby building social and intellectual capital, and also to identify areas in which practice could be enhanced as well as mechanisms to achieve this, thereby supporting leverage and impact. However, as with most things, the 'Bananarama principle' (named after the famous pop song) applies – that is, 'it ain't what you do it's the way that you do it' – meaning that peer review can be used as either a formative and developmental learning process, or as narrow accountability tool. For example, Greany (2020b) analysed three case studies of peer review between partnerships of schools, assessing whether and how these reflected the three forms of isomorphism (coercive, mimetic and normative) – or homogenization – identified by DiMaggio and Powell (1983). He shows how, in some cases, school leaders used peer reviews to benchmark their own school against others that they saw as more legitimate (i.e. because they have an Outstanding Ofsted inspection grade) at a time of significant uncertainty around how best to respond to England's changing policy and accountability requirements. These leaders used the findings from the reviews to prepare for their next Ofsted inspection, often by setting an agenda for internal change that focused on emulating the structures and processes in place at the higher-performing schools that had undertaken the review. However, 'dragging and dropping' structures and processes from one school to another in these ways did not lead to improved school performance except in cases where it was combined with wider processes of professional learning for all staff.

Our case study of Aotearoa also offers examples of successful leverage and, as detailed in Chapter 4, evidence of the potential for improved outcomes as a result of partnership working. Despite the current moratorium on the formation of new Kāhui Ako networks, it appears that where these networks already exist they are being normalized as the mechanism for enacting new priorities and securing leverage, irrespective of what the desired output might be. One recent example of this came from a Radio New Zealand segment aired as we were writing this chapter, which focused on inclusion and support for students with complex needs. All of the commentators made reference to the capacity-building they were involved in in schools, which they were developing via Kāhui Ako.

The focus on high-leverage strategies has been scaffolded by the Ministry in New Zealand through the introduction in 2016 of a Development Map and Toolkit. This runs to thirty pages and draws on Education Review Office School Evaluation Indicators, the Investing in Educational Success Working Group reports, and a wide range of academic evidence on the intersection between collaboration and enhanced outcomes for learners. The Map is not prescriptive, and is not intended as a mechanism to measure network progress, but it does offer a clear framework to lead a network from establishment, through developing, onto embedding and then to fully functioning:

> fully functioning stage is very different to how teaching and learning is organised today. Progression against some domains may take years before a Kāhui Ako is in the fully functioning stage. Not every Kāhui Ako will necessarily have the goal to progress to fully functioning.
>
> (Ministry of Education 2016b: 2)

Leverage here is through six domains: teaching collaboratively for the best learning outcome for every child, leading for progress and achievement for every child and every teacher, evidence guiding practice and actions, pathways developing and connecting along the whole educational journey, partnering with parents, employers, iwi and the community and, finally, building a thriving Kāhui Ako. At this stage it is too soon to make a definitive statement as to the difference Kāhui Ako are making, other than the anecdotal evidence from those who are involved in networks and understand their investment in them. Conversations during our research for this book suggested that, in Christchurch, possibly 40 per cent of Kāhui Ako were 'high performing' with leadership that was impactful and had changed education for the children in that Kāhui Ako. Estimates were made that a further 20 per cent were moving towards 'high performing'. But for some, there was still a great deal of work to be done to identify their high-impact strategies and flow these through the network. For these Kāhui Ako, it seemed to be a case of:

> We can't quite figure out what's going wrong. Something's not right. It's not happening for us.

These examples all highlight the level of nuance required for successful leverage and improved outcomes across partnerships. Leverage is about far more than a technical process of implementing evidence-based interventions: rather, it describes how leaders align a complex set of factors which, together, work to build capacity, social and intellectual capital, and thereby improve outcomes.

Conclusion

The chapter has explored the facets of Hargreaves' framework, but has also sought to show how it might be developed, for example to incorporate more recent work on epistemic communities and on learning systems. The chapter shows clearly that networks in all four countries are geared towards school improvement and effectiveness, certainly in the eyes of policymakers and also for most school leaders. But it also reveals wide differences in how these networks are shaped and operate to secure improvement. These differences partly reflect the different national contexts and frameworks, for example in how far school evaluation and accountability mechanisms operate summatively or formatively, but these differences do not explain differences between otherwise similar networks within each country. This is where Hargreaves' theory-based model helps to illuminate key themes, for example allowing us to interrogate how leaders conceptualize key issues such as the development of intellectual capital and the enactment of shared theories, codes and tools across network schools.

Throughout this chapter we have revealed a range of implications for network leadership when viewed through a school improvement and effectiveness lens. For example, using Hargreaves's terminology, we show how leaders in networks work to identify the capacity needs of individual schools and the overarching collective, and to then build capacity through structured approaches to sharing expertise and joint practice development. The more sophisticated network leaders work to achieve leverage and impact by strengthening intellectual and social capital across the group, for example by adopting routines which support the development of shared theories, language and tools for teaching and learning across schools. Importantly, we show that the leadership qualities and skills required to achieve these network outcomes are not always present, and that leaders in each country must work flexibly to respond to the needs and dynamics of their system and their particular partnership. This is why we argue in Chapter 9, where we discuss the implications for network leadership in more detail, that leaders must be skilled in three particular areas: working with paradox, sense-making and an ecosystem perspective.

6

Analysing Networks through the Lens of Governance Theory

Introduction

Governance theory draws on a range of theoretical traditions aimed at opening up 'the black box of the state' (Bevir 2011: 1). In education, as in other areas of the public sector, policymakers have commonly adopted New Public Management (NPM) approaches with the aim of making schools and school systems more responsive to the needs and wants of parents and more efficient, effective and accountable in their use of public money, although – as we explored in Chapter 2 – these approaches have been widely critiqued. Many NPM reforms in education seek to enact principles and practices derived from school effectiveness and improvement research: for example, where they increase school-level autonomy, focus school leaders on strengthening instructional capacity, and/or work to accelerate measured improvement in student test scores. However, governance theory recognizes that school effectiveness and improvement are not the *only* drivers of policy and practice in contemporary educational systems. Rather, policymaking and policy-implementation processes are frequently messy and multilayered, as a result of both established norms and expectations and the ways in which different stakeholders exercise their power (Ball and Juneman 2012; Skelcher 2000). In addition, policymakers frequently wrestle with 'wicked' problems that cannot be fully understood, can be in tension with each other, and to which proposed solutions depend on ideological preferences as much as evidence, making policymaking and implementation a complex and adaptive endeavour (Burns and Koster 2016; Rittel and Webber 1973).

Partly as a result of these issues, the state is seen to be adapting in many contexts, moving away from command and control towards what Jessop (2011) terms 'meta-governance'. This indicates how governments seek to achieve their goals by 'steering at a distance' (Hudson 2007), in particular by mixing and matching hybrid combinations of four coordinating mechanisms – hierarchy, markets, networks and community – as defined in Chapter 2. Each of these mechanisms is seen to have strengths but is also prone to common dysfunctions (Adler 2001): hierarchies can depress lateral relations and innovation; markets can erode trust and reproduce inequalities; networks can become exclusive and self-referential, while communities can struggle to cohere and to address multiple agendas in tandem. Hybrid combinations of these mechanisms can align successfully (Tenbensel 2017), but these combinations can also create tensions and paradoxes which can be passed through to frontline leaders to resolve (Greany and Earley 2017). As we explore below, one such tension seen commonly in marketized and network-based school systems is that schools are expected to compete against each other whilst also engaging in collaboration, requiring leaders to manage 'co-opetition' (Muijs and Rumyantseva 2014).

This chapter is structured in three main sections, addressing hierarchy and markets separately and then networks and community together, followed by a brief conclusion which seeks to draw out the key implications for network leadership. The hierarchy and markets sections focus mainly on system level developments across the four countries, while the networks and community section explores how these system level factors play out in the specific contexts of Bampton (England) and Aupaki (New Zealand).

Hierarchy

Greany and Higham (2018) define 'hierarchy' in terms of the formal authority of the state, which is exercised through statutory policies and guidance, national, regional and local bureaucracies, and performance management and intervention. In this section we explore similarities and differences in how hierarchical governance has developed and operates across our four case study countries, focussing on aspects that relate most strongly to inter-school networks, although we acknowledge that – for reasons of space – this treatment is necessarily selective and brief.

Each of our four case study countries has a distinctive reform trajectory, reflecting a range of factors such as historical development, differences in size and geography, and socio-economic, political and cultural factors. These differences make comparative analysis challenging (Scott et al. 2016), but it is possible to identify two common themes across the cases while recognizing that these play out differently in each system. Firstly, the schools we focus on in all four systems are publicly funded and accountable, meaning that hierarchical steering is an enduring feature, but while all four systems operated as relatively 'traditional' bureaucracies until the 1980s they have all sought to move away from that model in subsequent decades. This has included degrees of decentralization in all four systems, in which schools have been granted increased autonomy in relation to key areas, such as budgets, staffing and/or classroom pedagogy (aka school-based management), with parallel efforts to reshape local and national bureaucratic oversight structures. Secondly, partly as a result of decentralization, all four systems have encouraged the development of inter-school networks, often utilizing a combination of hard and soft governance mechanisms to incentivize these.

The country case studies (Chapters 1, 3 and 4) provide details on how public funding and accountability for schools – a core aspect of hierarchical oversight – operate in each system. As we see, there are some significant differences in what this means in practice. For example, Singapore's small and highly orchestrated system is described by local experts in terms of 'centralised-decentralisation' (Ng 2010) or a 'tight-loose-tight' approach (Toh et al. 2016), reflecting tight central prescription over aspects such as the curriculum and required student outcomes, together with a looser level of control over how schools operate to achieve these outcomes. Singapore has had just one party in power since independence, enabling both radical change (such as the Teach Less Learn More reforms) and significant continuity in how policies have been developed and enacted. This combination of change and continuity has been made possible by Singapore's collective focus on nation-building, its culture of pragmatism and tight levels of alignment across a small number of policy and practice bodies, such as the Ministry of Education and the National Institute of Education (NIE). Professor Pak Tee Ng from the NIE describes the dialogic and sometimes messy network governance model that supports this level of alignment:

> The officials from MOE, teachers from schools and teacher educators from NIE are constantly interacting through official and invisible networks about educational policies, school practices and teacher development. Such discussions are not always harmonious ... [but] change emerges through a process of advocacy, nudging, and mutual understanding, by parties united by a common purpose of education and nation-building.
>
> (Ng 2017: 180)

The size and diversity of our other three countries can make it hard to achieve and sustain Singapore's tightly orchestrated approach. For example, Greany (2018b) compares the experience of leading the national school leadership development colleges in Singapore and England (i.e. NIE and National College for School

Leadership),[1] showing how England's cluttered and fast-moving educational landscape requires its CEO to focus on strategic engagement with multiple different stakeholders, making it harder to retain a consistent focus when compared with the NIE. One aspect of the complexity in England, New Zealand and Chile is political change as a result of elections, and in Chile's case the ending of Pinochet's dictatorship. However, while changes in political power can certainly lead to significant shifts in educational policy, it seems that governments on both the left and right in all three countries have been relatively consistent in their focus on improving school quality and raising student outcomes, in line with the principles of NPM. For example, we saw how a left-leaning Labour government in New Zealand introduced the *Tomorrow's Schools* reforms in the 1980s, characterized as the 'closest in the world to the application of "economic rationalism"' (Easton 1994: 78). These market-oriented reforms had their parallel in both England and Chile in the 1980s, where right-wing governments under Thatcher and Pinochet introduced similar changes aimed at increasing choice and competition. Similarly, elected governments on both the right and left in all three countries have since sought to moderate the impact of markets and to increase the role of networks and collaboration, often with a particular focus on improving equity. For example, Chapter 3 described how a succession of centre-left Labour governments in England (1997–2010) introduced a range of networking initiatives, laying the ground for the 'Self-Improving, school-led system' agenda pursued by right-wing Conservative-led governments since 2010. Similarly, Chapter 4 explained how the right-wing National government in New Zealand introduced the Kāhui Ako |Communities of Learning programme in 2013, which has continued (although has not been expanded), with some widening of acceptable achievement challenges, under Jacinda Ardern's two Labour-led governments.

Critically, these generational shifts towards markets and, more recently, networks are never absolute and the role of hierarchical steering continues to be significant. For example, Montecinos, González and Ehren (2021: 201) conclude that although the network reforms in Chile represent 'a distinct break' from past, they nevertheless retain 'a managerial approach and hierarchical control by the Ministry of Education', not least through the influence of the accountability framework. Similarly, Greany and Higham (2018) show how, despite claiming to be 'moving control to the frontline' (DfE 2016: 8), the 'Self-Improving, school-led system' reforms underway in England since 2010 have actually served to intensify hierarchical governance and extend Labour's NPM reforms, with the system becoming more centralized as local authorities are rolled back and with sharper forms of accountability and intervention for schools judged to be underperforming.

New Zealand's approach represents an interesting comparison with England and Chile. As in those countries, the New Zealand government funds schools, sets national expectations regarding the curriculum and assessment and reviews school performance. However, these mechanisms do not have the same 'high stakes' implications as in England or Chile and the state does not undertake statutory intervention in individual schools, except as a point of 'last resort' or on the request of a school's board – a model we characterize as 'hierarchy-light'. Two developments are key to this: first, the Treaty of Waitangi has, over recent decades, gained increasing status. The Treaty now represents a legal and institutional framework that privileges the collective over the individual, thereby limiting any sense that the state can impose a single 'best' model for education (Macfarlane and Macfarlane 2019; O'Toole and Martin 2019); second, the sheer radicalism and extent of the *Tomorrow's Schools* reforms swept away local districts and established wholly self-managing schools, with no direct mechanisms for government control (Wylie 2012a, 2012b). For example, Section 75 of the 1989 Education Act states that 'except to the extent that any enactment or the general law of New Zealand provides otherwise, a school's board has complete discretion to control the management of the school as it sees fit'. More recent reforms, developed since 2017 by Jacinda Ardern's Labour-led governments, have sought to redress this balance and to strengthen the level of hierarchical coordination, although fierce resistance from some of the high-status schools that have benefitted most from autonomy has led to some of the more ambitious aspects of the reforms being removed or watered down. Nevertheless, the planned new Education Service Agency will have a purposeful regional presence as part of a redesigned Ministry of Education, offering support to schools but with the option of more direct influence, thereby aiming for 'greater alignment and coherence; clearer accountability; and rights of redress' (Ministry of Education 2019: 14).

Thus, hierarchical forms of coordination have evolved over time but have remained significant in all four systems. The agenda in all these systems has spanned left/right political divides and has remained aligned to NPM principles, seeking to reduce 'traditional' forms of bureaucratic oversight and to strengthen agency, accountability and responsiveness at school level. This focus on decentralization and school autonomy has been particularly obvious in England, Chile and New Zealand, with significant implications for both the 'middle tier' that has traditionally operated between schools and central governments, especially in larger systems (for example school districts and local education authorities), and for school-level leaders, who have faced increased pressure to demonstrate improvement along with vastly expanded workloads (Bonne and Wylie 2017; Gronn 2003). As noted above, New Zealand's reforms went furthest and fastest, with the wholesale removal of districts and the move to self-managing schools in the 1980s. In England, schools became self-managing in the same period, but local authorities – which form part of wider democratic local government structures – continued to play a role in overseeing local systems and addressing school performance concerns until the large-scale expansion of centrally funded academies after 2010. These recent changes have reduced the role and capacity of local authorities but have not eliminated them altogether (Cousin and Crossley-Holland 2021; Greany 2020a).

The shift towards school autonomy and the parallel reduction in 'middle tier' oversight in each system reflects similar, although locally nuanced, drivers and debates. For example, in New Zealand, three competing policy strands are seen to have shaped the initial reforms (Robinson and Ward 2005). First, a democratic-populist strand demanded continued parental participation in school governance. In this, the 'running of learning institutions … should be a partnership between the teaching staff (the professionals) and the community' (Department of Education 1988: xi). Second, a managerialist strand positioned local governance as a means to enhance effectiveness and efficiency of school management by 'freeing' actors from central bureaucracy. Third, a market-oriented strand was intended to increase the responsiveness of professionals to parents by encouraging competition for student enrolments (Fiske and Ladd 2000). However, in practice, research indicates that boards of trustees in New Zealand tend to approach governance as a procedural compliance activity in which the maintenance of cordial relations is prioritized over accountability and challenge, and when this is coupled with the limited educational expertise of most lay trustees there is insufficient focus on capacity building (Robinson and Ward 2005).[2] Furthermore, the shift to school autonomy and self-governance in New Zealand was seen to reflect three assumptions that were not borne out in practice (Wylie 2012a): that there was sufficient capability and capacity to identify needs and respond to them at individual school level; that competition was systemic and could somehow drive quality; and that school closure, where necessary, would be politically easy.

These challenges with school autonomy in New Zealand have strong echoes in England and Chile, where some schools have thrived, but others have struggled and become isolated in the context of inter-school competition and limited 'middle tier' coordination and capacity building (Montecinos, González and Ehren 2021; Greany and Higham 2018). One response in each system has been to try and reinvent the 'middle tier' (Lubienski 2014). For example, England has established a new model for hierarchical oversight through the expansion of MATs, although many schools and academies sit outside these arrangements and the system remains highly fragmented.³ Similarly, New Zealand is creating its regional Education Service Agency, while Chile is replacing its 345 municipalities with seventy Local Public Education Services (SLEs). However, in each case, the aim is not to simply replace one form of bureaucratic oversight with another, but to generate new ways of working in which schools retain their autonomy while also collaborating laterally, sometimes characterized as a process of 'middle out' change (Munby and Fullan 2016) which we explore in more detail in Chapter 10.

In parallel with restructuring the 'middle tier', therefore, policymakers in all three systems – and indeed in Singapore's more tightly orchestrated system – have sought to encourage the development of inter-school networks. In Table 6.1, we list the main strategies used by hierarchical policymakers to increase inter-organizational networking across the four countries and assess the benefits and common pitfalls of each approach. Clearly, this list is not exhaustive and the approaches are not mutually exclusive.

Table 6.1 Hierarchical strategies for fostering networks

Strategy	Examples	Benefits	Pitfalls
Incentives: Most commonly, offering time limited funding that groups of schools (and, sometimes, other partners) can bid for. Usually with a requirement that the partnership accounts for the use of the funding and reports specified outputs/outcomes.	Kāhui Ako |Communities of Learning – New Zealand. Teaching School Alliances – England.	Voluntary nature means that schools must commit to some level of collaborative working. Can encourage shared accountability for funding and outcomes – a focus on collaborative action.	Voluntary schemes achieve partial coverage – some schools unwilling or unable to participate. Risks of shallow/narrow collaboration. Time limited funding means impact may not be sustained.
Capacity building: Offering practical support and tools which help partnerships to become established – for example training programmes, expert facilitators, evidence/data packs to identify common challenges, partnership audits and so on.	Facilitators for Strategic Group – Bampton. Expert Partners – New Zealand. Clusters and networked learning communities (NLCs) – Singapore.	Builds capacity and commitment within schools. Can help jump-start new partnerships – avoiding 'rabbit holes'. Can support more effective forms of knowledge sharing.	Risks of over-reliance on the external facilitator. Partnership development processes can become time consuming and fail to secure genuine shared commitment/action.

Mandated: Networking is a legal requirement for some or all schools, often with specific expectations around governance structures, stakeholder involvement and so on.	School Improvement Networks (SINs) and Local Public Education Services (SLEs) – Chile.	Avoids risk of partial coverage. Specifying stakeholder and governance expectations can help avoid the 'dark side' of networks.	Risks of shallow/ formulaic collaboration. Focus on fulfilling technical requirements can stand in way of developing genuine shared commitment/ action.
Exhortation: Networking is encouraged – for example in ministerial speeches – and linked to moral purpose. 'System leadership' designations offer status and wider benefits to network leaders (for example income generation opportunities).	National Leaders of Education – England.	Creates normative climate/ expectations that schools will/should collaborate. 'System leader' designations can help identify network leaders and give them a degree of authority to initiate action.	Risks a focus on income generation (selling expertise across the network) over lateral knowledge exchange. 'System leadership' designations encourage internal hierarchies within networks.
Pressure: Existing forms of support for schools are removed, while new policies and expectations create pressure for change. Accountability frameworks might assess/report on network-level outcomes.	'Self-improving school-led system reforms' – England.	Creates genuine motivation to engage with networks as a source of information, exchange and mutual support. Shared accountability might help to reduce focus on individual school outcomes.	Can create a climate of fear, leading to instrumental focus on 'dragging and dropping' perceived best practices from higher-performing schools. Can encourage closed/exclusive networks and reduce equity – the strong supporting the strong.

In conclusion, this section has explored why and how hierarchical steering has become more complex in recent decades as policymakers have sought to mix hierarchical, market, network and – to a lesser extent – community forms of coordination in pursuit of enhanced school quality and learning outcomes. One interpretation is that there has been a shift over time from traditional forms of bureaucratic oversight (including via the 'middle tier'), to market-based coordination via school autonomy and parental choice, to lateral networks. However, we have shown that the reality is considerably more complex, as hierarchical and market forms of coordination continue and evolve, intersecting with each other and with network forms of coordination. This meta-governance model enables the state in all four systems to maintain a level of control, even if this is sometimes circumscribed. In these contexts, networks must, inevitably, operate at least to some extent 'in the shadow of hierarchy' (Scharpf 1994), but the ability of hierarchical strategies to initiate and shape networks is far from straightforward.

Markets

Greany and Higham (2018) define markets in terms of incentives and (de) regulation aimed at encouraging choice, competition and the commercialization of knowledge and expertise. As we outlined in the country case studies and explored further in the previous section, NPM-inspired reforms in all four countries have sought to increase school autonomy and to encourage parental choice and competition between schools, in the belief that this would drive up quality and increase responsiveness. However, countries that have introduced such market mechanisms have seen very limited evidence that competition leads schools to focus on improving teaching quality or to differentiate themselves through innovation strategies: rather, competition generally encourages schools to compete by cream-skimming the most 'desirable' students, leading to increased socio-economic stratification and inequality (Waslander et al. 2010; Lubienski 2009). For example, we saw how Chile's voucher system enabled aspirational parents to select private subsidized schools, leading to a collapse over time in the numbers attending public municipal schools. The impact of parental choice on school composition has been less brutal in New Zealand and England, but it nevertheless continues to shape local landscapes and to influence decisions around where and how to collaborate.

In New Zealand, *Tomorrow's Schools* introduced a deliberately marketized system. School home zones, which preserved the right of students to attend a local school, were abolished in 1991. This 'de-zoning' had a dual intent. In keeping with the broader context of neoliberal reform, it enabled enhanced parental choice while ostensibly increasing quality through fostering competition for students (Stubbs and Strathdee 2012). Competition was also linked to arguments of increased social mobility: underprivileged students would be 'empowered' to avoid what were deemed to be failing schools (Lauder et al. 1999). However, this marketization was complex in its manifestation. Thomson (2010) described the situation as a 'static universe', given the lack of desire of some schools to avail of the opportunity to broaden their student base: schools and students were differently positioned in regard to utilization of choice opportunities (Lauder et al. 1999). By 2000, given these dynamics, legislation was enacted by an incoming Labour-led government to protect the right of students to attend local schools, even where these were oversubscribed. Schools were permitted (but not required) to draw up a zone and selection system, subject to Ministry of Education approval, and working only to a loose definition that a school be a 'reasonably convenient school' (Rae 2002). Thus, schools were empowered, if they wished, to define the community they would serve, and the priorities under which any non-zone students would be selected (Pearce and Gordon 2005). More recently, under Jacinda Ardern's Labour-led reforms, control of school zones is shifting to the Ministry of Education.[4]

Similarly, in England, parental choice of school and the principle that funding follows the learner were introduced in the late 1980s. Subsequent research has shown how schools operate within local status hierarchies, in which schools at the top of the hierarchy are seen as the most prestigious and popular, while schools at the bottom are more likely to be undersubscribed and to serve higher proportions of disadvantaged children and/or those with additional needs. Schools in the middle of the hierarchy must compete against each other by enhancing their status, for example by achieving a higher Ofsted grade in order to signal to local parents that the school is successful. Greany and Higham's research (2018) included an analysis of national Ofsted inspection outcomes for all schools in England over a ten-year period (2005–15). This revealed a relationship between hierarchical inspection grades and the changing socio-economic composition of schools nationally. Schools that sustained or improved their judgement to Outstanding in the 2010–15 period saw, on average, a reduction in the percentage of students eligible for Free School Meals, while schools retaining or being downgraded to a Requires Improvement and Inadequate judgement saw, on average, an increase in free school meal eligibility. However, Greany and Higham's qualitative research also revealed that school status is determined by far more than Ofsted grades and is rarely a straightforward reflection of 'school quality'; rather it reflects a complex mix of factors that include the school's context, composition and history, together with its perceived performance, ethos and educational offer in relation to other schools locally. These findings fit with international research which indicates that parental choices are shaped by a complex range of factors, including considerations of social class and, to a lesser extent, race as much as by questions of school quality and academic outcomes (Waslander et al. 2010). Furthermore, in England, the playing field is not always level: since some schools can select students at entry, for example on the basis of faith or academic ability, while other schools have opted to exclude large numbers of 'harder to teach' children, who are more likely to be disadvantaged and/or to have special educational needs (Timpson 2019).

Three overarching findings can be drawn from Greany and Higham's (2018) research in relation to the influence of markets on collaboration in England:

- first, local patterns of competition and collaboration reflect three factors – the history of local relationships, the context of individual schools and the agency and values of leaders – but school leaders must always weigh up collaborative opportunities with an eye on how they might influence the school's positioning within the local status hierarchy;
- second, these issues play out differently between phases (for example primary versus secondary) and locales (for example rural versus urban);
- third, the reduced ability of local authorities to oversee place-based arrangements for student admissions and exclusions since 2010 has contributed to a wider sense of 'winners and losers', as schools that were already towards the top of local hierarchies have been able to benefit and entrench their position (for example by becoming a Teaching School or forming a MAT), while schools at the bottom have faced additional challenges.

In summary, policymakers in all four systems have seen networks as a means of counteracting some of the pitfalls associated with markets, for example by encouraging schools to share expertise and to collaborate to meet the needs of disadvantaged students. However, layering partnerships onto an existing stratified and competitive system is challenging. The fact that inter-school networks have formed in all four countries despite these competitive pressures does indicate that 'co-opetition' is feasible, but we have also outlined evidence (in Chapter 1) that many partnerships fail and/or develop in inequitable ways, partly as a result of competitive pressures (Armstrong et al. 2020; Paniagua and Istance 2018). Overall, we argue that networks in all four systems, but particularly Chile, England and New Zealand, operate 'in the shadow of markets' as well as 'the shadow of hierarchy' and that individual school leaders cannot be expected to overcome competitive pressures without active support combined with wider efforts to mitigate their impact, for example through hierarchical interventions to enforce more equitable models for school admissions as seen in Chile and New Zealand.

Networks and community

In Chapter 2, we set out the distinction between network and community forms of coordination: where 'networks' co-ordinate action on the basis of trust and are typically encouraged in public services through incentives for inter-organizational collaboration, while 'communities' foreground self-reliant solutions by citizens and providers based on shared values, identities and accountabilities. This distinction between network and community forms of coordination helps us to analyse different forms of partnership, although the distinctions are not always clear-cut. For example, in New Zealand, many pre-existing partnerships have chosen to become officially supported Kāhui Ako (i.e. networks), but others have chosen not to apply for the initiative – potentially remaining closer to self-organizing communities. This might reflect a political choice to retain the autonomy inherent under *Tomorrow's Schools*. Equally, it might reflect a lack of understanding of the eventual flexibility around achievement challenges that was won within the Kāhui Ako programme, or a view that the dedicated roles established for Kāhui Ako have insufficient flexibility. Certainly, similar concerns around the implications for existing networks of becoming formally recognized can be observed in England. Greany and Higham's (2018) study revealed that when existing 'community' networks chose to become formally recognized Teaching School Alliances, they were changed in the process. For example, because the model requires that one high-performing school is designated as the official Teaching School, this can disrupt an existing partnership that is built on equal and reciprocal relationships, with the lead school now taking a more dominant position, even if this is not its overt intention. For these reasons, we argue that networks operate more clearly 'in the shadow of hierarchy', while community-style partnerships are more able to operate independently but can also be more fragile and dependent on individual relationships and agency.

All four systems have encouraged the development of inter-school partnerships, drawing on combinations of incentives, capacity-building, mandated requirements, exhortation and pressure (Table 6.1). How these strategies are combined and deployed has important implications for the partnerships that form in each context. For example, New Zealand's Kāhui Ako policy offers funding tied to what can appear to be a bureaucratic set of requirements around role appointments, whereas England's system leadership models and Singapore's innovation hub schools have relied on identifying successful schools and encouraging them to design and lead lateral networks within a relatively non-prescriptive framework. All three models rely on voluntarism, with schools choosing whether or not to opt in, resulting in a patchwork of engagement and action, whereas Chile's mandated approach seeks to ensure that all schools participate in networks over time. The composition, size, depth and breadth of partnerships also vary widely, sometimes because of market-driven competition, but also in relation to the aims and approaches adopted by different partnerships. For example, Hung et al.'s (2016) analysis in Singapore distinguishes between partnerships that are 'designed deep' and those that are 'designed wide', reflecting differences in the types of innovation being scaled, with associated differences in network size, peer-learning approach and support requirements.

England's partnership landscape is described in Chapter 3, highlighting that most schools are engaged in at least one partnership. This showed how partnership working became more important to schools after 2010, as a result of rapid hierarchical changes which served to remove existing support while increasing central accountability pressures. Different localities across England responded to these developments in different ways, so Bampton provides just one example, although it is not untypical (Greany 2020a). The previously strong Local Authority effectively disintegrated in the period after 2010, leaving school principals feeling isolated. They formed the six local collaboratives to provide peer support as well as shared capacity and ideas on how to manage externally driven change. Six Teaching School Alliances were also formed, led by local schools, while around ten principals were designated as National Leaders of Education. School leaders felt intense pressure to perform well in Ofsted inspections, but the weakened Local Authority had limited capacity to support them, leading to a loss of trust locally. Partly as a result, many schools became academies at this time: higher-performing schools converted voluntarily, thereby freeing themselves up from Local Authority oversight, while lower-performing schools were forced to become sponsored academies within one of the twelve MATs that began to operate in the town. Three of these MATs were large, national chains, while the remainder were run by higher-performing local schools based in Bampton or neighbouring authorities. By the end of the decade, the Local Authority had begun to re-establish itself in a new, more facilitative role, thanks to the arrival of the new Director and the attempt to establish the Bampton Education Partnership. However, the continuing poor performance of schools together with high levels of poverty in the town led the national government to designate Bampton as an Opportunity Area, investing significant money into a place-based approach to improvement. This was by no means an attempt to re-establish the Local Authority as a 'middle tier': academies and MATs retained their autonomy and the time-limited programme was governed and operated separately from the Local Authority, staffed by civil servants seconded from the national Department for Education. Nevertheless, the Opportunity Area Board and leaders came to recognize that some level of local strategic coherence would be required if the impact of the programme's work was to be sustained over time. This led them to work with the Local Authority to initiate the Strategy Group which shaped and then launched the new Bampton Alliance.

Bampton's story reveals several important points about how school and system leaders respond to hierarchical and market pressures as they work to form network and community partnerships:

- Firstly, we see that the collapse of the Local Authority does lead schools to work together to form the six collaboratives, an example of 'bottom up' community governance. Each collaborative had a different form and focus, reflecting the agency and priorities of the leaders who shaped them. However, chairing the collaboratives was frustrating – 'you feel like you are the owner of something, but without the power, it's all buy in' – and there was a view that competitive pressures combined with wider developments prevented them from moving beyond a superficial level of partnership working – 'it's all around competition and league tables'. Some principals did value the collaboratives as a forum for mutual support, but others had been disbanded as schools moved off into different MATs. Meanwhile, some schools had formed stronger community partnerships – such as the Swan Partnership – and had chosen not to become a MAT or Teaching School Alliance; however, the limited coverage of such partnerships meant they were not a place-based solution for all schools.
- Second, Bampton was awash with designated 'system leader' Teaching Schools and NLEs, but this had not provided sufficient capacity or impetus for area-wide improvement. One issue was the design of the scheme: Teaching Schools received some limited core funding from the government, but there was always an expectation that they would generate additional income by selling improvement services to other schools across their alliance (DfE 2010). This drove what Greany and Higham (2018) characterize as a 'new economy of knowledge', in which high-performing

schools were encouraged to plug the gaps in provision created by the loss of local authorities by commodifying and selling their expertise, for example through leadership and professional development programmes. Market pressures thus shaped the work of these system leaders, pitting them in competition with each other and preventing a collective focus on place-based priorities.

- Third, competition now operated at the level of the town's twelve MATs, in addition to school level. MAT leaders in Bampton, as elsewhere, were being encouraged by officials from central government to grow, by taking on new schools – a way of securing economies of scale (Bernardinelli et al. 2018). However, the scope for growth was limited, since all except one secondary school in the town was already in a trust. One MAT – formed by the highest-performing secondary school in Bampton – had been able to grow by gaining government funding to open a new 'free' school. As a church school, the new school would be able to select 50 per cent of its intake based on parental faith criteria. Other local MAT leaders feared the new school would attract the most aspirational parents, given the strong 'brand' of the founding school and its faith-based admissions code, effectively cream-skimming potential students from their own schools' catchments.

These issues all played into the development of the Bampton Alliance as a place-based meta-partnership. The new Alliance represents a pragmatic attempt to combine hierarchical and network forms of governance, in order to moderate local competitive pressures and to secure sustained, joined-up action in pursuit of town-wide improvement for all children. Paradoxically, the Alliance was forged through a partnership between the central government's Opportunity Area and the Local Authority – that is, a Conservative (right wing) government that is fiercely committed to academization and the roll-back of Local Authorities, and a Labour-controlled (left wing) local authority that has come to accept the realities of an academized landscape. The Alliance seeks to engage all schools, academies and MATs across the town and describes itself as 'school-led', not least because it will need to rely on schools paying membership fees to fund its work beyond the start-up phase, although it can hardly be characterized as a bottom-up community initiative. Seen positively it might be positioned as an example of 'middle out' change (Munby and Fullan 2016). Certainly, there are equivalent locality partnerships operating in several other contexts across England, indicating the potential of the model. Gilbert (2017) explains that all of the local partnerships she studied across England had been 'birthed' by their Local Authority, indicating the need for hierarchical support at the outset. Whether Bampton's Alliance succeeds or not remains to be seen but, in initiating the work, the Opportunity Area Director was clear on two things: first, 'the status quo wasn't tenable', and second, despite the town's numerous MATs, system leaders and a reinvigorated LA, no one had felt willing or able to step forward to initiate an area-wide approach until the Opportunity Area itself intervened.

Turning to New Zealand, the presence of both network and community forms of coordination are equally evident, as are the drivers – individual, social, economic and political – that influence decisions as to where a given collaboration positions itself. Again, several features are worth highlighting:

- First, education in Aotearoa, as a system, is accountable to the principles derived from the Treaty of Waitangi: partnership, participation and protection. All educators are trained, and work within, the requirement to engage with and embrace a Māori worldview – one that is fundamentally collective (Macfarlane and Macfarlane 2019; O'Toole and Martin 2019). Partnerships can and do still operate in the shadow of hierarchy and markets, but there is a nationwide, mediating force for collaborative engagement. For example, an important aspect of Aukapi Kāhui Ako's work has focussed on strengthening links with local iwi and hapū [tribes and sub-tribes].
- Second, as we outline above, Aotearoa's hierarchical accountability framework is less 'high stakes' than England's, arguably giving schools greater latitude to engage in partnerships. However, hierarchy impacts in other ways – for example, the Kāhui Ako framework brings significant money but is also relatively prescriptive, requiring defined roles and a focus on agreed 'achievement challenges'. Interestingly, in our research for this book, respondents noted that some school leadership teams were disconnected from the work of their wider Kāhui Ako, as were some boards of trustees. It seems that some school cultures were better able than others to make internal and external collaboration 'real', and that the prescribed nature of the Kāhui Ako roles was, at times, not able to overcome this.
- Third, the impact of *Tomorrow's Schools* and the market-based approach it ushered in continues to resound. Some teachers and principals have had no experience of any system other than that of self-managing schools. However, this normalization of competition is not preventing schools from collaborating, stimulated by events such as the Christchurch earthquakes

and 2019 Mosque shootings, and by growing commitment to the Treaty of Waitangi. For example, we saw in Chapter 3 how Linwood's roll dropped by around 25 per cent in the years after parental choice was introduced in 1991, as aspirational parents sought higher-decile schools. Linwood's roll dropped further after the 2011 earthquake, exacerbated by internal discord, potentially making it an unattractive partner for the higher-decile Bays Cluster of primaries. The appointment of an experienced principal at Linwood as it exited statutory management, together with government investment for a complete rebuild of the College, has generated new collaborative opportunities which are, in turn, being leveraged through Linwood's active involvement in two local Kāhui Ako.

Conclusion

This chapter has explored the ways in which hierarchical, market, network and community forms of governance operate, separately and in combination, to shape the work of schools and school leaders in our four case study countries. We argue that partnerships of publicly funded schools must, inevitably, operate in the shadow of hierarchy, but we also show how hierarchical oversight continues to evolve as governments across the political spectrum pursue improvement and equity by applying the broad principles of NPM in their national context. From the 1980s onwards, this has included a focus on markets, most obviously through an emphasis on school autonomy and parental choice, but also through the encouragement of markets in school improvement services, particularly in England. More recently, governments have adopted a range of strategies to encourage networks and, less commonly, 'bottom up' community-style partnerships of schools. One significant outcome from these changes relates to the 'middle tier' that operates between central government and schools – a topic that we return to in Chapter 10.

Drawing out the implications for network leadership, we show how leaders in all four systems must acknowledge and navigate hierarchical and market pressures if they are to forge successful partnerships. At times, addressing hierarchical requirements might appear relatively straightforward – for example, deciding whether to accept government funding, or not – but leaders must also appreciate and address the consequences of hierarchical engagement. For example, we saw how existing, bottom-up partnerships in England that chose to become Teaching School Alliances were changed in the process, as the designated school took on the status of 'first among equals'. Similarly, in New Zealand, we saw that some existing networks have chosen not to become Kāhui Ako, presumably because they want to retain the autonomy and shared identity of a 'community' network. Markets add a further level of complexity for network leaders to navigate, in particular as a result of the inter-school competition and local status hierarchies which flow from parental choice policies. In Bampton, we see how local competition now operates at MAT as well as school levels; for example, as MAT leaders work to grow their trusts by opening new 'free' schools or by taking over existing schools. This MAT-level competition partly explains why the existing Bampton Education Partnership has struggled to achieve place-based coherence, so the work of the Strategy Group sought to acknowledge these tensions and to overcome them through commitment to a collective moral purpose as well as the pragmatic need to address shared challenges. These issues, which stem from overlapping and sometimes conflicting governance mechanisms, require leaders to prioritize things that can be in tension; for example, the needs of their own school and the needs of the collective. This is why we argue in Chapter 9 that network leaders must be able to work productively with tensions and paradox, to engage in collective sense-making and to adopt an ecological 'whole system' approach.

7

Analysing Networks through the Lens of Complexity Theory

Introduction

In the first chapter of his book *School Leadership and Complexity Theory*, Keith Morrison defines complexity as a theory of 'survival, evolution, development and adaptation'. Early in the chapter, Morrison (2002: 5–6) invites the reader to consider the example of a teaching principal in a small, four teacher, rural primary school in a remote 'introverted' area of the UK with few employment opportunities for adults. Morrison's school 'enjoys good relationships with parents' but these are limited to 'formal meetings' and visits on the occasion of special events. Disenchanted with government reforms and sensing that there is little likelihood of change, the principal takes early retirement. A new principal is appointed. She decides the students will need to be equipped for the changing world, and this likely involves exploring opportunities that lie beyond the local. Her aim is to extend the horizons of the local populations, including placing a greater emphasis on digital technologies, and to position the school as a community resource. She consults with teachers, and arranges a series of open meetings with parents, around how the school could move forward. Over time, out of hours classes in information technologies are developed for adults, the school becomes a centre of advertisement of employment opportunities and all the teachers shift their pedagogy to make the curriculum both digitally based and learner-centred. A small building programme is implemented, resulting in a learner-resource suite. As well, parent-assistants become a regular part of school life:

> within one year the school has changed from a slightly sleepy, if well-intentioned and friendly, place, into a vibrant community with links and connections to the outside community and beyond. In the school, teachers 'share' classes and work

together far more closely, and involve parents in decision making on curricular and pedagogic matters – the school has moved from benevolent autocracy to participatory democracy. Children and parents have raised aspirations.

Morrison goes on to analyse this shift using complexity theory. The departure of the former principal acts as a critical bifurcation point: in other words, events had reached a state where there was no option other than to find a new 'resolution'. This bifurcation results in a new principal for the school. The new principal is open to exploring the changing environment, and the need to build 'external connectedness'. New forms of external connectedness in turn demand changing forms of 'internal connectedness'. This contributes to – but is also an effect of – the principal's leadership which involves a facilitatory focus, with careful regard to communication. Morrison argues that 'the school has changed through self organization… a new organization has emerged in the form of team-based teaching… . Further, the school has become an open system', which has had an impact on the local environment, changing the opportunities for community members. Each of the chapters in *School Leadership and Complexity Theory* elaborates on processes of self-emergence. For Morrison, complexity theory is not just an interesting lens through which to understand how schools survive, evolve, develop and adapt, or not. Rather, he notes Fullan's argument that to be successful 'beyond the very short run' organizations including businesses and schools '*must* incorporate moral purpose; understanding of complexity science; and respect, build, and draw on new human relationships with hitherto uninvolved constituencies inside and outside the organization' (2001: 70, our emphasis). Twenty years later, these imperatives towards a moral purpose, a necessary understanding of complexity science, and the forging of new internal and external relationships speak directly to the growing uptake of educational networks as a global policy instrument (Azorín 2020).

Our intent in this chapter is to draw on examples from our case studies to illustrate how insights from complexity theory can inform our understanding of education networks as systems and subsystems that sustain themselves within evolving environments. In this chapter, we build on elements in the two preceding chapters both of which gave an oblique nod to the presence of complexity in the context of individual schools, and in networks of schools and other entities. Our discussion is mindful of the five subsystems of education identified by Hawkins and James (2018): the teaching staff system, the ancillary staff system, the student system, the parent system and, finally, significant other systems, such as governance organizations, inspection and accreditation agencies, policymaking entities and so on. Our approach is to explore the presence of Davis and Sumara's (2008) four complexity conditions – internal diversity, internal redundancy, neighbour interactions and decentralized control – before moving to consider the implications of self-organization and emergence for understanding education networks and their leadership.

Four complexity conditions

Internal diversity

The first complexity condition articulated by Davis and Sumara is *internal diversity*. This refers to the representational diversity within a network, and how this diversity acts as a source of innovation in responding to emergent circumstances. As we detailed in Chapter 1, internal diversity cannot be assumed in education networks. Rather, homophily is evident: people with like characteristics tend to be connected in bonded, often closed, networks. Here, social capital is evident in the norms – the isomorphism – that closed networks facilitate (Greany 2020b). There is, in this, evidence of the paradox of networks. Networks, including education networks, function most effectively by being simultaneously highly clustered in their strong links, which provide the basis for complementary cognition, while also benefitting from weak links, which can help to ensure diversity and access to wider influences and resources (Granovetter 1973). In this, successful education networks likely take the form of small worlds (Kamp 2013b; Buchanan 2002).[1] Within this, the whole-in-action is able to leverage individual resources in ways that generate innovation beyond what can be achieved by an individual school, thereby reaching the highest possible degree of complex behaviour (Nowotny 2005). Internal diversity shifts the focus from the human capital of individuals to the social capital of groups: what is able to be imagined through combining diverse insights in pursuit of shared goals which, for Fullan, would be framed around a moral purpose. It also shifts the focus of those in positional roles: rather than managing conflict by lessening it, the aim is to see the boundary work inherent in diversity as a resource (Arena and Uhl-Bien 2016).

This internal diversity and its powerful potential are evident in the context of Kāhui Ako in Aotearoa. Here, the literature suggests that even at the point of policy development, some educationalists were willing to 'get into the tent' to voice their concerns. This helped mediate some perceived limitations in the policy proposal (Thrupp 2018).[2] The need to name, and work productively with, conflict is a leadership task at all nested levels of the system. As such, it might involve lead advisors in the Ministry, lead principals, and/or across and within school teachers, as well as those who do not take on a named role but who focus their professional efforts through the structure of the Kāhui Ako. In Aupaki, the Bays Cluster from which the Kāhui Ako evolved did exhibit homophily and strong bonds generated through twelve years of cooperation. In moving into the opportunity for further support generated by *Investing in Educational Success*, the focus shifted to encompass collaboration around shared goals for the students in the broader community, including early childhood education and secondary. As Chapter 4 details, this has brought socio-economic and cultural diversity into play: Aupaki Kāhui Ako is focused on a moral purpose and achievement challenges that engage education providers working with communities who will transition into what is currently Linwood College, and who come from very different socio-economic communities than Linwood's current intake. The lead principal of the Kāhui Ako, and the principal of Linwood College, both see this diversity as offering opportunity for growth and innovation in the community as a whole. Yet this innovation through internal diversity is challenging work in a context where, for the past three decades, the system has been configured for schools to first and foremost, consider their immediate community. In our conversations in preparation for this book we were told:

> [There have been] Kāhui Ako where there's been higher decile or higher performing schools who have said, "Look, these are your problems and I can't take time out of my school to help you guys do this," and that's caused divisions. Those divisions were probably already there, but they were asked to come together to work together and they weren't able to get past that, and that to me has been really sad to see that happen; to see people actually stand up and say, "I'm not willing to help. My reputation is such that I don't want it tarnished with your school." That sort of conversation – that's been a big shame.

Internal diversity also has implications for the formation of trust. Trust is essential in a context of risk which is sustained, in part, by competitive funding mechanisms and relationships that lack a commitment to social investment. Our research in Aotearoa indicates that trust cannot be assumed, even in contexts where schools have cooperated over sustained periods through some form of shared identity, such as geographical location or being faith-based. In those contexts where new relationships form, the development of trust will take time. As we noted in Chapter 2, a critical point here is that one cannot know in advance as to the optimal membership to enable a network's 'appropriately intelligent action' (Davis and Sumara 2008: 39). Maintenance of diversity is critical even as the network settles into its work. This can present challenges. An example would be balancing a desire for representational diversity, through encouraging new members and new linkages, while at the same time seeking to establish the kinds of shared theories, language and tools required for an epistemic community (Glazer and Peurach 2015). As we argued in Chapter 5, there is evidence that educational networks benefit by establishing shared routines, boundary spanner roles, measurement tools and sense-making structures which allow diverse schools and professionals to build trust. As a respondent in Aotearoa noted:

> You have to start doing some work and start trusting each other and start building that routine of collaborative work, and then you can fine-tune it, but you have to start with something.

However, success is not guaranteed. For example, in Singapore, Toh et al. (2014: 835) note that despite a policy effort to 'actualize deep twenty-first century learning', the changes have resulted in 'short-lived ripples that fail to culminate into systemic impacts beyond the enclaves of individual schools'. As we sketched in Chapter 1, Singapore's 'success' in international rankings has been attributed to having fewer than 400 schools, tight central control exercized by a single political party and a pragmatic focus on efficiency and effectiveness. These very success factors might limit the kind of systemic work that Toh et al. argue is required for the task including establishing diverse connections within and across influential subsystems.

Internal redundancy

The second condition of *internal redundancy* refers to the necessity of overlaps, duplications and excesses within the system. These layers enable interactions through generating invitational moments when people encounter one another, share information and generate knowledge as a social learning system (Wenger 1998). They also compensate for system weaknesses, securing a network from failure at cutpoints when one node – be it an individual person or a group – is all that is holding the network together (McCormick et al. 2011). By definition, NPM with its pursuit of efficiency demands the removal of redundancy: the potential to maintain stores of internal redundancy in education cannot be taken for granted. Given this, the ability to foster and sustain internal redundancy warrants attention to who is appointed to positional leadership roles and whether they have the disposition and ability to open spaces for joint practice development and social learning, despite structural mechanisms and norms that can be contrary to the collaborative policy agenda.

In the context of Christchurch, educational spaces that enable internal redundancy are common, given the number of schools that have been repaired or rebuilt as modern learning environments, shared campuses and so on. The New Zealand case study indicated that, as experience of network leadership grows, so does diversity and redundancy, and thereby fitness for purpose. The Aupaki lead principal referenced his apprenticeship within another Kahui Ako prior to being appointed to the Aupaki role. Yet, in Kāhui Ako the policy stipulations as to who can apply for the leadership roles preclude one avenue towards internal redundancy.

> It became quite clear mid-roll out of the policy that the senior leadership team of [a] school had been completely isolated from the Kāhui Ako. They couldn't be leads and they couldn't be across schools teachers and they couldn't be within school teachers so they said, "This isn't something for us to be involved in".... One of those senior leadership people is going to have to step up and be the person that leads the school while the principal is leading the Kāhui Ako, so they actually take on more work that again isn't related to the Kāhui Ako and so they're out....They need to be in, they need to know what's happening and to be able to promote this at the department level and at the class room level where they're mentoring the other teachers and doing all that sort of thing, and if they're not involved and they're not invested, it doesn't have the same flow through the whole school.

Drawing from our English case study, Bampton is symptomatic of many localities in England ten years into the government's 'self-improving school-led system' reforms (Greany 2020a). Accordingly, it is replete in both diversity and redundancy – a context which offers significant opportunities for schools and leaders who are willing and able to grasp them, but which also leads to unhelpful levels of fragmentation, balkanization and inequality between schools (Greany and Higham 2018). The reforms were deliberately designed to disrupt the previous Labour government's universalist model in which *all* schools were encouraged, or even required, to engage with most new policies and expectations. The 2010 white paper stated that school leaders should 'feel highly trusted to do what they believe is right' (DfE 2010: 18), facilitated by reducing the co-ordinating role of local authorities. Higher-performing schools could thus choose whether or not to become an academy, form a MAT, or apply to become a Teaching School, but many schools were unwilling or unable to participate in these ways, creating a more diverse – even chaotic – system. One school leader interviewed by Greany and Higham (2018: 97) put it as follows:

> 'System' implies that there's a good degree of articulate design. And I think what's happening nationally is that there are all sorts of systems. The academization of secondary schools, more than primary schools, in fact, has meant that there has been a range of responses. And I don't think it was thought through politically, how to structure that with the loss – no one had really worked out what to do if you lost local authorities.... So, there isn't really a system, and I think there are lots of emergent means of managing the problem that was set up. But nobody knows what works.

By 2019, the impact of this approach was evident in Bampton, with six different Teaching Schools and twelve different MATs working independently and, at times, in a variety of sub-alliances. These developments were layered on to a deeper set of substructures and cultures, adding further levels of complexity; for example, with differences between schools by phase (primary/secondary), specialism (mainstream/special) and/or ethos (Catholic, Church of England, secular).[3] These issues had not prevented many schools from forming a variety of productive partnerships, with differing levels of homophily, internal diversity and redundancy: for example, in Chapter 3 we described the Swan Partnership, comprising eight primaries and one secondary school. However, other partnerships – such as the six local collaboratives – had largely dissolved in the face of increasing internal diversity, as member schools joined different MATs. Ultimately, the degree of systemic fragmentation, the evidence that shared priorities were not being addressed and that some schools had become unhelpfully isolated, led local system leaders to initiate the Strategy Group and to support the new Bampton Alliance.

The new alliance seeks to encompass a high level of internal diversity and redundancy, bringing together the various constituencies sketched above into an overarching place-based partnership, but the challenge with such diversity was to secure meaningful engagement from all schools. Helpfully, the Opportunity Area leader who commissioned and funded the work recognized the need to give time and space for the new solution to emerge, wanting to avoid 'surface commitment', 'we need to do a proper piece of work that really unpicks the problems, that people commit to the solutions that need to take place'. As in Aupaki, the first step was to articulate and commit, collectively, to the shared moral purpose inherent in providing the best possible education for all children in Bampton. Securing agreement on the 'case for change' and 'what are we trying to achieve' statements was important, facilitated by the deep commitment that all leaders in the group had to Bampton and its community. However, this commitment was not enough in itself to overcome the level of diversity and to galvanize action. While Bampton exists as a geographical place and its political and social history makes it meaningful in the eyes of the school leaders and teachers who work there, it is by no means a fixed or bounded system, reflecting the polymorphic and multidimensional character of socio-spatial relations (Gulson 2011; Jessop, Brenner and Jones 2008). Thus, Bampton is also part of a larger conurbation, part of England's national education system and part of a global educational community connected via Twitter and so on. In this sense, Bampton is a construct – which had been weakened by rollback of the Local Authority, but which the new alliance was seeking to reimagine and reinvigorate through both rhetorical commitment and practical action (Papanastasiou 2017). Building commitment to this new place-based alliance involved action on multiple fronts; for example, the visits to established place-based partnerships in other parts of England gave strategy group members confidence that change was possible, while bringing in high-profile speakers to the away days helped to give the work legitimacy. Meanwhile, more prosaic but equally important work behind the scenes helped to develop a sense of momentum: for example, the Opportunity Area Director explained how he worked to secure good attendance at the away days 'speaking to everyone every couple of weeks', doing 'the donkey work', because 'I need them to show up and contribute and commit'.

The attempt to build this sense of momentum around the potential for a new Bampton-wide alliance which could overcome the level of fragmentation in the system and generate new and productive forms of collaboration reflects what complexity theorists term the *snowball effect* (Mason 2016), similar to historical institutionalist work on path dependency and institutional change (Streeck and Thelen 2005). The snowball effect suggests that once the momentum of a phenomenon is established – for example, towards either fragmentation or productive collaboration in Bampton – it will tend to become locked in until a competing phenomenon results in a redirection of that path. It also signals the importance of positive feedback; indeed Mason (2016: 47) cites Waldrop (1993: 34) to explain that to complexity theorists, 'positive feedback seem[s] to be the *sine qua non* of change, … of life itself'. Thus, the aim is to establish the 'school-led' alliance and to achieve enough early progress to provide evidence that the new approach can add value, because this positive feedback will facilitate stronger commitment, which will enable the new ways of working to become locked in – the snowball will gather pace. Of course, as we explore in Chapter 9, success requires network leaders who can turn the excesses of place-based diversity and redundancy into a strength for complex coactivity (Davis and Sumara 2008), rather than always seeing these as a barrier.

Neighbour interactions

Internal redundancy creates a context for the third condition for complexity: *neighbour interactions*. By means of connection and being 'neighbourly', interactions enable new ideas as 'potentials to action' to be activated (Davis and Sumara 2008: 40). The key idea here, and one that we expand on in Chapter 8, is that while social networks and group interactions are 'undeniably important', they are not necessarily the critical component in networking, when viewed through the lens of complexity theory. It is, rather, the rubbing of one idea, hunch, question, insight against another that breaks thinking through to a new level, and the potential for system change in which both the actors and the structures move towards 'more sophisticated possibilities'. As we noted earlier, this condition is mediated to some extent by the need for a basis for interaction which, we suggest in Chapter 5, lies in a deliberate focus on creating the conditions for epistemic communities to develop, characterized by their shared theories, language and tools.

Davis and Sumara (2008: 40) argue that, in the academic context, these neighbour interactions would include 'conferences, seminars, journals, hallway interactions, visiting professorships, and wiki spaces' and so on. In the context of educational networks, the equivalent might be the 'sense-making structures' outlined in Chapter 5, which bring key leaders from across the network together to explore shared measurement data and to ask questions about what this tells them. However, if these sense-making structures are always instrumentally focused on school improvement and effectiveness there is a risk that they will not allow ideas to 'stumble' across one another (Davis and Sumara 2008: 41), in the ways that complexity theory suggests is valuable (we say more about sense-making as a network leadership quality in Chapter 9). This presents particular challenges for government instituted networks, given their tendency to focus attention on structures rather than processes and underpinning values. Our research from Aotearoa illustrates both aspects of this dynamic. On the one hand, case study leaders at both Ministry and network level clearly articulated the necessarily experimental nature of the work they were undertaking. They were hesitant to adopt a position of confidence in how one proceeded from day to day, and location to location. A Kāhui Ako member principal responded to a question as to whether they believed the Ministry would be confident of how the policy implementation was progressing:

> I doubt if they are confident. The smart ones won't be confident 'cos who would be confident with such a hairy beast that you're trying to wrestle with. You know? Far out.

Often, these leaders continue to work with policy instruments that were, in the decentralized education system of Aotearoa, largely considered too prescriptive. As some of our earlier research indicated, without change to align policy instruments at the macro-level with policy intent, the first-order business of neighbour interactions can be subservient to the second-order business of applying, approving and accounting around the use of public money and particular measures of success (Kamp 2013a, b). Policies, guidelines and procedures are, in themselves, neighbours who interact with particular effect and, once implemented, must be 'lived up to' (Ball 2000: 9). Yet macro-level policies can be mediated by instruments at the local level, with positive effect. Such local-level instruments focus less on structures, and more on creating opportunities for ideas to 'stumble across one another' (Davis and Sumara 2008: 40).

In Bampton, we saw how the strategy group's proposals for the new alliance were designed to bring the different phases and constituencies together to address shared challenges and to pursue a local vision for education. By the end of the process there was clear evidence that levels of neighbourly interaction between the members of the group itself had increased, despite all the divisions that systemic fragmentation and competition had accentuated. For example, the local authority's Director of Education explained that members of the strategy group had continued to meet on a weekly basis throughout the first six months of the COVID-19 pandemic, but now with a focus on addressing the public health crisis. In his estimation, this level of focused collaboration would not have been possible if the group had not built social capital in their work together during the preceding year. Equally, as we saw in Chapter 3, the new research breakfasts introduced as a result of the group's recommendations were described by one MAT CEO as 'the best thing that (we've) ever done'. Of course, these meetings and breakfasts could have been convened even if the Strategy Group had never existed, but the point is that the trust and social capital developed through the strategy group's work have facilitated a level of commitment and openness that would not have been possible otherwise.

Decentralized/dispersed control

The fourth condition to facilitate emergence – *decentralized/dispersed control* – extends this point. While the prior condition considers the need to let go of representational control, this condition focuses on leadership itself. We will return to this condition in detail in Chapter 9. For now, our focus is on how the role of the named leader is to create possibilities for emergence to occur. This brings us to the paradoxical context of needing leaders who, when acting in their role as a network leader, at times do so with minimal profile. In the context of education, members of subsystems of teachers, ancillary staff and parents and, in particular, students must be able to participate in decisions concerning their experiences (Davis and Sumara 2008). The complexity in this dance of being 'the' leader and spokesperson at some times and in some places, whilst fading into the background in others, is clearly evident in our case study countries. As we surveyed in Chapter 1, in Chile, a mindset of hierarchical leadership predominates, placing practice in tension with policy. In Singapore, too, hierarchical leadership is evident, yet to some extent at least is able to serve the network policy agenda given a centralized commitment for educational leadership to be nationally focused, even if not dispersed to staff, let alone students or parents, at the local level.

In Aotearoa, leadership might be said to be dispersed at times. Given the autonomy of schools, there is no one way that leaders are required to lead. During our research, a respondent noted that the way a principal leads a school is indicative of the way they would lead a Kāhui Ako. There is no structure or norm that demands hierarchy, yet the prestige attached to positional roles effects some influence as to how widespread leadership will become. A principal within Aupaki who is not the lead principal noted his attentiveness to ensuring that, in the context of any Kāhui Ako meeting, he very deliberately assumes his role as a middle (Ramsey and Poskitt 2019), letting the lead principal lead. In our discussion, we considered the limits of this process of respecting the positional role. We can consider here the potential of the Māori concept of ako, which refers to reflective and reciprocal nature of the teaching and learning relationship. In the context of leading education networks, an orientation of simultaneously leading and following has resonance. The intent of the collaborative policy agenda is to bring the forms of capital (Bourdieu 1986) held by the collective together in pursuit of the shared goal. The appointment of a Kāhui Ako lead principal is not to 'know' or 'do', but to create the conditions for emergence, in concert with all other leaders in the community. Foremost here would be each of the principals of member organizations. This again underscores a focus on trust being granted by the leader for others to step forward when they have insight, expertise, knowledge, connections or other sources of power that others do not yet hold.

In Bampton, the Opportunity Area Director was prepared to work behind the scenes, to do 'the donkey work', in order to ensure good attendance at the away days and, thereby, enable the possibility of dispersed control. The CEO of the existing locality partnership who was commissioned to help establish Bampton's Alliance, quoted in Chapter 3, provides another significant example. In order to overcome the issue of each of the city's various MATs wanting to negotiate its own bespoke arrangement with the partnership, he persuaded the MAT CEOs to work together to present a single proposal for how they would engage with it. This is one of several examples of how he co-constructs dispersed control to balance the need for coherence and ownership. Maintaining the right level of coherence is critical, and dispersed control is not the same as everyone doing their own thing. Shifting the path of the snowball from fragmentation towards productive collaboration and a sufficient level of coherence requires nuanced leadership that can work productively with the raw materials of complexity to facilitate emergence.

The implications of emergence

In Chapter 2 we engaged with the key concept of emergence: the understanding that new properties emerge from the collective behaviour of system components. Davis and Sumara's (2006) four conditions for the facilitation of emergence were used to explore the potential for emergence in our case study networks. Here we consider the implications of this potential, drawing on Hager and Beckett's (2019) detailed overview of complexity in education. Hager and Beckett argue that a number of major difficulties feature in accounts of education and its practice, all of which have resonance for our interest in education networks. First, there is a 'near universal assumption' that the individual human is the appropriate unit for analysis in considering the practice of education. Second, there is a tendency to seek to understand human performance by breaking it into parts, assuming that the sum of these atomized parts will be equivalent to the whole. This atomization tendency 'black boxes relations', thereby impoverishing our understanding. Third, there is an 'equally prevalent tendency' to focus on cognitive aspects of practice, resulting in 'thin' understandings that do not consider factors such as 'affect, know-how, the role of judgement and the various influences of context' (Hager and Beckett 2019: 127). In responding to these issues with 'traditional' education research, Hager and Beckett use theories of emergence to explore relationality in the work of what they introduce as the 'co-present group' (2019: 133–4).

We believe we can use this concept of the co-present group to explore relationality in education networks. The key dynamics of such groups are evident in our case studies, as we have sought to illustrate above. Co-present groups focus on a shared process towards a shared goal. A 'goals paradox' demands both congruence and diversity in goals that enable shared investment at the same time as forging synergistic advantage (Vangen and Huxham 2012: 732). Co-present groups are oriented towards the relationships of the group rather than the individuals who are members of the group. There is a holistic, rather than purely cognitive, appreciation of the group experience that contributes to an understanding of relationship and shared experience as constitutively social: the shift from individual human capital to collective social capital. While all members are important, Hager and Beckett suggest that groups are not necessarily egalitarian: hierarchy is present in some groups. This hierarchy could be seen to reflect greater practice experience, positional or political influence, or mana [authority or influence] in Aotearoa New Zealand. Thus equity, rather than equality, of participation is evident; the nature of participation is expected to ebb and flow as the practice of the group evolves. As well, while the presence of affect is crucial, this too will differ within and across networks at different stages in their practice.

Co-present groups are characterized not by structure but, rather, by six main features: affective functioning, a sense of place-in-time, particularity and accountability, participation and non-linearity, distributed participation (including through virtual means) and deliberation governed by the norms associated with the purpose of the group (Hager and Beckett 2019). While education policy commonly institutes networks through articulations of structure and governance (as evidenced in the introduction of Kāhui Ako in Aotearoa or the detailed discussions around how the Bampton Alliance should be legally constituted), complexity thinking perceives structure as the outcome of action (Cilliers 2001). When they emerge, network structures like all structures can be 'stable and long-lived … [or] volatile and ephemeral' (Cilliers 2001: 140). The potentially ephemeral characteristic of complex systems is problematic for government-instituted networks. The features of co-present groups cannot be anticipated in advance of emergence but, when they present themselves, may create a force for change to both formal and informal policies and procedures. This can create pressure for systemic change, without any impulse from government-level entities. Yet the macro-level of education can be resistant to systemic change. In earlier research on networks in Australia, a respondent noted that the first priority for governments is to be re-elected and this by necessity mediates the scope for systemic change in a context premised on NPM (Kamp 2006).

Two other implications of emergence merit comment: attractors and boundaries. Attractors provide our networks with their purpose and sustain them in their functioning, and particularly their affective functioning – the emotional investment in the collective purpose. For Kāhui Ako, while the achievement challenge could be argued to act as an attractor it is, from our perspective, more likely that to all intents and purposes the moral purpose of schooling is the attractor for all our networks.

> Attractors are associated with the system's functional purpose, which, commonly, is to live. For instance, bird flight patterns, such as starling murmurations, provide safety in numbers as well as enabling the most efficient use of the available air currents. Likewise, schools of fish move in patterns that minimise their chances of being taken by predators. Such patterns, which can be understood as multiple 'variations on the theme' of the attractor, demonstrate the flexibility that makes living complex systems adaptive and reflect the inherent cohesive wholeness of function of these systems.
>
> (Hager and Beckett 2019: 180)

This reference to murmurations merits a further observation concerning emergence and governance: complexity requires entities, including networks, to have the *freedom* to self-organize. This suggests that networks that are implemented by government, as well as community networks that gradually take on some kind of fixed form, should dictate, or establish the *minimum* critical specifications to enable their function, 'leaving others to find their own form' (Morgan 2006: 110). Such an orientation to governance would echo complex systems from nature: a murmuration achieves synchronicity through three simple rules – keep a minimum distance from other birds, fly at the same speed as other birds, move towards the centre of the flock.

Finally, boundaries are a critical consideration for appreciating the benefits of complexity theories, and for understanding networks. As Cilliers notes, 'rather than separating one thing from another, boundaries are something that constitutes that which is bounded' (Cilliers 2001: 141). The boundary is necessary for the network to understand itself, as well as being a necessary starting point for collaboration: that which is not first separate cannot form alliance. The boundary enables the measurement of progress towards new futures, and focuses our attention on the peripheries rather than centres (Cilliers 2001). In the vignette we cited at the opening of this chapter, this enabling potential of boundary-work is evident in the post-bifurcation assemblage created by a new head teacher: the school extends it horizons beyond its own, and the community, boundary. Technology is used to forge weak links that are unconstrained by time and place. Parents become a fully functioning component of the school whereas once they were occasional visitors and so on. In our case studies, the routine secondment of principals into the Ministry in Christchurch is an example of a productive means of working with boundaries. In Aotearoa, a former lead advisor for Kāhui Ako who became a principal was clearly a boundary-spanner in mobilizing the network agenda. In each of our cases, there will be numerous boundary spanners (Williams 2012), that contribute to the work of emergence, and the realization of network agendas. By contrast, in Bampton, the need was to reimagine the boundary: to reinvigorate the idea of Bampton as a meaningful educational as well as geographic entity, and to overcome the sense that a commitment to local place had lost ground as the Local Authority retreated and schools joined non-geographically bounded MATs. Equally, whereas MAT leaders had not engaged with the Bampton Education Partnership, they agreed collectively which members of their group would sit on the governance board for the new Alliance, thereby acting as symbolic and practical boundary-spanners for the new network.

Conclusion

As we discussed in Chapter 2, education acts as a complex system that evolves through dynamic interactions (Jacobson, Levin and Kapur 2019; Morrison 2002; Lemke and Sabelli 2008). The increasing complexity of education is in concert with increasing global complexity (Urry 2005) evident in theses such as the network society (Castells 1996), the risk society (Beck 1992) and the runaway world (Giddens 2002). There is, it seems, no turning back to simpler times. Complexity theory with its principle of requisite diversity and redundancy – internal complexity needing to meet environmental complexity – underscores why networks in education have been taken up as an important mechanism for knowledge generation and dissemination, for greater responsiveness to increasingly diverse student, parent and community needs, for broader curricular offerings that meet twenty-first-century demands, for providing emotional and practical support to education professionals and for securing innovations and so on (Suggett 2014; Hargreaves 2010, 2011, 2012a, 2012b). To realize this perceived potential of education networks, system change must be attentive to the patterns shaping the school-environment system, and the subsystems it contains. For schools to survive, evolve and thrive in their changing environments, they must understand themselves, the nature of their boundaries, and the possibilities and constraints within their environment (Maturana and Varela 1980). Mike Radford (2008: 518) suggests that should this thesis be 'persuasive it will have radical effects at all levels in terms of how we understand and manage the education system.' For Radford, complexity theory has the potential to reduce the tendency towards a 'praise and blame' culture where teachers and leaders are held responsible for success, or otherwise, of schools. Rather, there will be understanding of the 'complex of other factors that characterize the local and distinct nature of each education setting.' School improvement, when it occurs, reflects more than the 'agency of any particular variable within the system.' In Chapter 8, we will complement the insights offered by complexity theory by taking up Actor-Network Theory to explore the notion of actants and actors in education.

We finish by drawing together the implications for network leadership that emerge across this chapter. First, network leaders must find an appropriate balance between tight knit networks characterized by homophily, trust and the shared norms and collaborative culture that characterize an epistemic community, with the need for internal diversity and weaker ties which give access to a richer breadth of expertise and ideas than would otherwise be possible. Second, network leaders must find ways to maximize the potential for internal redundancy and neighbourly interactions, so that new ways of working can emerge and be translated into real-world advantages for all members. Achieving these outcomes requires a degree of dispersed control, but the trick is to balance this with commitment to network goals and shared moral purpose – as core attractors – and to embed routines and boundaries which require network members to constantly re-commit to the achievement of these goals and the re-statement of shared values. Emergence requires that network goals remain flexible and open to new possibilities, so leaders must work to set the snowball on its path and to identify positive feedback loops that can help to accelerate and/or adjust its direction, whilst acknowledging that this direction might shift.

This constant realignment is essential given the ambiguous and complex nature of the challenges that networks are seeking to address; however, there are risks that some network members might not understand the need for change or might resist its implications, so there is a need for continual collective sense-making in addition to consideration of the eight core features of networks outlined in Chapter 1. We develop these arguments further in Chapter 9, in which we suggest that network leadership involves working productively with tensions and paradox, collective sense-making and an ecological 'whole system' approach.

8

Analysing Networks through the Lens of Actor-Network Theory

Introduction

In Chapter 2 we introduced Actor-Network Theory as the fourth theoretical lens for undertaking our analysis of case studies of England, New Zealand, Singapore and Chile. We emphasized that Actor-Network Theory is not a 'classic' theory; it does not comprise a coherent, identifiable, theoretical framework of the kind applied in the last three chapters. Rather, it offers a sensibility to reading the practice of education in ways that forego any preliminary assumption about what it is that makes us act.[1] Thus, schools, students, teachers, the education system, social factors, curriculum, rankings and all the other educational entities we encounter are effects of continual processes of assemblage. The work of Actor-Network Theory is to track 'actants' – the full range of possible actors – as they create, advance or frustrate a collective task (Latour 1991). In networks, this range of actants goes far beyond relationships between individuals, or groups of individuals, as suggested by Popp et al. (2014: 18) and surveyed in Chapter 1. Thus, in our analysis of educational networks, Actor-Network Theory suggests we 'follow' the actors introduced in the proceeding chapters to see *how* it is that they instigate action, whoever – or whatever – they may be.

The value of this analysis is, at the most basic level, in the challenge it poses to the immediacy of reaching for social explanations for educational phenomena such as the persistence of educational inequities. While Bernstein could argue in 1970 that 'education cannot compensate for society' (1970: 344), Actor-Network Theory pauses to explore *how* both 'education' and 'society' are assembled in a given place and time, and to what effect. By tracing and articulating the ways in which heterogeneous actants – classrooms, funding, culture, parents, policy documents, school zones, beliefs, international rankings, geography, uniforms, digital devices, 'disadvantaged' students, earthquakes, the education system, lesson plans, qualification and inspection regimes and so forth – form an assemblage and become an accepted, often unquestioned, part of the 'real' world, the potential for systemic change appears. In understanding how 'things' are assembled, and what holds them together, the potential that they '*might be* assembled anew in some given state of affairs' becomes apparent (Latour 2007: 5 original emphasis). As a theory of agency (Law 1992) the opportunity for practical insights into the potential of educational networks through analysing their formation, organization, operation and leadership, is apparent: the work of leading educational networks involves a focus on assemblage, an understanding of how to acquire, and maintain, allies.

For policy purposes, the complexities of using networks as surveyed in Chapter 1 are mediated by the sensitivities of Actor-Network Theory. Despite the shift to network governance, research suggests the failure to embrace network insights in public administration beyond their use as a metaphor or conceptual scheme reflects the difficulty in conceptualizing precisely how to research, or measure the success of, networks (Alexander, Lewis and Considine 2011). Networks – envisaged as assemblages of nodes, ties and boundaries – are often 'read' through their nodes and these nodes, in turn, tend to be organizations (Diani 2003). Such a 'join-the-dots approach' to conceptualizing, visualizing and governing networks is highly problematic if the intent is to engage with the problems of education that, despite any number of policy initiatives, have defied resolution. Kamp (2013b) completed ethnographic research inside one of thirty-one government-instituted networks covering the state of Victoria in Australia to explore what it takes to move beyond connecting stable entities in the pursuit of more integrated and efficient forms of educational provision. If what is required is *not* more of the same – is, rather, an ability to move beyond existing practice, finding responses to problems not fully understood – then a different conceptualization of networking is demanded. This form of networking would be that which is 'inopportune' (Rabinow 2009), able to disrupt accepted objects such as 'school', 'teacher', 'curriculum' and, thereby, changing a school's connectivity and directionality (Kamp 2013b). Such a shift moves beyond a modernist world view, denying any duality between structure and agency (Landri 2021; St. Pierre 2004).

In this chapter we focus on our case study networks and the analysis in the preceding three chapters to consider how ANTian sensibility can progress our understanding of education networks and the implications of that understanding for their leadership. Landri's (2021) analysis of educational leadership, management and administration through Actor-Network Theory provides the most detailed and up-to-date account, so we follow his structure. Our hope is to contribute further to this work by complementing Landri's Italian focus with our four case countries. Accordingly, this chapter involves four sections that engage with four ANTian principles. First, the principle of *symmetry* between human and non-human actors that broadens the analysis from a predominantly humanistic impulse to reconsider who and what is the source of action. Our discussion here will proceed through two necessarily brief examples: performance technologies, and the presence, or not, of digital devices as network actors. Second, the principle of *translation* that illustrates how mediation occurs. Our discussion here will explore how actors are enrolled in, and become prime movers in, networks. Finally, the notion of *network*, or more evocatively, *net-work* which enables us to foreground learning as critical to the action orientation of networks. In this, we will engage with what Landri refers to as processes of 'network stabilization' (2021: 15) to explore black boxing and boundary crossing as networks move towards some form of 'realness' in our case study contexts. In the concluding section of the chapter, we draw together key insights and reflect on the implications for network leadership.

Symmetry

> Apart from a "naïve" belief in "super-heroic" leadership or in the charismatic quality of headteachers and teachers, other perspectives (such as distributed leadership for example) suggest considering how actors are imbricated in complex social relationships that are essential to the (*sic*) agency. In those cases, however, there is no doubt about who the "actors" are: they are humans.
>
> (Landri 2021: 39)

In previous chapters, we have encountered a number of non-human actors that are brought into closer focus in the present chapter to acknowledge the concept of generalized symmetry. Symmetry does not only concern humans and non-humans. It also problematizes any dichotomy: micro and macro, nature and culture, big and small (Landri 2021: 41). Reflecting on previous chapters, our focus would also problematize notions of hierarchy and markets, hard and soft governance, as well as organic and instituted networks. Here, all of these 'things' are analysed as network effects.

Standards, as a form of performance technology, are an outstanding example. Globally, there is a growing body of literature that demonstrates how the OECD Programme for International Student Assessment (PISA) is a fully fledged non-human actor (Addey and Gorur 2020; Piattoeva 2020; Fenwick 2010). Yet there is nothing linear in PISA's action: in each of the case study countries the standards assemblage acts differently. Our two primary case studies – England and New Zealand – are relatively close in the 2018 OECD rankings, with New Zealand appearing twelfth and the UK fourteenth; both achieve above the OECD averages for reading, mathematics and science.[2] Singapore's rank is second (a drop from first in 2015) while Chile's is forty-third. In England, the publication of PISA results every three years might stimulate some media debate, particularly if England has moved up or down in the rankings, but the impact on the daily work of schools and teachers is minimal when compared with the 'high stakes' nature of annual national student assessments. However, PISA has had numerous indirect effects in England: for example, in an attempt to emulate the perceived success of 'high performing' East Asian nations, not least Singapore, Ministers have invested vast sums in efforts to import 'maths mastery' approaches into the curriculum and teaching practices of schools (Boylan et al. 2019). In New Zealand, a small nation-state devoid of any formal national school ranking system, and with a commitment to the Treaty of Waitangi, the PISA rankings act without durability: the network of intermittent PISA rankings, educational commentators and media reporting is insufficiently durable.

Singapore – like New Zealand an island nation with a similar-sized population but vastly fewer schools – is, as we detailed in Chapter 1, enacted through this particular actor-network as a global education success. Reading the Country Report for Singapore (OECD 2018) through the lens of Actor-Network Theory gives some indication of the range of actors involved in this assemblage of success. Thus, student and parent competitiveness, prestigious schools, timeliness, fear of failure, ability grouping, extensive preschool learning, intercultural exposure, multilingualism, educational resources, staffing levels, pedagogical skills in working with digital devices, supportive virtual learning platforms and portals (and, presumably internet capacity and power) and homework rooms in schools are all present, and acting with students. Singaporean students are enacted as successful yet are simultaneously highly subject to schoolwork related anxiety and exposure to bullying (Ministry of Education 2018b). An actor-network reading of Chile would highlight a different assemblage. Here, a distant actor in terms of the marketization reforms of the Pinochet regime continues to act, in assemblage with other actors. These include, but are not limited to, the sheer volume of schools, continued deregulation that sustains inequality, teacher qualifications, recruitment and remuneration, emergent (compulsory for public schools) networks, intentionality for improvement, social poverty, coverage by *El Mercurio* of the efforts of Fundacion Chile, private sector employers, the Chilean

Education Conflict and theories of school improvement and effectiveness (Levin 2011). Thus, our critique of international large-scale assessments that appear as 'immutable mobiles' (Latour 1987) whose meanings remain stable is more productively undertaken with attention to the full range of actors that force, privilege, mobilize, encourage, undermine, stall (and so on) particular forms of practice in particular places and times. This, in turn, gives more possibilities to 'act back' against homogenizing education policies that become privileged allies for such performance technologies and, potentially, are counterproductive to socially just and nurturing education for all.

In his discussion of symmetry – drawing on the work of van Dijck and Poell (2018) – Landri details the increasing role of non-human actors, both digital and paper:

> Analogue technologies do not disappear from the scene but are placed in the background. Formerly at the core of a school manager's bureaucratic tasks, the printed paper remains, and while there is a policy of dematerialisation, translating into a renewed call for the digitisation of everything, documents, circulars and so on are made present in paper form, often by using and printing digital versions for a specific purpose. Paper and pen are still used as technologies of writing and, in particular, in the practice of taking notes to record everyday activities.
>
> (Landri 2021: 47)

Diverse analogue and digital platforms are not simply a tool used by a human actor. Rather they are clearly involved, sometimes even setting the agenda. For example, while schools in our case study countries may have in-principle autonomy in establishing self-evaluation processes, in practice attention is directed by non-human actors that embody models of knowledge that reflect the school improvement and effectiveness literature (Landri 2021). Thus, Singapore's School Excellence Model (described in Chapter 5) allows schools to establish goals and measure progress against them, but all criteria require evidence of systematic planning and measuring against appropriate benchmarks (Ng 2007). In Bampton, England, the role of paper-based forms in school reviews is significant. As explained in Chapter 5, accredited head teachers are commissioned by the Bampton Education Partnership to visit each Local Authority maintained school every term, using the prescribed forms to structure the conversation and capture information on school and pupil performance or on specific areas of risk, such as safeguarding. Following these visits they decide on a rating, with schools judged 'amber' or 'red' prioritized to receive additional support. This process is intended to ensure consistency and fairness, by capturing 'hard' data (for example on pupil performance) and 'soft' intelligence (for example on staff and leadership capacity) on each school, and to ensure that schools will not fail an Ofsted inspection due to inadequate record keeping. In practice, the process is seen by most interviewees to be overly 'compliance based, they don't get into classrooms', preventing a focus on more developmental conversations and 'real' work which could support actual improvement ('I don't get very much out of it really'). Meanwhile, the growth of digital platforms is creating new challenges. For example, the twelve MATs operating in Bampton use a number of different digital platforms to store and analyse pupil data, but these platforms do not always 'talk to' each other, which can make it difficult to share data between MATs and with the local authority. As one MAT CEO explained:

> There's lots of data going in. As a MAT we have fed in our assessment data. The LA has asked for it, but their system doesn't align with our approach, so it's become an industry.

For Landri, therefore, 'platforms are not merely a neutral tool, as they orient the ways schools define themselves', reinforcing an 'epistemology of seeing' (2021: 52–3) and thereby acting as a form of soft governance.

However, digital platforms have potential to act as a 'prime mover': an enabler of a more stabilized assemblage that may generate positive outcomes to all the actors in an event. An example from New Zealand is illustrative. One of the Christchurch Kāhui Ako – Ōtākaro Community of Learning – clearly demonstrates the mobilizing agency of non-humans in collaborative endeavours. Ōtākaro Kāhui Ako includes seven schools – two secondary (one girls' and one boys'), two intermediate and three primary – and thirteen early childhood education providers. Over 2,500 of the students in the network study on one campus. A geological actor was central to this network opportunity. As part of the earthquake recovery we described in Chapter 4, the rebuild of Avonside Girls' High School and Shirley Boys' High School is on a co-located site, Orua Paeroa. This spectacular, colourful campus enables each school to retain its culture, identity and teaching spaces while facilities such as administration, auditorium, gym and cafe are shared by both schools. There are physical bridges that link the two teaching 'wings', Shirley Boys' on the left and Avonside Girls' on the right as you enter the campus. Each school is visually distinct, yet closely intertwined given the way the architecture acts. There are multiple Kāhui Ako-funded 'within' and 'across' school teacher roles on the campus and thus the chance for 'casual conversations and then the opportunities that arise from those happen much more often'. One across-school teacher spoke of the need for an array of mechanisms to, first, manage the risk of 'being invisible' and, second, to build social capital and, thereby, a foundation for joint practice development that does not elevate existing demands. Thus 'colleagues' is reframed to 'everyone working together' within the Kāhui Ako, including non-members such as the university and, potentially, local employers. This across-school teacher began by doing relief teaching for Kāhui Ako members, noting other non-human actors: 'I got out of this suit because you can't be a [kindergarten] teacher if you're in a suit'. He worked in both early childhood and primary schools, observing and talking with teachers. This gave visibility but left the question 'how can we continue to grow that?' The answer to this question was to develop podcasts for shared professional development that was:

> short, sharp, relevant.... They didn't need to ask their principal's permission, they didn't need to book a time with me; we didn't need to align our calendars or whatever. They could click on Spotify, they could click on Apple, they could go on their phone. They're at the gym, on their way to school, and they could listen to a conversation and be part of that collaborative conversation.

We can conceptualize this as a highly productive assemblage of humans in the form of the Kāhui Ako roles and non-humans in the form of digital platforms, mobile phones and such like. Such a productive association with a prime mover is one that has the potential to win the 'trial of strength' against the 'anti-programs': all those actors such as markets, time pressures, bureaucracy and so forth that counter the emergent collaboration (Landri 2021: 7).

Another example of a digital platform acting as both a 'prime mover' and, for some participants, an 'anti-program' comes from an evaluation that one of us undertook of networks established for rural church schools in England. Most rural schools in England are small and many are geographically isolated, making it hard for staff to come out of school to participate in face-to-face networks. Schools were recruited to join the proposed new networks from September 2019 on the basis that most meetings would take place online, via Zoom, run by an external facilitator. However, during that first term both the facilitators and many school leaders struggled with the online format. Some participants lacked the necessary kit or had poor internet connections, several did not have a private office so had to join from a shared office, while many simply did not feel confident using the technology. As one facilitator put it, 'every meeting someone can't log on or can't see or can't hear'. Perhaps due to participants' lack of confidence, this human-non-human association changed how people acted: meetings suffered from a lack of 'flow', with awkward 'gaps and silences'. 'It's hard to tell how what you are doing is being received and it is discouraging', explained one network facilitator. Furthermore, some important dimensions of communication were seen to be lost online; for example, one school leader felt the absence of casual contact, noting that the best sharing can 'come out of having a chat over a cup of tea in the break'. However, this rather bumpy start was seen by those who persisted to have paid off after England was placed into its first national lockdown in March 2020, in response to the COVID-19 pandemic. Schools were largely closed (except for the children of 'key workers') and the majority of children were learning at home. Not surprisingly, participation in the networks decreased during the lockdown period, as school leaders grappled with a huge number of COVID-related challenges, but around half of the participants did attend at least one online meeting before the end of the summer term in July. One facilitator described these meetings as 'the best yet', while several participants argued that the networks had been 'ahead of the curve' in their use of technology and that this had helped them enormously when they had been forced to switch to online learning and home working during lockdown.

Translation

> The word 'interaction' was not badly chosen; only the number and types of 'actions' and the span of their 'inter' relations has been vastly underestimated. Stretch any given inter-action and, sure enough, it becomes an actor-network.
> (Latour 2007: 202)

In Chapter 2 we introduced one of the seminal ANTian frameworks that provided the 'basic vocabulary of the approach' (Landri 2021: 8): Callon's (1986) four non-linear moments of translation. Here, we use this framework to give a flavour of how an assemblage takes form as human and non-human actors attempt to associate with one another. The New Zealand case study and, particularly, the introduction of Kāhui Ako, offer an apt illustration of using the principle of translation to explore the enactment of network policies.

Problematization is the point at which there is articulation of a problem or issue. In New Zealand, as we articulated in Chapter 4, from the introduction of *Tomorrow's Schools* there had been research and advocacy that questioned the consequences of New Zealand's radical approach to self-managing schools. There had also been, over the decades, a number of small-scale network initiatives that might be able to be scaled up. The fifth National Government was a prime mover in initiating problematization through establishing the *Investing in Educational Success* Working Group and consequent policy. With a significant allocation of the Vote Education budget allocated to the policy, the problem of atomization and its consequences was articulated in such a way to become a key player in the education landscape. An obligatory passage point was established: a 'single locus that could shape and mobilize the local network' and 'have control over all transactions' (Bijker and Law 1992: 31).

In the second moment, *interessement* is the process whereby an entity acts to stabilize the identity of the other actors encountered in the problematization. For Kāhui Ako, the introduction of endorsed achievement challenges as an actor achieves this moment. Securing an endorsed achievement challenge within the assemblage formalizes the existence of the network, bolsters its focus and, potentially, precludes engagement and investment in other actor-networks. Yet such action is always subject to negotiation: translation foregrounds the cracks and spaces in which actors exercise agency (Kamp 2013b). We can see this through the third moment of *enrolment* where negotiations take place and formal roles begin to appear. What form does 'negotiation' take in the context of our case studies of educational networks? In New Zealand, Kāhui Ako have a clearly articulated right – indeed an obligation – to negotiate. With the establishment of the Education Support Agency, that right will be further elevated, with the Education Work Programme giving Priority A status (i.e. aiming to achieve progress within the next twelve to eighteen months) to 'the Kāhui Ako model providing more flexibility in clustering arrangements and achievement challenges, and in the use of staffing and funding resources' (Ministry of Education 2019: 43). Negotiation strengthens the network but can equally weaken it: actors 'may connect in ways that lock them into a particular collective, or they may pretend to connect, partially connect, or act disconnected and excluded even when they are connected' (Fenwick 2010: 120). In the Aupaki network, the opposite is evident. Linwood College, already a funded member of Tamai Kāhui Ako, formed a connection as an 'associate member' of Aupaki, thereby bringing no resourcing. Yet this tenuous connection has opened the way for a shared future involving both Kāhui Ako which could not have been imagined previously:

> One of the great advantages of Kāhui Ako is that type of language and understanding is now part of the narrative. ... it just wasn't even on our understanding then, let alone talking about it. Now it is part of the dialogue.

However, as our analysis in Chapter 6 indicates, the formalization of roles has also undermined the shared agenda by introducing funding as an actor in the assemblage. Teachers who are appointed to formal roles are granted staff release time that can readily slip towards a perception that the formation of social capital and joint practice development is 'their' responsibility, rather than the shared responsibility of all members.

The fourth moment of *mobilization* we might analyse as the point where social capital becomes an actor: enabling other actors to be mobilized in ways that were not possible prior to translation. In Aupaki, the Linwood principal referenced building trust with the Aupaki principals. The next phase of this mobilization will be trust between the Aupaki and Tamai principals, at a level sufficient for fully collaborative actions: committing staff and engaging in joint projects across two Kāhui Ako. However, an Actor-Network Theory analysis of social capital of necessity involves both human and non-human actors (Salomão Filho and Kamp 2019). Not only do norms of reciprocity and trust become evident here, networks can enrol non-human actors in formal roles. Here too, as Bourdieu (1986) anticipated, the network gains voice and has recognized spokespersons. These spokespersons may be human, may be documentary, may be digital but, regardless, a network is established from precarious prior connections (Fenwick 2010). The extent to which a network retains this sense of 'realness' depends on a sustained effort to attract allies: 'the more *attachments* it has, the more [the network] exists' (Latour 2007: 217, emphasis in original). The aim must be to become 'more and more durable'; for networking to be 'routine practice' (Landri 2021: 79).

The formation of the Bampton Alliance can be seen to have followed a similar messy combination of *problematization, interessement, enrolment* and *mobilization*. The Opportunity Area Director was perhaps the first to observe that 'the status quo was not an option', leading him to enlist the Local Authority Director, to commission the external facilitators and to work with them to recruit the carefully selected Strategy Group. That broader group then went through its own, parallel, multistage process of acknowledging the issues (represented in the formally agreed 'case for change' and 'what we are trying to achieve?' statements), negotiating agreement on the need for specific, shared actions and then beginning to mobilize to launch the new Alliance. As we acknowledge in Chapter 3, this process was sometimes fraught and discussions sometimes moved backwards as well as forward, reflecting the presence of actors such as fragmentation, competition and a sense that deep-seated poverty and inter-racial tensions across the town would always overwhelm any attempt to achieve real change. This association of actors made progress challenging, constantly threatening to overwhelm the best efforts of network leaders.

We focus here on the impact of one non-human actor on these four processes: namely, the hotel in which the four Strategy Group away days were held. The hotel was selected for several reasons, including because it was seen as one of the better-quality (but still affordable) venues locally, and because it was geographically near to Bampton, but not in the town itself. The hope was that Strategy Group members would see it as an attractive and comfortable venue, and that they would commit more fully if they could not 'pop back' into school at the start or end of the day. These aspirations – coupled with dogged work behind the scenes by the Opportunity Area Director – were largely fulfilled, with good attendance at all four away days. However, the hotel's design and operation amplified the impact of pre-existing cliques and factions within the Strategy Group dynamics. For example, the away day sessions were held in a large, reasonably airy, but often poorly heated room in the hotel conference centre. The hotel would not serve a buffet lunch outside the conference room, so group members needed to walk down several long, dreary corridors to reach the restaurant. The restaurant did serve a buffet lunch, so the guests collected their food and then seated themselves at a small table in one of two separate dining rooms. This whole process took a considerable amount of time, but more importantly broke any sense of group dynamic that had developed during the morning sessions, as well-established subgroups sat themselves together. As a result, progress often faltered or moved backwards in the afternoons, for example if members of a particular subgroup that had *'re-mobilized'* over the lunch together raised new objections or problems. The hotel thus played a key role as a non-human actor in the overall assemblage. Yet this also highlights how cliques and subgroups within a network can engage in parallel processes of *problematization, interessement, enrolment* and/or *mobilization* in parallel with – or sometimes in opposition to – the wider process.

Network

> What is important in the word network is the word *work*.
>
> (Latour 2004b: 83)

In the preceding sections of this chapter we have, using ANTian concepts, made the case for a closely attentive reading that gives symmetry to human and non-human actors in networks. We have also introduced the principle of translation, using its 'specialized meaning: a relation that... induces two mediators into coexisting' (Latour 2007: 108). Here, in considering 'network', the emphasis is not on structure but, rather, on the work the collective is encouraged to do, on the basis of the entities which are part of the collective (Latour 2004b). As Landri (2021: 83) explains, 'In ANT, the word network does not qualify a closed thing but a dynamic assemblage of entities, a set of successful translations'. When this dynamic assemblage gains some sense of stabilization and begins to act 'as one', it can be thought of as a 'black box' (Latour 1987: 131). Black boxes are 'low maintenance' and, in this, appeal as being something we can 'rely on' (Harman 2009: 37). While policy narratives might speak of education networks as if they were a black box, this does not serve us well given its suggestion of some form of closure or completion (Landri 2021). Given the preceding analysis, and the introduction of this notion in Chapter 2, the idea that an educational network could stabilize, become 'one' and no longer require maintenance forecloses on important insights into how networks actually 'work'.

As an alternative, Landri (2021: 85) introduces the notion of an ecological perspective, arguing that 'the strength of this approach lies in foregrounding the way that cooperation of many worlds does not imply a consensus'. An ecological perspective on networks with its recognition of necessary dissent (Thrupp 2018) takes up the concept of boundary objects as a means of translation. These objects are both 'plastic' and 'robust', 'they are weakly structured in common use and become strongly structured in individual site use... their structure is common enough to more than one world to make them recognizable, a means of translation' (Star and Griesemer 1989: 393 cited in Landri 2021: 85). Boundary objects are thus open, 'flexible enough to be filled and adapted to local needs' (Landri 2021: 86), thereby facilitating cooperation as a preliminary to collaboration. They are also a critical component of social learning systems (Wenger 2000) of the kind that can magnify joint practice development; multiplicity and tension are energy sources for the kinds of knowledge work required in networks that can learn and, thereby, effect change (Kamp 2013b, 2019b).

If we accept this analysis, it suggests that the approach in Aotearoa New Zealand and Singapore, where the government predominantly works through guidelines, rather than prescription, is appropriate for policies concerning the implementation of educational networks. The implementation of Kāhui Ako was critiqued for its 'stifling' specifications (Kamp 2019b) and, moving forward, the intent is for less prescription to realize the potential of networks (Ministry of Education 2019). In Chile, the introduction of compulsion for publicly funded schools and the mandated nature of network formation are both acting in ways that could be counter to the ambitions we might hold for educational networks. In England, Teaching Schools have worked within loose government guidelines which do not prescribe the size or operational model for Alliance networks: as a result, Greany and Higham (2018) identify three distinct TSA trajectories – *exclusive, marketized and hierarchical* – while also showing how these trajectories overlap and interact in hybrid forms. England's TSA policy guidelines thus act as boundary objects, enabling coexistence, but remaining 'flexible enough to be filled and adapted to local needs' (Landri 2021: 86).

The differentiated forms of mediation articulated within Actor-Network Theory are all valuable in tracing the development of the eight core features for networks that we rehearsed in Chapter 1. Firstly mediation as interference aligns with our thesis that successful networks reflect a shared goal. This shared goal, however formally or informally articulated, is a mechanism whereby each agent interferes with, or translates, the original goal of the other. In the process, heterogeneous actors move from cooperation to collaboration. Our second core feature was related to the degree of commitment and contribution of network members: the issue of investment in the network. This speaks directly to the four moments of translation: articulating the issue and clarifying the identity of those humans and non-humans who have a role to play in resolving the issue before enrolling and mobilizing actors. Here, our English case offers an interesting example of tensions around interessement – the point when an association between actors is, in theory, strengthened and actors are precluded from engaging in other actor-networks. In our English case, principals spoke about the difficulties of balancing the dynamics of 'multi-belonging' where they might belong to both a MAT and one of the local collaboratives. In such instances, the investment in network may be in excess of the return from diluted investment unless network leaders have, or are prepared with, the insights and expertise to work effectively with complex co-activity, as we discussed in Chapter 7.

Third, we addressed the issue of shared values, practices and attributes. This, too, is a mechanism of translation, using the notion of composition and the way that the composite goal – be it an achievement challenge, a vision or a diktat from government – becomes the common achievement of each of the actors. We argued that the fourth core feature of networks is their embedding within wider societal contexts. From an ANTian perspective, we can use the concept of opening the black box of 'structure' and 'societal context' to take a close-up reading to see how the entities that form the structure or societal context come together in some form of co-existence to become a durable form. Being attuned to black boxing is also a means by which we can better engage with our sixth core feature: the design principles upon which we base our understandings of network effectiveness. Having opened the black box of 'successful networks' to better understand the complexity that inheres within the network and the techniques that hold the network together in some form of coherent assemblage, we can more effectively understand and articulate what kinds of 'design principles' will best serve our purposes, and those of policymakers.

Our fifth core feature concerned the tensions in enough-but-no-more governance and management structures over the life course of a given network. We referred to the notion of a network spectrum and the need for models of governance that were fit for purpose. Clearly, this feature intersects with the preceding feature and the extent to which a network is compelled, or not, to work in connection with wider governance contexts. This is the work of interessement. Thus, in Aotearoa we can see networks that refuse this stabilization of their identity, despite the evident potential for Kāhui Ako to become an obligatory passage point for collaboration in education across Aotearoa.

Knowledge and diffusing innovations are the seventh core feature we propose. Here, we can use the language of translation as delegation to explore the way that both understandings and actions related to educational networks are, and can be, delegated to non-human actors. In this, the potential for a radical expansion in knowledge generation and diffusion becomes apparent, even in the absence of human actors. Finally, we acknowledged forms of leadership and management as being a core feature of educational networks. This will be the focus of our exploration in the following chapter.

Conclusion

In this chapter we have used an array of principles and concepts drawn from Actor-Network Theory's various iterations to explore educational networks as contextual, tenuous enactments. From an ANTian perspective, a network 'does not connect things that already exist, but actually configures ontologies' (Fenwick 2010: 119); to be a 'realistic whole' is not the starting point but, rather, a provisional achievement of a composite assemblage (Latour 2007: 208). All of this fluidity seems to sit in tension with the tenets of new public managerialism, and rightly so: from the perspective of Actor-Network Theory there is 'no straightforward determinism through which technologies and materialities make the social durable' (Landri 2021: 87).

A key insight from the analysis in this chapter is the privileging of practice over structure. In considering the formation and operation of educational networks, a great deal of attention goes to the formation of connections between existing entities: how many entities, of what kind, how many links, how to 'network' and so on. Actor-Network Theory prefers to draw attention to the constant process of enrolment and mobilization in a dynamic assemblage of entities that cohere around a given practice. This has implications for how we might lead educational networks, and how we might prepare human actors for such leadership. We stated above that the work of leading educational networks involves a focus on assemblage, an understanding of how to acquire, and maintain, allies. An important insight from the perspective of Actor-Network Theory here concerns symmetry. Questions of what makes us act are central to Actor-Network Theory. In our ANTian exploration of where and how leadership acts in an educational network we, of necessity, reject a focus on an individual leader to explore leadership as diffused, shared and exercised by humans and non-human actors in complex interrelationships. In the following chapter we build on these insights to consider both existing leadership constructs, such as distributed and systems leadership, as well as three network leadership practices which, we argue, are apparent across all four of our theoretical lenses: working productively with tensions and paradox, collective sense-making and an ecological 'whole system' approach.

The Theory and Practice of Network Leadership

Introduction

As the opening scenario of this book illustrated, the challenges of contemporary education have generated increasing interest in the potential of networks. This, in turn, has implications for how we think about and undertake leadership. In Chapter 1 we outlined eight core features of networks, the last of which highlighted the importance of leadership, but also noted that such leadership is not always successful and that leading a single school is not necessarily a good preparation for leading across a network. And yet, in education the orientation of leadership most often continues to focus on a role-based function – particularly a head teacher or principal – linked to a specific job, a specific organization or some 'heroic' individual who 'stepped up' at an 'extreme moment' (Riley 2009: 216). Given the context surveyed in Chapter 1, such an orientation to leadership is limiting. Even within individual organizations, rarely is leadership practised in such isolation. The focus of leadership thus needs to move beyond single leaders and single institutions (Preedy, Bennett and Wise 2012). This does not mean there are no overlaps between leading successfully within a school and leading across a network: both contexts require many similar leadership qualities and skills, such as integrity, the ability to communicate well, to think strategically and to facilitate group decision-making and commitment, although it seems likely that such qualities become even more essential for leaders who cannot rely on positional authority (Hill 2008). For Riley, what is required is that we conceptualize leadership as occurring in layers: 'of, and with, a school community; of, and with, the local community; and of, and with, the broader locality'. This rhythm – 'of, and with' – serves well for thinking about network leadership here.

In this chapter we draw on both organizational and education theory to develop a position on how the leadership of educational networks might best be conceptualized and undertaken, seeking to build on and synthesize the analysis in the preceding chapters. Organizational theory is a school of thought in which competing paradigms often co-exist, rather than one supplanting another (Morgan 2006). However, a functionalist managerialist paradigm remains dominant. This paradigm assumes the world is both knowable and consistent, and it is oriented to the production of order and regulation. Such a paradigm appears to fit well with schools given their apparently functional orientation. It is evident in the governance framework of NPM that the leaders in our case studies encounter. It sustains the influence of school effectiveness and improvement research on policy and efforts by governments to 'steer' from a distance. The organizational unit is thus the individual school, and school-level actors are vested with high degrees of autonomy while working within a 'performative' context (Ball 2000, 2003) that involves regulation through targets, indicators and evaluations. These tools encourage leaders to focus internally and to see inter-organizational collaboration as, at best, a nice-to-have option. Thus, it seems that leadership occurs in a context premised on collaboration but governed by comparison and commerciality.

As early as 2004 Paul Skidmore argued for the need to move away from old paradigms of management and leadership towards approaches that would be better aligned to the logics of networks and the tensions of the current environment. He framed this new model of leadership as 'leading between'. For Skidmore, the undermining of the legitimacy and effectiveness of traditional institutional frameworks, coupled with the increasing complexity of the context, demands increased leadership. Skidmore references the advent of 'superheads' in education as being an example of old theory that dies hard: individuals being brought into challenged schools and given authority, resources and remuneration 'on the assumption that they will personally be able to reverse the decline, often with very mixed results' (Skidmore 2004: 93). In this, Skidmore is referencing the work of Ronald Heifetz (1994) who argued that conventional models of leadership and authority perpetuate the idea that leadership is about influence and persuading people to follow a vision. Heifetz notes that, by contrast, leadership *without* authority – within and beyond organizations and communities – has a long history that includes particular forms of disobedience to mobilize 'adaptive work'. Adaptive work is about confronting the gap between the call to action that consolidates a network and the capacity of the network to achieve that action. What are the characteristics of network leaders from Skidmore's perspective? First, network leaders lead from the outside in, meaning that they start with the needs of the communities they serve, and then consider how available resources and capacity might best address these. Second, network leaders mobilize disparate supplies of energy. Third, network leaders foster trust and empower others to act. Fourth, network leaders help others to grow outside of their comfort zones. Fifth, network leaders are 'lead learners' rather than professing to know all the answers. Finally, network leaders nurture other leaders including, in school contexts, students and their extended family and communities. In this, Skidmore (2004: 99) adopts a system orientation to network leadership:

> [Network leaders] understand that most systems – from organisations to cities to biological ecosystems – are too complex and unpredictable to be controlled from the top-down. Yet they display an underlying tendency towards self-organisation and order, leading to what Briggs calls 'meaningful patterns of uncertainty'. This self-organisation can be shaped in purposeful ways, provided we can develop leadership models that distribute leadership across organisations.

This chapter engages with these ideas and considers their implications in light of the evidence and analyses we have developed throughout the book and, particularly, the eight core features of networks that we articulated in Chapter 1. We begin by reviewing what Thomson, Gunter and Blackmore (2021: x–xi) term the Transnational Leadership Package (TLP). They suggest that, in the context of the twenty-first century, the TLP is the dominant paradigm in educational leadership. Not surprisingly given the points we make above, the focus of the TLP has been on the leadership of single schools, but we explore two areas – distributed and system leadership – in which this focus has broadened out in recent years as school systems have grappled with the need for more adaptive forms of leadership. We then detail the key concepts and practices that we see as key to successful network leadership in our case study contexts. This analysis sets out three core approaches which, we argue, apply across all four of our theoretical lenses: working productively with tensions and paradox, collective sense-making and adopting an ecological approach. We conclude by drawing out the implications, building on the eight core features of networks identified in Chapter 1.

A Transnational Leadership Package

Thomson, Gunter and Blackmore (2021: x–xi) argue that, over time, the leadership industry in the field of educational leadership, management and administration has evolved to suggest that there is 'one-best way to do leading and leadership and to be a leader'. This leadership 'package' derives from diverse settings, intellectual and practice traditions, including Taylorist principles of scientific management, the human relations movement, the contemporary focus on quantitative evidence and data-driven decisions and, sometimes, more socially critical perspectives. These paradigms have now converged, contemporaneously with the neoliberal agenda that is 'virtually enforced' by bodies such as the International Monetary Fund, the World Bank and the OECD.

From this convergence, preferred models of leadership have been articulated. An example is the notion of transformational leadership which is 'simultaneously about delivery, an emotional commitment to the delivery and predictive evidenced-based process to delivering the delivery!' (Thomson, Gunter and Blackmore 2021: xii–xiii). In this, 'tactical and pragmatic' mediations do occur at the local level but for the most part the paradigms of educational leadership, management and administration 'inform and communicate vision and mission for localized implementation'. 'Good' leadership thus becomes normalized in particular ways, as does the development of leadership training, standards for leadership and principal certification, as we explore in the next chapter.

To contextualize the evolution of the TLP, we can consider the trajectory of leadership discourses beyond education. For example, in his review of collaboration in public policy and practice, Williams (2012) provides an overview of leadership for collaboration in the public sector more broadly, developing the work of Parry and Bryman (2006). In this overview, trait theory is dominant up to the 1940s. The main characteristics of trait theory are that leaders have physical traits, individual abilities and personality characteristics that distinguish them from non-leaders. From the 1940s to the 1960s, the focus moves from traits to behaviours, with two dominant behavioural styles apparent: first, consideration for subordinates and second, initiating styles. The emphasis here is on training rather than selecting leaders. From the late 1960s to the 1980s, contingency theories come to the fore, placing a focus on the situational factors that affect leadership effectiveness. Williams suggests that since the 1980s, theories of 'new leadership' have become dominant. These theories and their focus on leaders as managers of meaning, as transformational and visionary continue to be influential. New leadership theories were complemented by concerns for dispersed leadership that became popular from the 1990s. Dispersed leadership is concerned with mediating perceptions of leadership as heroic and, in the process, giving focus to leadership as dispersed across organizations. This body of theory aims to nurture leadership capacity in individuals and teams in organizations. From the turn of the century, according to Williams, theories of collaborative leadership have gained dominance, alongside continuing interest in transformational and dispersed leadership theories. Collaborative leadership theory 'reflects context which is interdependent, diverse and collaborative; demands styles which are facilitative and empowering; catalytic and connective' (Williams 2012: 101). However, it is important to highlight that other authors do not see 'collaborative leadership' as dominating recent thinking in the way that Williams does. For example, Pendleton and Furnham (2012) provide a similar summary of trends in leadership thinking over time, but they characterize the period since 2000 in terms of 'organic leadership', where the emphasis is on buy-in, mutual sense-making, and authentic and distributed leadership.

These differences indicate why such overviews risk oversimplification and misinterpretation, but they are helpful in highlighting two points relevant to the discussion that follows: first, conceptions of leadership are not fixed, rather they evolve in line with wider societal and institutional shifts; second, at any one point in time, there is likely to be a dominant discourse for leadership which shapes and is shaped by research, policy and practice. The current dominant discourse – the TLP – might focus on leadership for improvement and efficiency within individual schools, but we argue the case for leadership that is collaborative, capable of working productively within the reality of complex ecosystems in order to achieve broader and more equitable outcomes for children and families.

Leading within and beyond schools – the emergence of system leadership

The TLP notion reflects a coalescing of research and thinking in relation to school leadership within individual schools in recent decades, informed by a series of systematic and meta-reviews which synthesize empirical research in this area (Liebowitz and Porter 2019; Robinson and Gray 2019; Hitt and Tucker 2016; Robinson, Hohepa and Lloyd 2009). One influential example of these reviews is Leithwood, Harris and Hopkins' (2020) update to their 2008 article *Seven Strong Claims about Successful School Leadership* (Leithwood, Harris and Hopkins 2008). The authors confirm their earlier analysis which suggested that all school leaders draw on the same 'repertoire' of leadership practices across four domains: setting directions, building relationships and developing people, redesigning the organization to support desired practices and improving the instructional program. Within the twenty-one specific practices set out within these four domains, only three speak to the kinds of practice arguably required for educational networks, and only the third of these is genuinely outward-looking: first, build a collaborative culture and distribute leadership; second, structure the organization to facilitate collaboration; third, connect the school to its wider environment (Leithwood, Harris and Hopkins 2020). This highlights the extent to which 'good' school leadership has come to be seen as domain-specific, with a relentless internal and instructional focus on improving student achievement and attainment (Earley 2021). However, within this overarching picture, two concepts have emerged which reflect a broader and more open set of perspectives on leadership and organizational development.

The first is distributed leadership (Spillane 2006), which has developed – alongside transformational and instructional leadership (Gumus et al. 2018; Marks and Printy 2003) – as one of the core models for educational leadership within schools (Bush 2019). From the 1990s, Pearce and Conger argue, 'conditions were finally right for the acceptance of [distributed leadership's] seemingly radical departure from the traditional view of leadership as something imparted to followers by a leader from above' (2003: 13). Distributed leadership allows us to understand leadership as a collective, rather than individual, property – an idea that is key to understanding leadership in networks. Leithwood, Harris and Hopkins (2020) argue that leadership within schools has greater impact when it is distributed because this facilitates greater ownership of improvement efforts across teams and allows for diverse forms of expertise to be drawn upon. Higham et al. (2009: 66) suggest that distributed leadership is one of a triad of leadership concepts required for collaborative capacity-building. Leadership of learning sits at the base of their model, while distributed leadership sits above this and focuses on developing and empowering 'a wider cadre of staff to act and think more strategically'. System leadership then sits above distributed leadership, enabling networks that reach beyond individual institutions. It is immediately possible to see how these ideas have informed the design of networking schemes: for example, in the Kāhui Ako model three core network roles are funded – one 'system' leader (Kāhui Ako lead principal), and two distributed roles (across-school and within-school teachers).

As a normative discourse for educational management and leadership, distributed leadership has not been lacking in critique (Lumby 2018; Harris 2013). Peter Gronn (2002a, 2008) was an early proponent, arguing that distributed leadership offered the potential to recognize important dimensions of leadership which so often go unrecognized in the mainstream literature, such as distributed cognition, reciprocal influence, diffusion of leadership and power, and conjoint agency. However, more recently, Gronn (2016: 172) has come to suggest that distributed leadership 'has lost the analytical gloss that once it may have had'. Instead, he sets out a persuasive argument for leadership configurations as hybrid, always existing on a set of continua (i.e. individualism and collectivism, informal and formal, emergent and designed) in ways which change over time and in response to contextual demands. This notion of hybrid leadership has also been applied to network leadership; for example, Townsend (2015) argues against seeing leadership as a set of binary alternatives, suggesting instead that network leadership requires the ability to combine collective and individual activity, knowledge generation and knowledge transfer, emergent and designed features and so on.

We turn now to the second educational leadership concept which helps shed light on network leadership – system leadership. In a 2004 report for the National College for School Leadership in England, Michael Fullan argued that systemic change would be necessary to effect a meaningful challenge to the normative models of educational leadership. Using as his example the initial impressive achievements of the National Literacy and Numeracy Strategy in England, Fullan noted that while there were lifts in achievement, these soon plateaued. According to Fullan, teachers and principals did not 'own' the strategy and this had an impact on innovation, accounting for the inability to sustain progress on literacy and numeracy, and on other dimensions of teaching and learning that were argued to be in need of systemic reform. Fullan argued that system reform requires a focus on adaptive challenges rather than technical solutions (Heitfetz and Linsky 2002). Adaptive work gets to the heart of the conflicts in collaborative endeavours; it is 'the learning required to address conflicts in the values people hold, or to diminish the gap between the values people stand for and the reality they face' (Heifetz 1994: 22). In this work, leadership focuses on a range of behaviours: setting the context, encouraging organizational members to function as 'tags' (people who are effective followers, exercising influence that moves others towards action), establishing ethical standards, engaging in adaptive work, developing cultural proficiency and creating adaptive capability (Hickman 2010). These behaviours, and the kinds of contexts that sustain them, are of necessity underpinned by systems thinking and its related concept, system leadership.

System leadership is a slippery concept, made more complex given 'system' can reference an array of assemblages: an education system, a local authority system or a network of schools (Harris, Jones and Hashim 2021). System leadership is more than simply involvement in network activity (Hopkins 2007). Hopkins and Higham (2007) argue that system leaders in education are those individuals who invest in the improvement of both their own, and other, schools. While endorsed as a component of the Transnational Leadership Package at the start of the twentieth century (Pont and Hopkins 2008), some jurisdictions have developed an overt systemic focus to leadership, including England and Singapore as we saw in earlier chapters. In their review of the literature, Harris et al. (2021) suggest three distinctive but interrelated interpretations of system leadership. First, as evidenced in Singapore, system leadership *as* system change. Here, leaders within the system and its subsystems collectively operate as system change agents. Second, as evidenced in England, system leadership, where designated leaders of education are responsible *for* system change. Third, system leadership *through* system change. Here, Ontario is offered as an example where system change results in the emergence of system leaders.

England's model of system leadership – in particular the government-designated National Leaders of Education model (NLEs – see Chapter 3) – has been evaluated most comprehensively (Armstrong et al. 2020). Early assessments of the approach were largely positive (Pont and Hopkins 2008; Hopkins and Higham 2007) and David Hargreaves (2010, 2012b) argued that system leadership would be fundamental to the development of a successful 'self-improving' school system. Subsequent evaluations did indicate positive impact where system leaders and their teams were brokered to support struggling schools (Muijs 2015a). However, independent research has also highlighted significant issues with the concept as it has become tied into England's wider reform framework. For example, Cousin (2019: 19) positions system leaders as 'part of the increasingly networked, complex governance system', holding degrees of power as a result of their credibility in leading successful schools, but nevertheless acting as agents of a new order that is ever more centralized and demanding in its NPM-driven accountability and performance expectations. In a similar vein, Greany and Higham (2018) characterize system leaders as a 'co-opted elite'. Cousin's qualitative, longitudinal approach allows her to identify the ways in which this co-optation occurs, as leaders subtly shift their language and behaviours over time. For example, she shows how two system leaders became less distributed and more directive in their approach as the system's demands on them ramped up, and how the language of 'moral purpose' gradually falls out of the narrative. Policymakers in England may not have been overly concerned by these critiques, but they have becoming increasingly dissatisfied with the school-to-school support model that NLEs undertake, turning instead to the permanent 'structural solution' offered by Multi-Academy Trusts (MATs – see

Chapter 3). The result is seen in the fragmented complexity of Bampton, where NLEs, Teaching School leaders, MAT CEOs and various other 'system leaders' are working to secure change in a variety of ways, but with little overarching coherence or impact, requiring the new Bampton Alliance as a means to try to build coherence.

Turning to our other three case study systems, we see a range of approaches. In Singapore systems thinking is overt and embedded within formal leadership development programmes, as we explore in the next chapter. Many leadership positions and responsibilities in Singapore are rotated, with school leaders spending time on secondment at the Ministry of Education and successful leaders moved periodically to high-need schools, helping to generate collective commitment and awareness of cross-cutting issues (Ng 2017). By contrast in Chile, the policy shift towards mandated networks has equipped formal system leaders with a restricted frame of action, a frame that ultimately folds the focus of principals back to individual school success (González, Ehren and Montecinos 2020). In Aotearoa, while there is not a discourse of system leaders, an orientation towards system leadership is implicit in the move towards Kāhui Ako initiated through *Investing in Educational Success* coupled with mandated system-wide commitments to the principles of the Treaty of Waitangi. For example, qualities of manaakitanga (respect and care), pono (values), ako (reciprocal learning) and awhinatanga (empathy) are deemed essential for educational leaders, while a Māori world view is fundamentally concerned with whakawhanaungatanga, that is, relationality between humans and embedded in the connectedness of all things (Ruwhiu and Elkin 2016).

This brief review of system leadership in our four case study countries highlights the limitations of models that are tied too closely to individual 'superheads', the approach that Skidmore critiqued at the start of this chapter. Furthermore, building on our analysis of networks through the lenses of governance and complexity theories (Chapters 6 and 7), while there are clear pitfalls in positioning system leadership as a mechanism for securing hierarchical requirements, we equally cannot assume that system leadership will automatically emerge, bottom up, to address every complex challenge in systems that remain predicated on the performance of individual schools. Based on their review of evidence, Harris et al. (2021) propose four observations to realize the potential of system leadership. First, seniority or years of experience within education cannot be the main criterion for recruitment and selection to formal system leader roles. Second, leaders within a system cannot be assumed to be system leaders. Third, system leaders need to have the status, recognition and skills to lead both 'thought' and 'practical' work. This might suggest, in connection to Fullan's (2005) argument detailed above, that such leaders work with *both* adaptive challenges and technical solutions. Fourth, these leaders must hold a theory of action and the ability to model 'next practice' rather than 'existing or best practice', adding value to the system itself. In David Hargreaves' (2012b) term, these system leaders must be 'analytic investigators'. Furthermore, in addition to developing professional capital within schools, as proposed by Andy Hargreaves and Michael Fullan (2012), we suggest that system leaders must build *systemic* capital.

Leadership within and across networks

Distributed and system leadership provide two helpful concepts for understanding leadership within and across inter-school networks. Distributed leadership helps us to see leadership as a collective, shared property, with all the complexity that comes with a move away from individual, positional roles. System leadership helps us to move beyond the focus on individual schools and to see leadership as focussed on addressing systemic and collective issues and priorities, as we explore further in relation to a place-based approach in the next chapter. Equally, as we state above, leadership within schools remains important, while established leadership constructs such as transformational and instructional leadership can contribute to our understanding of leadership in networks. For example, if we consider the experienced principal of Linwood College, who is involved in two very different Kāhui Ako, we can see clearly that part of his success in building trust and initiating change across the partnerships derives from his skills in co-developing a compelling vision founded on moral purpose (i.e. transformational) and his ability to initiate and embed collaborative routines which help teachers to learn and improve (i.e. instructional). We therefore take these insights as our starting point as we explore the distinctive nature of network leadership in education.

In Chapter 1, we argued that leading and managing networks requires sophisticated and widely distributed skills and qualities, but also that network leadership can be learned and developed (a proposition that we return to in the next chapter). We cited Popp et al. (2014: 33), who suggest that network leaders must nurture a culture that 'addresses competing interests, politics and power differentials; and that promotes trusting relationships, curiosity, conscious interest in gaining different perspectives, and respect for diversity of views among organizations.' But we also referenced Vangen and Huxham's (2003) notion of 'collaborative thuggery', which can be required to gain and maintain momentum in networks. Our research for this book, interviewing and observing a range of leaders involved in the Aupaki Kāhui Ako and Bampton Alliance case studies, provides numerous examples of such leadership in action. We draw on many of these examples to inform our analysis in the earlier chapters. This analysis shows that these leaders can and do work nimbly and pragmatically to address the NPM-driven demand for school improvement and effectiveness within single schools, but that this does not prevent them from also engaging productively in networks and, often, addressing complex cross-cutting issues. This is what we mean by 'of, and with' – leadership can be hybrid and configured in multiple nuanced ways. However, this is not the same as saying that leadership can be all things to all people; there will always be trade-offs and hard choices to make, which is where a degree of pragmatic 'collaborative thuggery' becomes necessary. For example, at the start of the process in Bampton, the Local Authority Director wanted the strategy group's work and membership to encompass wider stakeholders and issues that stretch beyond schools, such as the new family health and well-being centres that were being established across the town at that time. The Opportunity Area Director argued that embracing this broader focus and membership created a risk that the core issues in the school sector – that is, the fragmentation and factionalism – would not be fully addressed. In the event, the latter view prevailed and the group maintained a narrower – but still ambitious – focus on generating alignment and coherence in the school sector. Seen through a complexity lens, this decision could be seen to have limited the scope for internal diversity and neighbourly interactions, thereby reducing the potential for a genuinely joined-up set of solutions that could meet the real world needs of children and families to emerge. Our purpose here is not to suggest that one or other approach might have been 'better', simply to observe that network leadership will always require trade-offs – or, in more academic language, dealing with paradox.

Building on these foundational observations, our research highlights three particular aspects of network leadership that appear distinctive and significant: working productively with tensions and paradox, collective sense-making and adopting an ecological approach. Critically, we argue that these three areas emerge as relevant and necessary for network leadership across all four of our theoretical lenses, although the exact nature and extent of leadership in each area differ as we look through each particular lens.

Working with paradox

Paradox 'denotes contradictory yet interrelated elements... [which] seem logical in isolation but absurd and irrational when appearing simultaneously' (Lewis 2000: 760). Various observers have noted the tensions and paradoxes that lie at the heart of many networks, particularly where they are funded by government. For example, networks face demands for measurable 'results' despite the reality that relationship-building takes time, that network outcomes can be hard to measure and that individual schools are held accountable for their own, separate results while also being encouraged to work in networks. We noted Townsend's (2015) suggestion above that network leadership is hybrid, operating on a series of continua that are not mutually exclusive. Embracing paradox involves a similar recognition that leaders can respond to system complexities without needing to fully resolve conflicts to the point of nonexistence (Bowers 2017: 45–6). O'Reilly and Reed (2011) suggest that taking up the lens of paradox allows leaders to adopt an and/and approach – or the 'of, and with' rhythm with which we started this chapter – rather than assuming what is good for one network member must always be at the cost of another.

An engagement with paradox underpins Vangen and Huxham's practice-oriented theory for managing, leading and governing networks (Vangen and Huxham 2012). For Vangen (2017), the embrace of diversity involves five aspects. First, leaning towards bespoke learning around culture (and away from generic learning). Second, leaning towards flexibility in member organization structures to accommodate the needs of the collective (and away from rigidity where partners retain privileged inward-looking needs). Third, leaning towards autonomy, so that individuals in network roles can act to accommodate the needs of the collaboration (and away from the constraints of accountability to their organizations). Fourth, leaning towards leadership that seeks to embrace diversity and complexity (and away from simplifications). Finally, partner-specific communication, where communications should be sensitive to individual partners' culturally determined needs, rather than generic forms of communication that enact the collaborative agenda.

On first reading, this idea of partner-specific communication might seem counter-intuitive and inefficient. Yet, consideration of our case studies shows this mechanism in action. For example, in Chapter 3 we saw how the CEO of a locality partnership in England approached the challenge of 'being the glue in the system'. He argued that it was essential to sustain meaningful engagement with all schools and MATs across the city, since without this there could be no collective learning and improvement. However, sustaining engagement was in tension with the formal role the partnership had been given to challenge schools judged to be underperforming. In these cases, there was a temptation to draw on bureaucratic forms of communication, such as official warning letters, but the CEO explained that such approaches were counterproductive if it meant these school leaders lost trust and stopped engaging with the network. Instead, he adopted a more relational and bespoke partner specific communication approach.

Collective sense-making

Our second network leadership theme is collective sense-making. We touched on this idea in Chapter 5, where we outlined the concept of epistemic communities in which teachers share: theories, or mental maps, about teaching and learning; professional language to describe and analyse their practice; and tools, such as a curriculum, to structure their work. We argued that fostering an epistemic community across a network of schools could support richer forms of collaboration, and that this can be developed through the adoption of enabling routines, boundary spanner roles, shared measurement tools, a culture of improvement-oriented peer evaluation and challenge and, finally, sense-making structures. Sense-making is a concept propounded by the organizational theorist Karl Weick, who is perhaps best known for suggesting that schools are *loosely-coupled* systems (Weick 1976). Bauer (2019: 119–21) explains that Weick eschews 'the noun *organization*, in favour of the more active *organizing*', his point being that 'the world – including both organizations and their environments – are being constantly enacted by individuals and groups'. It is straightforward to see how this can apply to networks and *networking* as much as organizations and *organizing*. Within Weick's work, sense-making is a rich concept that has been interpreted in different ways (Eddy-Spicer 2019; Johnson and Kruse 2019), but we focus here on a core aspect, that sense-making involves an interaction of activity and interpretation. Key points that flow from this for school and network leaders are that 'meaning is apt to *follow* action, and that ambiguity can never be eliminated entirely (or, by extension, our predictions cannot help but be fraught with uncertainty)' (Bauer 2019: 129). Furthermore, organizing – and, we argue, networking – emerges in communication. Or as Bauer (2019: 133) puts it 'what leaders lead is the sharing of knowledge, ideas, and perspectives.... Leading is a *social process of learning together*'. In Weick's words, leaders are poets who speculate, ask questions, follow hunches and 'talk airy nothing into being' (Weick 2011: 9), but they do this collectively, thereby generating shared meaning. Sense-making thus has similarities with Steve Munby's (2021) outline of invitational leadership, part of which involves generating 'a misty vision' and then inviting others to help to shape the thinking, including through collective reflection on actions and events that have already taken place. We see various examples of collective sense-making in Bampton and Aupaki. The most impressive network leaders in these contexts do not only consult in superficial ways; rather, they are problem finders who are prepared to ask difficult questions and to confront underlying issues, they can articulate how these issues relate to the wider goals and values of the partnership, and they adopt a consistently invitational social learning approach in order to make sense of ambiguity and generate shared ways forward.

Eco-leadership

The third network leadership concept is eco-leadership, in which the leader 'looks both ways: internally at the organizational network and externally at wider ecosystems (social, technology, and nature)' (Western 2019: 309). An ecological perspective exercises the patient and 'complicated forms of association between beings' (Landri 2021: 35); this implies countering the anthropocentrism of dominant leadership models and suspending the universalizing logic of the TLP. Leading an ecosystem requires a 'radical' distribution of leadership (Western 2019), committing to 'a long-term agenda of enrolling, including and enabling other players with an interest in learning; in the work of schools, and incorporating other learning modalities in a much more central way – in short, becoming "open"' (Hallgarten, Hannon and Beresford 2015: 50). Eco-leadership is, of necessity, focused on ethics and underpinning values. Rupert Higham (2021) argues that existing approaches to leadership reflect underpinning assumptions (for example, that adults have the moral right and/or duty to pass on their ethical codes to children) which no longer hold true in today's world, given that we are faced with catastrophic threats to our climate, economies and democracies. On this basis, Higham argues for a radically different approach to systemic reform as well as leadership practice, one that recognizes and fosters the role of young people as partners and leaders in change.

Eco-leadership is holistic, so it can be hard to 'spot' within the messy reality of our case study sites, but it is nonetheless apparent. Toh et al. (2014: 836) analyse networks and leadership in Singapore through the lens of ecosystems. They conclude that in a 'favourable socio-political climate that encourages collaboration ... leaders can forge ecological coherence', in part through 'a form of leadership which had an intrinsic ecological belief for the collective good'. These leaders had specific knowledge and skill being 'fluent implementers, communicators of vision and contextually astute mediators who were able to manage the multiple tensions of policy and teacher enactments on the ground level' (2014). These principals are also collective sense-makers, with the ability to 'corral deep conversation ... at critical milestones (ensuring) a more profound understanding of decisions made' (Toh et al. 2014: 841). Critically, this work also stretches into the classroom, where teachers were, simultaneously, involved in their own work to forge ecological coherence across the network: 'as the teachers debated on pedagogical decisions, provided solutions to enactment dilemmas and made attempts to frame problems collectively, the embodied human capital was tapped, philosophical thrusts of the innovation internalized and camaraderie built over time through the shared meaning-making process' (Toh et al. 2014).

Implications in relation to the eight core features of networks

Leadership is essential to gaining ecological coherence and, thereby, creating the conditions for educational networks to achieve their aspirations. The management and leadership of networks are rightly described as being challenging. Successful leadership in these contexts is multifaceted and contingent, so there is no one 'right' way to lead networks. Nevertheless, we suggest that in addition to a number of aspects that have been previously explored (certainly distributed leadership and system leadership, but also aspects of educational leadership within schools, such as transformational and instructional/learning centred leadership, that can be reimagined across a network context), three aspects stand out from our research as particularly important across all four of our theoretical lenses: working productively with tensions and paradox, collective sense-making and adopting an ecological approach.

Building on this, Kamp (2012) suggests five strategies for achieving collaborative goals, drawing on the work of Brian Massumi (1992). First, leaders need to model disconnecting from habitual ways of pursuing the collective goal given habit fosters resistance to change. Second, leaders need to identify, and work in, the cracks and spaces in the actual world to try out innovations. Third, leaders need to 'pass' in the system as it is, so innovation must sometimes be camouflaged so that it appears acceptable to the system as the system changes. Fourth, in a related action, leaders need to weave between the actual and what is becoming possible, until such time as the fifth strategy of 'coming out' is possible. This is the point where the new ways of working are presented as the new normal, thereby enabling even greater transformational potential.

In Table 9.1, we revisit the eight network characteristics from Chapter 1, drawing out the leadership implications that are now evident as we look across the analysis through the four theoretical lenses.

Table 9.1 Eight core features of networks and their leadership implications

Eight core features of networks from Chapter 1	Leadership implications
Successful inter-organizational networks reflect a shared goal or interest, although organizations can have multiple motivations for engaging – for example s*afety, effectiveness* and s*tatus* – which can be in tension with each other.	Leaders work together to define and address shared goals, with a focus on the needs of children and families. There is a recognition that some valued outcomes cannot be easily measured, and that innovation, complexity and emergence mean that some outcomes cannot be predefined.
	Leaders understand that tensions and paradox are necessary components of educational networks and that these do not necessarily need to be resolved for the collective to achieve its aims.
Network impact relates to the level of commitment and contribution of network members reflecting shared ownership and benefits. Network members' ability to commit to network processes can wax and wane in line with wider factors.	Network facilitators are invitational and skilled at co-design – they seek collective engagement and benefits from networking. Leaders find ways to unlock and grow collective capacity so that networking achieves impact.
	Leaders' awareness of complexity theories enables them to work flexibly with the ebbs and flows of member commitment, including by adopting partner specific communication needs.
Successful networks generally share values, practices and attributes, which take time to build.	Leaders work together to define and realize their shared moral purpose, including a core focus on meeting the needs of all children and families.
	Leaders focus on the critical importance of relationality or, in Aotearoa, whanaungatanga [kinship].
	Leaders seek to foster trust and social capital, but they also recognize the limits of tight bonds and so seek to connect beyond their existing boundaries.

Inter-organizational partnerships are embedded within wider societal contexts and interact with the multiple social networks that intersect the organizations involved. Networks can be seen to have four dimensions – structure, function, strength and content.	Leaders continually 'read' their eco-system and, in the process, anticipate interrelationships and identify where, and how, to intervene in feedback mechanisms to move the collaboration forwards.
Many networks develop formalized governance and management structures over time as they grow, believing this will improve efficiency, but such structures can risk reducing levels of ownership for (some) members.	Leadership involves identifying the minimum specifications for effectiveness and accountability and, where necessary, working collaboratively with stakeholders, including government, to negotiate how these can work to facilitate the other core dimensions outlined here.
	Leaders are pragmatists, able to engage in 'collaborative thuggery' where necessary in order to move the agenda forward.
A number of design principles or features are important for network effectiveness, such as the availability of resources (including time) and the use of shared protocols and routines to guide action.	Leaders are aware that these non-human actors can, and do, act as leaders in their own right.
	Network leaders maintain focus on how to form assemblages with all actors, both human and non-human. By implication, network leaders are also attentive to assemblages that do not mobilize the collaborative agenda, and act to remove, or at least impede, those assemblages.
Networks in education often focus on generating and diffusing knowledge, although the extent to which such knowledge benefits from formal codification or not is debated.	Leadership prioritizes social learning and sense-making, the principles of epistemic communities and learning systems are embedded into the daily work of teachers and leaders across all member schools, so that knowledge and expertise are continually developed and shared to support network learning.
Leading and managing networks requires sophisticated skills and qualities from lead facilitators and wider participants.	Leaders model system leadership, so that it becomes a resource and expectation for all.
	Leadership is distributed. There is a focus on ensuring that teachers and wider staff have regular opportunities to engage in networking and to develop as network leaders.

Conclusion

This chapter has illustrated the ways in which network leadership is not the purview of a single leader in a formal leadership position, despite the introduction of such roles into the networks established by government in our case studies. Leadership is more organic and diverse, and grows across a network. In collaborative networks, effective leaders view their role as 'leader as host' rather than 'leader as hero' (Wheatley and Frieze 2011). Hosts invite all parts of the network to participate and contribute. They trust in others' creativity and commitment. They know people are supportive of that which they have played a part in creating. They invite people in, ask questions and support risk-taking. They invest in meaningful conversation to secure new insights and action possibilities. This notion of 'leader as host' resonates with ecological approaches to leadership that acknowledge complexity and interdependence. In Chapter 10, we move to consider the implications of these insights for policy and practice in relation to leadership development and the operation of the 'middle tier' across local school systems.

10

Leading Networks: Implications for Policy and Practice

Introduction

The previous chapter focused on the implications of the analysis throughout this book for how we conceptualize educational leadership within and across networks. This chapter builds on that analysis, first by providing a synthesis of the key messages and implications that emerge and, second, by drawing out a set of strategic implications for policy and practice. In undertaking this assessment we assume that schools and school systems globally will continue to foster inter-school networks as they seek to enhance educational quality, equity and innovation, although we also seek to challenge the dominant NPM-driven focus on choice, efficiency and effectiveness. We do this in particular by arguing the need to reconceptualize the purpose and role of the 'middle tier' in larger education systems (where the 'middle tier' – or meso-level – refers to any form of statutory or non-statutory support and influence operating between individual schools and central government) and in our proposals to strengthen collective forms of leadership development.

As we have emphasized throughout the book, we are not suggesting that networks are straightforward or a magical solution for every educational challenge, even if they are sometimes presented in that way (Grimaldi 2011). Rather, we have tried to illustrate how and why networks are invariably messy and often problematic, both for the practitioners who work within them and for those in policy or strategic roles who seek to understand and facilitate their development. We argued in Chapter 1 that networks can have a 'dark side'; for example, if they reproduce unequal power relations, are closed and exclusive in their membership, encourage groupthink and/or are motivated by risk, fear and suspicion. We have not focused extensively on these darker aspects in our analysis in Chapters 5–8, but they have been discernible in the background. For example, in Chapter 6 we explored the impact of local status hierarchies, which emerge in response to market pressures coupled with intensive hierarchically imposed performance requirements in some systems. This combination of intense pressure to demonstrate school performance in the context of competitive status hierarchies can lead schools to form or join networks that exclude certain members, such as lower-status schools that do not enhance the 'brand' or that are seen to require more intensive support (Greany 2020b). In a similar vein, in Chapters 3 and 8 we examined how the collapse of the Local Authority in Bampton, England, led to a loss of trust and fragmentation, with multiple cliques and networks emerging, some of which reproduced unequal power relations (for example, where a high-performing school was brokered to support a poorly performing school, which it then took over as part of a MAT) and others of which were motivated by fear and suspicion.

Given this complexity, it is challenging and potentially risky to synthesize the findings or to draw out specific implications for policy or leadership development practice in this area. However, on balance, we think it is valuable to overlay and compare the analyses and to identify overarching themes and questions which, we hope, can help orient readers towards the areas and issues that most require attention.

The chapter is structured in three sections. The first provides a synthesis of the analyses undertaken in Chapters 5–8, using the four theoretical lenses, and draws out key implications for policy and practice. The second focuses on the nature and role of 'middle tier' in relation to networks, a topic we touched on in Chapter 6. Finally, the third section addresses the theme of leadership development for networks and network leadership in education.

Synthesis – what do the four lenses tell us?

Existing influential analyses of school systems and school leadership have tended to ignore or underplay the importance of networks (Barber et al. 2010; Barber and Mourshed 2007), although some more recent studies do address their role within wider policy and practice frameworks (Ehren and Baxter 2021; Greany and Earley 2021; Cousin 2019). Nevertheless, our detailed focus on networks and network leadership across four systems is unique and reveals a number of important cross cutting implications for policy and practice.

In Table 10.1, we summarize key points from Chapters 5–8 in relation to the four lenses and then, in the right-hand column, draw out implications for

Table 10.1 Synthesis of key concepts, arguments and implications from the four theoretical lenses

Theoretical lens	Summary points	Implications for networks and network leadership
School Effectiveness and School Improvement (Chapter 5)	David Hargreaves' 'capital theory' (2001) emphasizes four interrelated concepts – intellectual capital, social capital, leverage and institutional outputs – and highlights the importance of trust and reciprocity between colleagues. His later work (2010, 2012b) positioned inter-organizational networks as central mechanisms for school and system improvement, fostered through joint practice development, co-creation, collective moral purpose and peer evaluation and challenge. These concepts can be observed, to different extents, across the case studies. In particular, we highlight the importance of shared intellectual capital as a platform for enhanced teacher learning, which supports capacity building and leverage. Securing shared intellectual capital requires leaders to focus on knowledge mobilization through the development of epistemic communities, characterized by shared theory, language and tools across schools. This requires a network-wide learning architecture, involving enabling routines, boundary spanner roles, shared measurement systems, sense-making structures and a culture of collaborative peer evaluation and challenge.	Leaders focus on effectiveness and improvement at the level of individual schools in all four systems. There are differences in how far accountability is formative and/or summative, with implications for network engagement (i.e. instrumental versus developmental). Network impact is easiest to observe in narrowly defined 'turnaround' partnerships. Network level 'improvement and effectiveness' is rarely defined or encouraged in systematic ways. Networks offer a means of unlocking and making available collective capacity, but this is not a given and success relates to the eight core features (see Chapters 1 and 9). Leverage is about more than implementing evidence-based interventions: it describes how leaders align a complex set of factors which, together, build capacity and improve outcomes. We pose three questions for leaders: • How best to engage with hierarchical and funding incentives, which can augment core capacity but can also introduce bureaucracy and create dependency? • How to develop capacity across non-homogenous partnerships? • How to assess capacity limitations, for example to know when a partnership arrangement is not the optimal solution?

Governance theory (Chapter 6)	Governance theory aims to open up the 'black box of the state' (Bevir 2011: 1). We analyse how hierarchy, market, network and community forms of coordination operate separately and in hybrid ways to steer the work of schools. NPM approaches aimed at securing efficient and effective performance (Hood 1991) have dominated education policy in recent decades. This has led to an emphasis on school autonomy and accountability and a reduced role for traditional 'middle tier' bodies (for example local authorities). An NPM focus on school quality and student outcomes is apparent in all four countries, even in the face of political swings to left and right, though there are differences in how this plays out. Generational shifts towards markets and decentralization and, more recently, towards networks, have occurred in all four countries. But hierarchical steering continues to be significant, through meta-governance. Policymakers have seen networks as a way to counteract pitfalls associated with markets. However, we show how networks operate in the shadow of both hierarchy and markets. We compare network and community forms of coordination. Self-formed community networks based on shared identities can have greater independence from hierarchical requirements, but these examples are limited. Where existing 'community' partnerships engage with hierarchically defined requirements (for example to access funding) they are changed in the process.	The context of the system (size, geography, racial and/or socio-economic stratification and so on) the history of relationships between schools and (local) policymakers, and the agency of key actors, all shape how networks develop. All four systems are seeking to combine hierarchical and network forms of coordination. Examples of 'self-improving' community networks are relatively rare. Hierarchical policy draws on combinations of incentives, capacity-building, mandated requirements, exhortation and pressure to stimulate networks. Too much prescription can make partnership working unattractive and/or can skew activities unhelpfully. Too little prescription could mean that partnerships 'reinvent the wheel'. Hierarchical accountability frameworks influence how schools engage in and with networks (see SESI above). Some systems have developed accountability models which differentiate between school and network-level processes and outcomes, which may help to strengthen commitment and joint action (Janssens and Ehren 2016). The mixing of different governance structures creates tensions and paradoxes for frontline leaders in local contexts. Layering partnerships onto an existing marketized and stratified system is problematic. 'Co-opetition' is feasible in some contexts, but many partnerships fail and/or develop in inequitable ways. Networks – and network governance – have a particular role to play in coordinating place-based (i.e. local) action. This requires attention to the nature and role of the 'middle tier'.

Complexity theories (Chapter 7)	Complexity theories allow us to explore network processes and their potential for supporting wider outcomes, such as knowledge generation and dissemination, as well as for generating adaptive responses to complex challenges. Complexity theories explore subsystems and how they dynamically interrelate in influential ways – an ecosystem perspective. We focus on Davis and Sumara's (2008) four complexity conditions. *Internal diversity* highlights a paradox – i.e. most networks benefit from both strong and weak ties simultaneously. Highly bonded core groups characterized by homophily should maintain strategic 'weak links' to ensure access to wider influences and resources. *Internal redundancy* – the necessity of overlaps and duplication within a network, offers potential for chance encounters and *neighbourly interactions*. *Decentralized/dispersed control* focuses on collective leadership. However, maintaining the right level of coherence is critical: dispersed control is not the same as everyone doing their own thing.	The focus on efficiency in NPM pushes against a need for redundancy. Network leaders must balance the requirement for homophily and diversity and find ways to foster trust and social capital across less tightly bonded networks. Our case studies reveal how leaders work to build on homophily, but also work to encompass greater socio-economic and/or cultural diversity in network membership. This is achieved by fostering shared moral purpose – i.e. a commitment to improve education for all children. Another case study shows how the network struggles to cohere in the face of too much diversity and redundancy. In these contexts, it is important to consider the attractors and boundaries which give shape to joint work. School leaders in this case committed 'in principle' to the shared vision (i.e. collective moral purpose), but overcoming fragmentation required additional action on multiple fronts over the course of nearly two years. Once established, this group was able to pivot to address a new complex challenge – the COVID-19 pandemic. The role of the named leader is to create possibilities for emergence to occur, often by working with minimal profile.
Actor-Network Theory (Chapter 8)	'In ANT, the word network does not qualify a closed thing but a dynamic assemblage of entities, a set of successful translations' (Landri 2021: 83). ANT seeks to track 'actants' – the full range of possible actors – as they create, advance or frustrate a collective task. *Symmetry* reconsiders who and what is the source of action. *Translation* refers to 'what happens when entities, human and nonhuman' come together and correct, changing one another to form links. Translation can involve four non-linear 'moments': problematization; interessement; enrolment; and mobilization (Callon 1986). Network stabilization' occurs through these moments as actors coalesce around a shared agenda, network processes become routine and, with sufficient allies, the network becomes 'real'.	We show how performance technologies (for example international pupil assessments) and digital technologies operate as network actors. These non-human actors are neither immutable nor neutral tools; rather, they shape how policymakers and school leaders operate and define themselves in ways that can narrow down or open up network potential. Network formation – or *translation* – is rarely a single, unified process. Rather, it can develop at multiple levels and in multiple ways simultaneously, not least due to non-human actors. In one case study, the overall flow is towards the launch of a new place-based alliance and stabilization of the network, but this masks the various eddies and whirlpools which disrupt the flow as various cliques and subgroups within the network engage in parallel processes of translation. The design and operation of the hotel in which the formative away days are held play a role.

networks and network leadership. This highlights a number of important points, both in relation to the individual lenses and as we look across the four lenses. For example, starting with the individual lenses, we see that:

- SESI – achieving leverage (i.e. impact) across a partnership requires sophisticated leadership, with a focus on generating an epistemic community characterized by shared theories, language and tools underpinned by enabling routines, boundary spanners and so on, since this provides a platform for collective learning and progression for teachers.
- Governance – it is important to align hierarchical and network forms of governance to ensure inclusive and equitable systems, since 'self-improving' community networks are relatively rare and can be exclusive. This requires careful attention to the 'middle tier' and how network development is facilitated, and to how wider system features (for example accountability, funding and so on) support this. As we explored in the last chapter, frontline leaders will need to grapple with tensions and paradoxes as they operate in networks, for example where network and market forms of governance are combined (co-opetition).
- Complexity – Narrowing impact down to measures of school quality and/or student outcomes (as in SESI) and focussing too narrowly on efficiency (as in NPM) risks reducing the potential for wider innovations to emerge. Network leaders must balance the requirement for homophily and diversity and find ways to foster trust and social capital across less tightly bonded networks.
- ANT – Network formation – or *translation* – is rarely a single, unified process. Furthermore, net-work is shaped by non-human as well as human actors, so leaders must pay attention to the full range of actors and must learn to appreciate and work productively within these overlapping processes if they are to achieve a productive level of stabilization through the 'moments' of translation.

In addition, as we look across the four lenses and four contexts, we see a number of wider themes and implications. One of these relates to levels of convergence and divergence in how global trends are interpreted and addressed across the four contexts. On the one hand, we observe how global forces and processes are driving convergence. For example, in Chapter 6 we argued that all four systems have adopted NPM, while in Chapter 9 we showed how they are all absorbed in transnational logics of practice around the leadership and management of education, the Transnational Leadership Package (Thomson, Gunter and Blackmore 2021). However, notwithstanding this level of isomorphism (DiMaggio and Powell 1983) apparent across the four countries, we can also see important differences in how they conceptualize and support networks. These differences appear to reflect more fundamental divergences in how school and system leaders in each context have interpreted and responded to these global forces, reflecting their distinctive contexts, histories and educational beliefs and values. For example, in New Zealand we explored the growing influence of the Treaty of Waitangi as the founding document of Aotearoa, and the commitments it demands to embrace te Ao Māori, a Māori world view that privileges the collective. This is a profound resource for Kāhui Ako which has resulted in guidelines that draw on both Māori and Western insights. In Singapore, we saw how policy has fostered a systemic focus on twenty-first-century learning, with school-led networks supported to pioneer and disseminate digital learning innovations. By contrast, in England, the focus of school-to-school support partnerships and policy has been narrower, aimed at addressing school turnaround and securing measurable improvements in student test scores.

These examples are suggestive of deeper contrasts and differences in how networks are conceptualized and positioned, which the four lenses help to illuminate. For example, the school improvement/effectiveness and governance literatures tend to view networks as tangible, practical and at least partially controllable, whereas the complexity and ANTian perspectives reveal them to be elusive, expansive and continually evolving. We are not suggesting that one or other perspective is more valid; rather, we argue that the extent to which policymakers and practitioners in any given system adhere to one particular lens – whether consciously or unconsciously – will condition how far they are able to appreciate the full potential of networks and how they work in practice to unlock this potential. At the risk of over simplifying, while a SESI perspective can provide focus and can, perhaps, reduce some of the messy and time-consuming complexity of networking, it can limit the potential for adaptation and innovation. Similarly, while a complexity perspective can create space for innovations to emerge, it offers far less predictability regarding the outcomes that can be expected or even whether particular constituencies will engage, potentially leading to investment fatigue and disengagement from some stakeholders. For these reasons, we urge school and system leaders to engage with multiple perspectives at once, recognizing that each has its strengths and limitations. Beyond that, as we indicate above, how any given leader, school, network or system chooses to engage with networks will relate to fundamental questions about how they see the purposes of education in the twenty-first century. We hope that Table 10.1 provides insights that can inform debates on these issues and help policy and practice audiences to conceptualize and develop networks in response.

In conclusion, two findings are worth emphasizing from the synthesis in Table 10.1. First, as we explored in the last chapter in relation to network leadership, networks are rarely straightforward and commonly create tensions and paradoxes that frontline leaders must work in hybrid ways to accommodate. Second, while networking can be learned, we cannot assume that leaders who have been trained and worked largely within individual schools will necessarily have the skills or capacity to lead successful networks. These points support our focus on the 'middle tier' and leadership development in the subsequent two sections.

Reimagining the 'middle tier' in networked systems

In this section we revisit the discussion of the 'middle tier' that we touched on in Chapter 6. Greany (2020a: 3) defines the 'middle tier' – or meso-layer – as encompassing any aspect of statutory or non-statutory support and influence which operates between individual schools and central government. This definition can encompass lateral networks, whether they be government funded or 'school-led' community networks, as well as networks that involve hierarchical (for example local or national government) and/or wider representatives (for example professional development providers). The definition does not assume that the 'middle tier' is necessarily place-based, but our focus here is on locality examples, given this is the context of our two main case studies – Bampton and Aupaki. In our experience it is in this place-based 'middle tier' space that networks are most often forged and operate and in which network leaders must address tensions and paradoxes, because this is where the needs and wants of different constituencies bump up against each other.[1] As a result it is in these local 'middle tier' contexts that leadership and attention to system learning are most obviously required, yet these complexities are often neglected by national policymakers. For these reasons, we argue that policy must consider the nature and function of the 'middle tier', the role of networks within this and how leadership will be developed and supported to address collaborative aims, at least as closely as any national or provincial framework for network development.

In Chapter 6 we showed how our case study systems have positioned inter-school networks as a means of addressing issues arising from wider changes to hierarchical governance. Moves to increase school autonomy – through decentralization – have had an impact on traditional 'middle tier' structures, such as school districts and local education authorities, which have historically provided the primary locus of place-based improvement and knowledge sharing in many systems. In New Zealand, boards of education were removed altogether as part of the *Tomorrow's Schools* reforms of 1989, while in England the role of local authorities has been progressively rolled back, and in Chile the municipalities are being replaced with a smaller number of Local Public Education Services (SLEs). These changes have been characterized by locally nuanced drivers and debates: for example, in New Zealand we outlined three strands – a democratic-populist strand around parental involvement in school governance; a managerialist strand geared towards effectiveness, efficiency and reduced bureaucracy; and a market-oriented strand aimed at increasing responsiveness and competition. Similar themes can be identified in England, along with debates around the rightful role of local democratic oversight for public education (Hatcher 2014). As we saw, Chile, England and New Zealand have all faced challenges as a result of decentralization and competition between schools, including increased socio-economic stratification in school admissions, isolated and struggling schools and limited mechanisms for sharing and building professional capacity. In response, policymakers have sought to develop new 'middle tier' arrangements, whether through the creation of new, collaborative structures within hierarchy (such as the incoming Education Service Agency in New Zealand, MATs in England and SLEs in Chile) and/or through lateral networks.[2]

In practice, making the shift from hierarchical and/or market-oriented frameworks and cultures to collaborative network-oriented systems is rarely straightforward. In Chapter 1 we cited González, Ehren and Montecinos' (2020) study of how one newly formed SLE team in Chile had worked to develop networks across its constituent schools. The researchers found that building trust and ownership among schools had proved challenging, due to 'a mindset where vertical and centralized coordination, associated with hierarchical governance, predominates over horizontal and distributed leadership, associated with network governance' (2020: 15). Similarly, in Chapter 3, we showed how Labour and Conservative governments' investment in networks in England from the late 1990s onwards had succeeded in shifting the earlier competitive culture, but that efforts to create a 'self-improving system' have been problematic, not least due to the historic and continuing role of hierarchical and market influences, with the result being a more fragmented and unequal system characterized by 'winners and losers' (Greany and Higham 2018).

A key challenge here is in conceptualizing the desired and actual role of any reshaped 'middle tier', and particularly the appropriate balance between hierarchical and network forms of governance. Greany (2020a) identifies four contrasting interpretations in the literature. The first suggests that existing 'middle tier' bodies can be reformed to support priorities set by national or provincial government, through 'tri-level' (i.e. centre, district, schools) efforts (Levin 2012). A second view is that local agency is fatally diminished in the face of 'highly centralized system steering' (Ozga 2011: 149), with data used to hold schools accountable and 'middle tier' bodies 'reconstituted as conduits of central information and policy' (Ozga 2011: 156). The third perspective sees space for local agency, whether for new or existing players, so long as they are willing and able to reform themselves to work within the new disintermediated environment (Cousin 2019; Lubienski 2014; Ball and Junemann 2012). Finally, the fourth group argue that diverse players, including schools, can collaborate around shared agendas to achieve productive 'middle out' change (Munby and Fullan 2016; OECD 2015). Hargreaves and Shirley (2020) develop this fourth perspective further by distinguishing between 'leading in the middle' and 'leading from the middle'. In this, the former is a more formalized connector and buffer between the centre and schools, whereas the latter implies a more fluid set of relationships bound together by moral purpose, collective responsibility and leaders from different organizations playing an active role in initiating, rather than just implementing, change.

If we apply these perspectives to our case study countries we can see how one or more can be perceived in each context. Chile's reshaping of its municipalities into SLEs is clearly an attempt to develop tri-level reform, as is Singapore's introduction of superintendents, clusters and zones. In both systems, however, these hierarchical changes are combined with efforts to generate lateral networks – SINs in Chile and networked learning communities (NLCs) in Singapore – highlighting the ambition to avoid a purely top-down relationship between local bureaucrats and individual schools, and to foster a degree of 'middle out' change. England and New Zealand's examples are less clear-cut, not least because school-level autonomy has been such a strong feature in both systems over the past thirty years. Nevertheless, certain features and trends can be identified: both systems have stripped back or removed the traditional 'middle tier' and have relied on national data and systems to monitor schools, while both have also been held up by different observers as exemplifying the third (disintermediation – Lubienski 2014) and fourth perspectives ('middle out' change – Munby and Fullan 2016; Fullan 2015). However, the fact that England and New Zealand's approaches have been compared does not mean they are necessarily developing similar 'middle tier' trajectories. England's move towards non-place based MATs is very different to New Zealand's continued commitment to individual self-managing schools linked together through voluntary Kāhui Ako and community partnerships. Inevitably, these differences create very different dynamics for leaders in each case. In England, the CEOs of the new MATs have complete authority over their member schools and many are using these powers to try to forge internally coherent approaches to improvement and knowledge sharing (Greany and McGinity 2021; Greany 2018a). This creates a challenge for place-based collaboration: indeed, as MATs become more coherent internally, collaboration *among* them may actually become more challenging, for example, if the teachers working in different MATs adopt very different terminologies and models of practice (Glazer et al. 2022). We saw how these issues play out in Bampton, where securing engagement from the twelve MATs was challenging in itself, an issue that was compounded by the fear among many non-MAT schools that they might be taken over by a trust. In contrast, New Zealand's Kāhui Ako leaders cannot rely on positional authority over their member schools, and while the Ministry of Education, and others, convene meetings which bring leaders from the city's various Kāhui Ako together, there is no impetus for a formalized place-based partnership equivalent to Bampton's Alliance.

These points highlight a related consideration for the 'middle tier' – the elusive nature of 'place' itself. In Chapter 7, we introduced the idea that sociospatial notions of place are important but nonetheless constructed, with networks playing in a role in this process (Papanastasiou 2017; Gulson 2011; Jessop, Brenner and Jones 2008). For example, the Bampton Alliance is seeking to reimagine and reinvigorate commitment to a local, place-based approach in the context of a reduced role for the Local Authority and as a counterbalance to the various ways in which schools are engaging in alternative networks and structures, including MATs. Aupaki Kāhui Ako reflects a different set of place-focused dynamics, influenced by both geography, historical loyalties to particular schools and declining rolls in the wake of the earthquakes of 2010 and 2011. Linwood secondary school's new campus is located some 10 kms away from the Bays cluster of primary schools, a similar distance to the oversubscribed Cashmere High in the more affluent area of Cashmere. As outlined in Chapter 4, Linwood has historically attracted a more socio-economically disadvantaged and more ethnically diverse intake than the Bays primary schools. Aupaki Kāhui Ako makes manifest an opportunity to reshape perceptions of opportunity across the locality in addition to – or even as a result of – working on shared improvement and learning priorities.

Drawing these insights together, we argue the need for policymakers to focus on how the 'middle tier' can best facilitate networks and network learning that meets the needs of all students, and schools, in a locality. At a macro-level, this requires clarity on the desired role of any reshaped 'middle tier', together with a continuing commitment to the importance of place if all schools – and therefore all communities – are to access and benefit from network developments. At a practical level, we argue that making this happen requires the adoption of a *local solutions* mindset and a *co-design approach* across all aspects of policy development and enactment. Bunt and Harris (2010: 32) define local solutions as combining local action and national scale:

> Instead of assuming that the best solutions need to be determined, prescribed, driven or 'authorised' from the centre, policymakers should create more opportunities for communities to develop and deliver their own solutions and to learn from each other.

Bunt and Harris argue that such 'mass localism' requires 'a different kind of support from government and a different approach to scale' (2010: 32). On the one hand 'it is not enough to assume that scaling back government bureaucracy and control will allow local innovation to flourish' (2010: 32). Rather, local solutions require an active but facilitative approach from the centre, geared towards defining core principles and then helping to stimulate networks and support local dialogue, learning and action, while accepting that different localities might have legitimately different priorities and ways of working. This is the core of the co-design – or co-creation – approach (Bransden et al. 2018), which goes beyond superficial stakeholder engagement and consultation, and instead seeks to actively involve key constituencies in shaping and addressing contextually appropriate plans of action and then supporting a continuing process of evaluation, learning and change.

We argue that a place-focused approach to developing the 'middle tier' which adopts a local solutions mindset and co-design methodologies will – in the process – also help to foster and support collaborative networks which can enhance students' education and outcomes. Practical questions, such as the ideal size and composition of localities, will depend on geographic factors as well as historic and current sociopolitical and community boundaries. The most important thing is that the local focus is meaningful to the education professionals who live and work there, and that there is the potential to generate shared moral purpose, joint practice development and meaningful collaborative action across the network. We see examples of what this means in practice in all four of our case study systems, even though we also highlight the ways in which NPM, markets, efficiency and so on can often overwhelm or subvert these efforts. Balancing and aligning hierarchical and network-based roles and capacity will thus be key, making sure that hierarchical leadership is geared towards facilitating network development, securing equity and engagement from all schools and supporting wider learning. This involves working in the ways outlined here, through local solutions and co-design, and considering how the eight core features of networks (Chapters 1 and 9) can be addressed.

In considering these possibilities, we encourage school and system leaders to address the following questions:

- What are we trying to achieve – in particular, what is the desired balance between improvement/quality, equity/inclusiveness and innovation/emergence?
- How well will any new framework ensure that professional knowledge and expertise is continually created, articulated, shared and embedded across local networks in ways which enrich children's education and learning?
- What are the respective roles of hierarchical, network and community forms of co-ordination in securing these objectives, in particular to ensure equity and inclusive development (and how might we minimize the impact of any historic emphasis on markets/competition)?
- How will decision-making and resources be distributed to the level of the locality, the network and/or the school?
- Where should responsibility for outcomes reside – at school-level, network-level and/or 'middle tier' level (NB: different outcomes might be pursued at different levels simultaneously) – and over what timescales?
- What forms of accountability are needed – formative and/or summative, vertical (to government) and/or lateral (to peers and parents) – and what are the minimum specifications?
- Do we need to define and support specific roles, processes or types of expertise – for example, network leadership, enabling routines, boundary spanners, shared measurement systems, sense-making structures?
- Have we allowed (sufficient) space for emergence (internal diversity, internal redundancy, neighbour interactions and decentralized control) and

have we considered sufficiently the role and influence of non-human actors, such as PISA?
- How can we best facilitate these developments given the need for a local solutions and co-design approach? For example, what are the implications for national or state-level ministry teams? How can we best unlock and facilitate local action, without creating a compliance or dependency culture?

Implications for leadership development

In Chapter 9, we explored the implications of networks for leaders and leadership, arguing that a network perspective requires moving beyond the 'classic' NPM-driven Transnational Leadership Package, with its narrow focus on school improvement and effectiveness and on individual leaders. Instead, we argued that leadership within and across networks requires attention to issues of culture, power and paradox, with an ability to navigate the eight core features laid out in Chapter 1. These arguments underpin our analysis here, where we consider the implications of all that we have explored for how leadership is developed and supported. Our analysis builds on the previous section, where we argued that policymakers must consider the boundary work involved in shaping place-based 'middle tier' spaces for network development and governance. Our assessment of the implications here is necessarily brief, so we focus on broad implications rather than specific recommendations for facilitators of leadership development. We start by briefly reviewing how our four case study systems have approached leadership development in recent years before examining why and how these approaches need to become more collectively focused and more fully embedded within the real work of leading complex and networked educational systems.

Approaches to leadership development

A number of studies have analysed the features of effective leadership development, both within the education sphere and more widely (Breakspear et al. 2017; Jensen et al. 2017; Pillans 2015; DeRue and Myers 2014; Barber et al. 2010; Glatter 2008; Darling Hammond et al. 2007). These studies provide a level of detail around how leadership skills and capacity can be developed that is beyond the scope of this chapter, but three points are worth highlighting. First, programmes should be 'philosophically and theoretically attuned to individual and system needs' (Fluckiger et al. 2014). Second, programmes should be purpose-designed for different career stages, highlighting the need to see professional development as a career-long continuum and to design programmes differently to meet the needs of different groups. Third, leadership development opportunities must be embedded within the day-to-day context of schools, so that leaders are reflecting on their contextual challenges and, in the process, are also working to achieve successful, and meaningful, change and improvement.

This evidence has informed the design of educational leadership development strategies and programmes globally. Reflecting the emphasis on school autonomy and school effectiveness and improvement that we described earlier, these initiatives have mostly focused on individual leaders – particularly aspiring and newly appointed school principals – and on developing the skills and knowledge required to lead improvement within individual schools. Many countries adopt similar approaches in terms of how leadership is defined and how individual leaders are identified and developed, with a reliance on competency-based standards linked to formal programmes and accreditation processes (Greany 2018b; Harris and Jones 2015; Pont et al. 2008). That said, Walker, Bryant and Lee (2013) reviewed the design and delivery model for principal preparation programmes in five countries (Australia, Canada, Hong Kong, Singapore and the United States), noting both high levels of convergence in many aspects, but also variations as a result of local contextualization, leading to some non-trivial differences. An example would be whether and how universities are engaged in providing and accrediting provision, and how significantly practitioner expertise is recognized and integrated.

Our case study countries broadly reflect this picture, although Singapore's approach stands out as more ambitious, as we outline below. England's National Professional Qualification for Headteachers (NPQH) was introduced in the 1990s and was briefly made mandatory for all newly appointed principals, though is now optional again. A wider suite of National Professional Qualifications (NPQs) is available for middle and senior leadership roles within schools and for 'executive leaders' (i.e. leaders across two or more schools, usually within a MAT context) (DfE 2020; Supovitz 2014). The Department for Education launched a new content and assessment framework for all the NPQs in 2020, each with a tightly prescribed set of domain-specific skills and competencies which address the government's knowledge-based curriculum and traditional (i.e. direct instruction) pedagogic approach. The NPQs for head teachers and executive leaders do include a 'working in partnership' domain (DfE 2020), but this is limited to a narrow set of areas geared towards raising pupil attainment and so bears little resemblance to the kinds of invitational network leadership we explored in the last chapter.

Chile has implemented several reforms aimed at enhancing the quality and capacity of leaders in state-funded schools. Before 2006, there was no Chilean legislation to regulate head teacher selection, meaning that heads were appointed without regard to technical expertise or qualifications (Galdames and Gonzalez 2016). A law changing this was introduced in 2006 and implemented nationally by 2011. In addition, the Ministry of Education has provided funds to improve working conditions and salaries for school leaders and for national professional development programmes, including through the launch of two national School Leadership Centres.

New Zealand's decentralized system has historically provided limited professional development support for aspiring and serving principals, although optional induction programmes have been available for newly appointed principals since 2002. As recently as 2018, the Education Council – now the Teaching Council – acknowledged that professional learning for experienced principals had been neglected. This stimulated the launch in 2018 of a Leadership Strategy and Educational Leadership Capability Framework[3] and proposals, now underway, for the Council to launch a government-funded Leadership Centre, which will develop 'leadership capability and capacity for every teacher, including those in role-based leadership roles but not limited to that' with a focus on 'principled, capable, adaptive and inspirational leadership' (Education Council 2020).

Finally, Singapore has a single, monopoly provider – the National Institute of Education – formed in 1991 as an autonomous institution within the Nanyang Technological University. The NIE is responsible for the key milestone programmes that teachers complete on their route to principalship, including the flagship six-month full-time Leaders in Education Programme (LEP) for aspiring principals. Launched in 2001, the LEP's content covers systems and futures thinking, organizational learning and dealing with complexity as well as more operational aspects of leadership. It includes a two-week visit to another country and a Creative Action Project (CAP), where participants propose and implement a 'value-adding change' in a different school to their own. Jensen et al. (2017) use the LEP as an illustration of how systems can look beyond rigid competency-based approaches to develop challenging, dynamic and open-ended learning experiences which foster genuine systemic thinkers for schools. However, other observers are less confident. For example, Dimmock and Tan observe that the NIE's programmes align with the Ministry of Education requirements generating 'high degrees of homogeneity and conformism' (2017: 336).

Leadership development for networked leadership

The overviews of leadership development approaches in each of the four countries in the last section highlight the dominant focus on individual leaders and on leading learning and improvement within individual schools. Clearly, this focus can have benefits and we are not suggesting that all such efforts should cease, but we do suggest that developing successful leadership within and across networks requires an additional emphasis on collective and place-based approaches, in line with our arguments above for local solutions and co-design approaches to network and practice development more widely.

Despite the convergence in approach across our four countries, we see differences in how far the different school systems and programmes focus on integrating leadership development into the everyday reality of leading schools. The more integrated and embedded programmes expect participants to undertake real-world tasks which challenge and stretch them, while also requiring them to reflect on their leadership with support from mentors and coaches. For example, Singapore's LEP programme involves undertaking a Creative Action Project in another school (Jensen et al. 2017). Programmes that are embedded in these ways offer greater potential to influence and shape the powerful leadership learning that occurs naturally in every school and locality: this learning develops through informal socialization and experiential learning as leaders work with and learn from their peers. This experiential learning is hugely important because it shapes cultures and norms in fundamental ways – for good or ill. Leadership practice and agency are then shaped and grown – or diminished – by these cultures and norms. Leaders will quickly learn from their role models and peers whether to collaborate or compete and will respond to whether the wider framework they operate within is enabling or punitive. Thus, in systems where trust and social capital are already high, where schools collaborate and share their expertise and capacity so that effective practice spreads, and where leaders have a voice in shaping policy and commit to achieving shared goals, then leadership agency will be increased. However, the opposite is also true; where leaders, teachers and schools are criticized and assumed to be underperforming, where they risk dismissal if the results in any given year are poor, and where they can see that the way to get on in a politicized environment is to game the system, then leadership agency will be diminished. For these reasons, we argue that leadership development designers must seek consciously to intervene on and influence school and system-level cultures and norms, whilst also building collective leadership capacity in the process.

Building on this insight, and informed by evidence from previous educational networking programmes (Jackson and Temperley 2006), research and practice outside education (Western 2019; Williams 2012), related approaches such as improvement science (Bryk 2015) and our own experience of facilitating networks, we argue that developing network leadership requires an embedded, place-based, facilitatory and capacity-building approach. In essence, this means that policymakers and leadership development designers should seek to build 'middle tier' and network-level leadership capacity by identifying and supporting local leaders to lead in the ways we outlined in Chapter 9. In line with the ethos of local solutions and co-design, this support would not impose a predefined leadership 'curriculum'. However, it would be underpinned by an agreed framework and theory of action for how networks might best develop in that context, since this would provide structure and avoid reinventing wheels. Examples of candidate frameworks that we have explored in this book include the concept of epistemic communities and network learning architectures (Chapter 5) and/or the four conditions for emergence (Chapter 7). Similarly, local leaders should be encouraged to reflect on how far their existing networks address the eight core features, summarized in Table 9.1, and to identify specific priorities for development from this. Critically, this local capacity-building work should be supported over an extended period of time by one or more skilled facilitators. These facilitators might be experienced school leaders who are also expert in coaching and the facilitation of adult learning, and they might work with university-based researchers to ensure that data and evidence informs discussions and developments in a sense-making model. The remit of these facilitators should be to work flexibly, responding to local needs and developments, but with the aim of building local leadership capacity so that their support can be withdrawn over time. They should certainly work with 'middle tier' and network leaders, but might also support wider groups – such as subject leaders who operate as boundary spanners – in order to build distributed capacity.

Conclusion

This chapter has synthesized key learning and implications, in particular for policymakers and leadership development designers in relation to networks and network leadership. In doing so it defines a broad and demanding agenda that will require significant change for many national and state-level ministries of education, which are often poorly equipped to lead in the kinds of local solutions and co-design ways that we outline, as well as for existing 'middle tier' leaders and for designers of leadership development. The prize will be that networks and network leaders will be better able to collaborate and work adaptively and to thereby achieve the kinds of joined up, place-based and systemic outcomes that contemporary education requires.

Concluding Thoughts

In the Introduction to this book we asked you to imagine a school leader who is facing an issue or challenge and to consider the networks she might turn to for emotional and/or practical support. Let us imagine now that she has read this book – what might she take from it and what might be the implications? Clearly, we hope that it has broadened and deepened her understanding of networks and their leadership, even if in doing so it has raised as many questions as answers. We hope too that she will see how networks could help her address her immediate challenge and might, over time, become a sustainable source of ideas, expertise, capacity and learning for her entire school – helping her and her wider community to develop, adapt and innovate. More ambitiously, the book might prompt our imaginary leader to ask new questions – about her own leadership and the extent to which leadership is a shared and collective property in networks, about her school's approach to change, improvement, effectiveness, hierarchy, markets, complexity, emergence, non-human actors and/or the 'middle tier', or about how her school might forge partnerships to address cross-cutting issues faced by students and families across the wider community.

Any or all of these outcomes appear possible, but we are clear that network development should not only be left to individual schools and leaders. Although we started by imagining an individual school leader, we could equally have imagined a policymaker, a leadership development adviser, a parent or young person. We have tried to draw out the learning and implications for these readers as much as serving school leaders, hoping that they too might take action in how they work to facilitate and support inter-organizational networks which can enrich education.

What do we see as this book's main contribution to knowledge? We consider this in three areas: the book's international scope, its methodological and theoretical contribution, and its application to policy and practice. The international scope is clear in our focus on four country cases and also our co-authorship, which combines our unique UK/New Zealand knowledge and perspectives, along with our experiences and insights gained in other jurisdictions. Through this we show that national cultures and contexts matter and, as a result, that network leadership is not always the same. However, there are common trends and implications that can be drawn out. A key methodological contribution, as we see it, lies in our parallel network-level and place-based case studies in Aotearoa New Zealand and England, in which we use common tools and approaches to allow for comparative analysis. Place-based socio-spatial research of this nature presents a range of methodological challenges, not least the foundational question of what different stakeholders interpret as 'local'? This becomes even more challenging when combined with networks, which are inherently fluid and often unconstrained by spatial considerations (Jessop, Brenner and Jones, 2008). In both Aotearoa New Zealand and England we interviewed a range of policymakers, network/system leaders and organizational leaders, sometimes on multiple occasions and over time, allowing us to develop a thick, multi-perspective picture of the dynamics at play. Turning to the book's theoretical contribution, we see this in the unique attempt to apply four distinct lenses to the country and network cases. This allows for a combination of depth and breadth of analysis; helping to reveal different aspects of networks and their leadership which – we argue – would not have been possible if we had adopted a single lens. The final two chapters then draw these perspectives back together, revealing both common themes and the ways in which they allow for differing interpretations and cross-cutting implications. One important aim here was to show how school improvement/effectiveness tends to be taken for granted – the water that we swim in – but that when we look at networks through other lenses, they can be seen in new ways and new insights can be gleaned. We hope that this work might come to be seen as a template for similar theoretical development in other areas of education leadership research. Finally, in terms of application to policy and practice, this reflects our particular interests and stance, which meant that we were always keen to ensure that the book would have applied relevance in the 'real' world. Heavy use of theory can stand in the way of such attempts, but in Chapter 2 we seek to make the lenses accessible, while the eight features of networks (Chapter 1) and Table 10.1 (which summarizes the main findings and implications from each lens) are examples of how we seek to draw out implications for policy and practice.

What about the implications of this book for future research? This is a question we focus less on in the book itself. Certainly, we think that the model of exploring networks and network leadership transnationally and through contrasting theoretical lenses is original and significant in terms of its contribution to existing knowledge. That said, this book is far from the last word, so it is possible to see how the methodology could be developed and applied to a wider range of countries, cases and/or lenses. The book also raises many wider questions and possibilities for further research – too many to capture in full here, but two stand out as priorities. First, how can we develop a more comprehensive understanding of the outcomes and benefits of networks across different contexts, particularly in relation to aspects that stretch beyond individual and/or collective school improvement and effectiveness to encompass cross-cutting issues, including equity and innovation? Secondly, to what extent do the network leadership skills and qualities that we identify here apply across a wider range of contexts, and – if they do – so what?

Our final reflection is on the process of writing this book and of collaborating across a twelve-hour time difference. When we first planned the book, we intended to spend time together during Annelies' periodic visits to England and to undertake case study research together in Singapore. In the event, none of that has been possible, due to the COVID-19 pandemic and associated travel restrictions and lockdowns. Instead, like many school networks, we have become more proficient in using technology – a non-human actor that offers rich advantages, but also acts on the nature of collaboration! Undertaking comparative research is always demanding and at times we felt that we had bitten off more than we could chew, but the process has been hugely stimulating and rewarding, like all the best partnerships.

Notes

Chapter 1

1. This definition is appropriate given our focus on schools as organizations, but we recognize that it builds on more fundamental definitions, such as Wasserman and Faust (1994) who describe a network as a 'set of actors and the ties among them'.
2. Rincon-Gallardo and Fullan (2016: 6) distinguish between networks as 'a set of people or organizations and the direct and indirect connections that exist among them', and collaboration as 'the act of working together with a common purpose'. Our focus on goal-directed networks addresses this distinction.
3. See also Hadfield and Jopling (2012), Chapman (2015, 2019) and McCormick et al. (2011) for wider discussions of theoretical perspectives on networks and their leadership in education. Hadfield and Jopling develop what they term a structural-pluralist perspective, while Chapman draws on socio-cultural theory (including the two dimensions of social cohesion and social regulation) and explores optimistic, pessimistic and realist perspectives on networking. McCormick et al. provide an in-depth review of literature, including SNA and ANT, as a context for their findings on teacher learning through networks in the UK.
4. See Révai (2020), Brown (2020), González, Ehren and Montecinos (2020), Armstrong, Brown and Chapman (2020), Azorín, Harris and Jones (2020), Hubers et al. (2018), Brown and Poortman (2018), Middlewood, Abbott and Robinson (2018), Sartory, Jungermann and Jarvinen (2017), Diaz-Gibson et al. (2017), Rincon-Gallardo and Fullan (2016), Ainscow (2015), Chapman (2015), Muijs (2015a, 2015b), Hargreaves, Parsley and Cox (2015), Suggett (2014), Muijs and Rumyantseva (2014), Kamp (2013a, 2013b), Muijs, Ainscow, Chapman and West (2011), Grimaldi (2011), Muijs, West and Ainscow (2010), Hargreaves (2010, 2011, 2012a, 2012b), Jackson and Temperley 2006), Earl et al. (2006).
5. The authors approached various networks in the United States but did not get responses to the survey.

Chapter 2

1. Each of these areas has a vast research base, reflected in multiple systematic reviews in each area, so we do not attempt to reference all of these here. The Education Endowment Foundation's Teaching and Learning Toolkit (see https://

educationendowmentfoundation.org.uk/evidence-summaries/teaching-learning-toolkit/) provides a good overview of evidence on teaching and learning, in particular for disadvantaged children. The EEF has also published various systematic reviews on wider areas, such as CPDL for teachers – see https://educationendowmentfoundation.org.uk/evidence-summaries/evidence-reviews/. For a recent review of evidence on the impact of school leadership on student outcomes, see Liebowitz, D. and Porter, L. (2019),' The Effect of Principal Behaviors on Student, Teacher, and School Outcomes: A Systematic Review and Meta-Analysis of the Empirical Literature', *Review of Educational Research* 89(5): 785–827.

2   Each master concept had two subsidiary concepts. Outcomes include cognitive and moral, educationally manifest in the formal and hidden curriculum. Intellectual capital includes knowledge creation and knowledge transfer, educationally manifest in learning, both formal and informal. Social capital includes trust and networks, educationally manifest in community, both moral and academic. Leverage includes innovation and evidence-based practice, educationally manifest in teaching, both didactic and modelling.

3   Hargreaves' full 'maturity model' for a self-improving school system (2012) includes twelve elements across three dimensions (professional development, partnership and collaborative capital). We do not outline the full framework here for reasons of space, but it can be found here: https://www.gov.uk/government/publications/a-self-improving-school-system-towards-maturity.

4   Actants are the full range of potential agents in the network; the actant may come to be seen as a source of action – an actor – or not.

Chapter 3

1   In recent decades, the Scottish, Welsh and Northern Irish assemblies have each taken responsibility for devolved education policy, meaning that the approach to education in England is now distinct from the rest of the UK.

2   According to 2013 data from nineteen OECD member states in the Luxembourg Income Study data set. Available online: https://www.equalitytrust.org.uk/scale-economic-inequality-uk (accessed 2 April 2020).

3   Department for Education (2017) 'Schools, pupils and their characteristics: January 2017' SFR 28/2017. Available online: https://assets.publishing.service.gov.uk/government/uploads/system/uploads/attachment_data/file/650547/SFR28_2017_Main_Text.pdf (accessed 2 April 2020).

4   Available online: https://assets.publishing.service.gov.uk/government/uploads/system/uploads/attachment_data/file/389388/School_Admissions_Code_2014_-_19_Dec.pdf (accessed 2 April 2020).

5 Available online: https://www.gov.uk/government/collections/national-curriculum (accessed 2 April 2020).
6 Three quarters of all primary academies and half of all secondary academies were part of a MAT in February 2020.
7 Once an academy has joined a MAT it ceases to exist as a separate legal entity, although the MAT board can choose to delegate some operational autonomy to individual schools at its own discretion. Most MATs do promote collaboration between their member schools (Greany 2018a). However, because a MAT is a single organization, individual MATs are not treated here as networks or partnerships (i.e. in the sense of a voluntary collaboration between three or more independent entities). The case study below focuses on a meta-network – the Bampton Education Alliance – that involves multiple MATs as well as LA-maintained schools.
8 The government has announced that a network of eighty-seven Teaching School Hubs will replace the previous network of around 750 Teaching Schools in summer 2021. Teaching School Hubs will be 'centres of excellence for teacher training and development', based in high-performing schools and MATs across the country. Available online: https://www.gov.uk/guidance/teaching-school-hubs (accessed 11 May 2021).
9 Schools could apply to become a Teaching School on their own or, less commonly, as a job-share (i.e. where the role and funding was shared between two or three schools).
10 All names in this case study are anonymized. Ethical approval for the research was secured through the University of Nottingham School of Education Ethics Committee.
11 Established in 2014, England's eight Regional Schools Commissioners (RSCs) represent the Secretary of State for Education, providing oversight and scrutiny of academy trusts' performance.
12 A former secondary head teacher and MAT CEO was subsequently recruited as interim Chief Executive for the Alliance.

Chapter 4

1 There are over 600 islands, with Stewart Island being the largest of the smaller islands.
2 The New Zealand Curriculum runs to over 150 pages in full. Eight principles 'embody beliefs about what is important and desirable': high expectations, Treaty of Waitangi, cultural diversity, inclusion, learning to learn, community engagement,

coherence and future focus, along with values to be 'modelled and explored'. The Curriculum details five key competencies for learners – thinking, using language, symbols and text, managing self, relating to others and participating and contributing. It also details eight learning areas: English, the arts, health and physical education, learning languages, mathematics and statistics, science, social sciences and technology. Each learning area has achievement objectives at eight levels which are not mapped to Year levels; this recognizes individual differences in progress.

3   The National Administration Guidelines set out the statements of desirable conduct for schools in Aotearoa New Zealand. Available online: https://www.education.govt.nz/our-work/legislation/nags/ (accessed 20 July 2021).
4   Decile 1–7 schools can receive extra funding if they do not ask for donations; 95 per cent have adopted this policy.
5   Labour won government in 1984, having been largely in opposition from 1949. The first Labour government 1935–49 had been highly interventionist. Subsequent governments of both left-wing and right-wing persuasions had engaged in limited market liberalization.
6   Commonly referred to as the Picot Report, after the Taskforce Chair, businessman Brian Picot.
7   While professional learning provision was originally contracted from universities by the Ministry of Education, the system has become increasingly fragmented over the past decade (Professional Development Advisory Group 2014).
8   In 2017, the incoming Labour Government acted on its manifesto and officially ended the reporting of National Standards by primary and intermediate schools, arguing that since the introduction of National Standards, reading levels had dropped to their lowest level on record. While schools no longer had to report on National Standards they could continue to use the assessment tools internally.
9   Iwi refers here to extended kinship group of people descended from a common ancestor and associated with a distinct territory.
10 For consistency, we use the term across-school rather than across-community, which is also used.
11 Available online: https://www.education.govt.nz/communities-of-learning/about/all-approved-kahui-ako-to-continue-to-receive-full-funding/ (accessed 2 March 2021)
12 As one component of that Conversation, the Tomorrow's Schools Taskforce (2018: 91) noted the need for more time to 'bed' the Kāhui Ako model in, and that further development was required to 'enable its potential benefits to be fully and

more easily realised'. A review concerning that further development is occurring at the time of writing.

13 Available online: https://conversation.education.govt.nz/conversations/tomorrows-schools-review/

14 Available online: https://www.education.govt.nz/assets/Documents/Ministry/Information-releases/R-Education-Portfolio-Work-Programme-Purpose-Objectives-and-Overview.pdf

15 C.E. Beeby was director of the New Zealand Council for Educational Research (NZCER), and Director of Education from 1940, initially under the First Labour Government.

16 The current principal is able to comment on this having been a teacher at Linwood College in the early 1990s.

17 At the time of writing, Linwood College had been relocated to the former Avonside Girls' High School site while the college is rebuilt. Avonside Girls was relocated to their rebuilt school, a modern campus that is shared with Shirley Boys' High School. Linwood's NZ$ 44 million rebuild was due to be completed by 2018; it is now anticipated the students will return to their Aldwins Road site in 2022. At that time, Linwood College will become Te Aratai College, translated as 'pathway to the sea'. Te Ngai Tūāhuriri is the local Rūnanga [tribal council] and gifted this name to the community. It acknowledges the connection of the school to its geographical location.

Chapter 5

1 Until recently, the Education Review Office approach did however imply a public performance grade in terms of the 'return time' set for reviews. Thus, if a school attracted a one-year return time, this might be used by stakeholders as an indirect indicator of the quality of the school.

2 These critiques, along with the fact that it had largely failed to engage the town's MATs, were the main reason that the Bampton Education Partnership was closed and replaced with the new Bampton Alliance, as outlined in Chapter 3.

3 England's designated 'system leader' schools, such as Teaching Schools and National Leaders of Education, arguably sit somewhere between these two models, given that they are designated on the basis of their high performance.

4 Strictly speaking, pairing up two schools to work together in this way does not meet our definition of a network, which we defined in terms of three or more legally autonomous organizations that work together to achieve not only their own goals but also a collective goal, however we consider them as partnerships here.

Chapter 6

1. The article also assesses Scotland's national school leadership college.
2. Similar findings have been identified in England – see, for example, James, C., Brammer, S., Connolly, M., Eddy-Spicer, D., James, J., Jones, J. (2013), 'The Challenges Facing School Governing Bodies in England: A "Perfect storm"?', *Management in Education* 27(3):84–90.
3. As noted in Chapter 3, MATs are hierarchical organizations and not networks in the sense of 'three or more legally autonomous organizations that work together to achieve not only their own goals but also a collective goal'.
4. Christchurch again provides an interesting case here, having already had experience of collaborative work between the Ministry of Education and the Secondary Principals Association to identify and transition to zones that contributed to the good of the community, rather than the good of the school.

Chapter 7

1. We focus here on networks that are successful in achieving beneficial educational aims. However, there is nothing inherently good in either small worlds or effective networks; both can be used for nefarious purposes.
2. In large part, these centred on the imposition of a policy of such scale with insufficient consultation with educationalists, and the high level of proposed prescription within the instruments. For Kāhui Ako, there has been sustained critique of the policy as implemented in its 'stifling' specifications and procedural requirements (Kamp 2019b).
3. In practice, of course, a school might locate itself within several of these categories at once, reflecting the nested and intersectional nature of organizational networks and identities.

Chapter 8

1. Following Fenwick (2010: 118) we used the term actor-network theory as a 'loose, contingent marker' rather than engaging with the periodization of the developments of Actor-Network Theory.
2. PISA 2018 results for England, disaggregated from the UK, are published separately – see https://assets.publishing.service.gov.uk/government/uploads/system/uploads/attachment_data/file/904420/PISA_2018_England_national_report_accessible.pdf

This analysis shows even closer alignment between England and New Zealand in the Reading and Science domains (within one PISA point each time), while England scores slightly higher than New Zealand in mathematics (ten PISA points).

Chapter 10

1. Clearly, it is possible for networks to develop in wider contexts, not least online. See Jessop, Brenner and Jones (2008) for a fuller discussion of 'place' and other socio-spatial concepts.
2. The reconfiguration of the middle tier is not unique to our case study contexts. For example, in the United States, the monopoly of the *One Best System* in which school districts ran schools has given way to a combination of Charter Management Organizations (CMOs), comprehensive school reforms, school support organizations, School Improvement Network, state-run districts and so on (Cohen, et al. 2018). This is perhaps most evident in post-Katrina New Orleans, where Bogotch and Bauer (2015: 182–3) conclude that: 'The evolution of charter structures in New Orleans does not erase the competition for external resources (i.e., funds and people)… (which) makes for a highly contested educational terrain of competing values… competition and cooperation drives the next reform. We note the emergence of cooperative clusters, some ad hoc, filling an administrative need of school site leaders so that they can survive and engage in school improvement. But we would point out that the ad hoc structures themselves – whether driven by internal city initiative or externally driven – both tend to reflect a pre-Katrina mindset/reality separating the haves from the have-nots'.
3. See Teaching Council for Aotearoa New Zealand website: teachingcouncil.nz

References

Absolum, M. (n.d.), *Building Effective Kāhui Ako*, Christchurch: Evaluation Associates.

Addey, C. and Gorur, R. (2020), 'Translating PISA, Translating the World', *Comparative Education*, 56:547–64.

Adler, P. (2001), 'Market, Hierarchy and Trust: The Knowledge Economy and the Future of Capitalism', *Organisation Science*, 12(2):215–34.

Ainscow, M. (2015), *Towards Self-Improving School Systems: Lessons from a City Challenge*, London: Routledge.

Alexander, D., Lewis, J. and Considine, M. (2011), 'How Politicians and Bureaucrats Network: A Comparison across Governments', *Public Administration*, 89:1274–92.

Amagoh, F. (2016), 'Systems and Complexity Theories of Organizations', in A. Farazmand (ed), *Global Encyclopedia of Public Administration, Public Policy, and Governance*, Cham: Springer International Publishing.

Annan, J. and Carpenter, R. (2015), 'Learning and Change Networks', *Kairaranga*, 16(20):8–17.

Arena, M. and Uhl-Bien, M. (2016), 'Complexity Leadership Theory: Shifting from Human Capital to Social Capital', *People & Strategy*, 39:22–7.

Argyris, C. and Schön, D. A. (1978), *Organizational Learning: A Theory of Action Perspective*, Boston: Addison-Wesley Publishing Company.

Armstrong, P. and Ainscow, M. (2018), 'School-to-School Support within a Competitive Education System: Views from the Inside', *School Effectiveness and School Improvement*, 29(4):614–33.

Armstrong, P., Brown, C. and Chapman, C. (2020), 'School-to-School Collaboration in England: A Configurative Review of the Empirical Evidence', *Review of Education*, 9:391–51.

Aupaki Kāhui A. (2017), *Aupaki Kāhui Ako Achievement Challenges*. Available online: https://www.education.govt.nz/assets/Documents/Ministry/Investing-in-Educational-Success/Communities-of-Schools/AC/99196-ACHCHA.pdf (accessed 29 July 2021).

Averch, H. A., Carroll, S. J., Donaldson, T. S., Kiesling, H. J. and Pincus, J. (1972), *How Effective Is Schooling? A Critical Review and Synthesis of Research Findings*, Santa Monica: RAND Corporation.

Azorín, C. (2020), 'Leading Networks', *School Leadership & Management*, 40:105–10.

Azorín, C., Harris, A. and Jones, M. (2020), 'Taking a Distributed Perspective on Leading Professional Learning Networks', *School Leadership and Management*, 40(2–3):111–27.

Baars, S., Bernardes, E., Elwick, A., Malortie, A., McAleavy, T., McInerney, L., Menzies, L. and Riggall, A. (2014), *Lessons from London Schools: Investigating the Success*, Reading, UK: CfBT.

Ball, S. J. (2000), 'Performativities and Fabrications in the Education Economy: Towards the Performative Society?' *Australian Educational Researcher*, 27:1-23.

Ball, S. J. (2003), 'The Teacher's Soul and the Terrors of Performativity', *Journal of Education Policy*, 18:215-28.

Ball, S. J. (2009), 'The Governance Turn!', *Journal of Education Policy*, 24:537-8.

Ball, S. J. (2011), 'A New Research Agenda for Educational Leadership and Policy', *Management in Education*, 25(2):50-2.

Ball, S. and Junemann, C. (2012), *Networks, New Governance and Education*, Bristol: Policy Press.

Barber, M. (2008), *Instruction to Deliver: Fighting to Transform Britain's Public Services*, London: Methuen.

Barber, M. and Mourshed, M. (2007), *How the World's Best Performing School Systems Come Out on Top*, London: McKinseys & Co.

Barber, M., Whelan, F. and Clark, M. (2010), *Capturing the Leadership Premium: How the World's Top School Systems Are Building Leadership Capacity for the Future*, London: McKinsey & Co.

Bauer, S. (2019), 'Karl Weick's Organizing', in B.Johnson and S. Kruse (eds), *Educational Leadership, Organizational Learning and the Ideas of Karl Weick: Perspectives on Theory and Practice*, 119-135, London: Routledge.

Bauman, Z. (2012), *On Education*, Cambridge: Polity Press.

Bautista, A., Wong, J. and Gopinathan, S. (2015), 'Teacher Professional Development in Singapore: Depicting the Landscape', *Psychology, Society and Education*, 7(3):311-26.

Beck, U. (1992), *Risk Society: Towards a New Modernity: Theory, Culture & Society*, London: Sage Publications.

Bernardinelli, D., Rutt, S., Greany, T. and Higham, R. (2018), *Multi-Academy Trusts: Do They Make a Difference to Pupil Outcomes?* London: UCL Press.

Bernstein, B. (1970), 'Education Cannot Compensate for Society', *New Society*, 15(387):344-7.

Bevir, M. (2011), 'Governance as Theory, Practice, and Dilemma', in M. Bevir (ed), *The SAGE Handbook of Governance*, 1-16, London: Sage Publications.

Bidart, C., Degenne, A. and Grossetti, M. (2020), *Living in Networks: The Dynamics of Social Relations*, Cambridge: CUP.

Biesta, G. (2007), 'Why "What Works" Won't Work: Evidence-Based Practice and the Democratic Deficit in Educational Research', *Educational Theory*, 57(1):1-22.

Bijker, W., and Law, J. (1992), *Shaping Technology/Building Society*, Cambridge, MA: MIT Press.

Bogotch, I., and Bauer, S. (2015), 'Katrina at 10 and Counting', in L. Mirón, B. Beabout and J. Boselovic (eds), *Only in New Orleans: School Choice and Equity Post-Hurricane Katrina*, Dordrecht: Springer.

Bogotch, I., Miron, L. and Biesta, G. (2007), '"Effective for What; Effective for Whom?" Two Questions SESI Should Not Ignore', in T. Townsend (ed), *International Handbook of School Effectiveness and Improvement*, 93–110, Dordrecht: Springer.

Bonne, L. (2016), *National Standards in Their Seventh Year*, Wellington: NZCER.

Bonne, L. and Wylie, C. (2017), *Teachers' Work and Professional Learning: Findings from the NZCER National Survey of Primary and Intermediate Schools 2016*, Wellington: NZCER.

Boocock, A. (2019), 'Meeting the Needs of Local Communities and Businesses: From Transactional to Eco-Leadership in the English Further Education Sector', *Educational Management, Administration and Leadership*, 47:349–68.

Bourdieu, P. (1986), 'The Forms of Capital', in J. Richardson (ed), *Handbook of Theory and Research for the Sociology of Education*, 241–60, New York: Greenwood Press.

Bourdieu, P. (1990), *The Logic of Practice*, Stanford: Stanford University.

Bowers, A. (2017), 'University-Community Partnership Models: Employing Organizational Management Theories of Paradox and Strategic Contradiction', *Journal of Higher Education Outreach and Engagement*, 21:37–64.

Boyask, R. (2020), *Pluralist Publics in Market-Driven Education: Towards More Democracy in Educational Reform*, London: Bloomsbury Academic.

Boylan, M., Wolstenholme, C., Demack, S., Maxwell, B., Jay, T., Adams, G. and Reaney, S. (2019), *Longitudinal Evaluation of the Mathematics Teacher Exchange: China-England – Final Report*, London: Department for Education.

Brandsen, T., Steen, T. and Verschuere, B. (eds) (2018), *Co-Production and Co-Creation: Engaging Citizens in Public Services*, New York: Routledge.

Breakspear, S., Peterson, A., Alfadala, A. and Khair, M. (2017), *Developing Agile Leaders of Learning: School Leadership Policy for Dynamic Times*, Doha: WISE.

Bronfenbrenner, U. (1996), *The Ecology of Human Development: Experiments by Nature and Design*, Cambridge, MA: Harvard University Press.

Brown, C. (2020), *The Networked School Leader: How to Improve Teaching and Student Outcomes Using Learning Networks*, Bingley, UK: Emerald Publishing.

Brown, C. and Poortman, C. L. (2018), *Networks for Learning: Effective Collaboration for Teacher, School and System Improvement*, London: Routledge.

Brown, S. (2002), 'Michel Serres: Science, Translation, and the Logic of the Parasite', *Theory, Culture, and Society*, 19:1–27.

Bryk, A. (2015), 'Accelerating How We Learn to Improve', *Educational Researcher*, 44(9):467–77.

Bryson, J., Crosby, B. and Stone, M. (2006), 'The Design and Implementation of Cross-Sector Collaborations: Propositions from the Literature', *Public Administration Review*, 66:44–55.

Buchanan, M. (2002), *Small World: Uncovering Nature's Hidden Networks*, London: Weidenfeld Nicolson.

Bunt, L. and Harris, M. (2010), *Mass Localism: A Way to Help Small Communities Solve Big Social Challenges*, London: NESTA.

Burns, T. and Koster, F. (eds) (2016), *Governing Education in a Complex World*, Paris: OECD.

Bush, T. (2011), *Theories of Educational Leadership & Management*, London: Sage Publications.

Bush, T. (2012), International Perspectives on Leadership Development: Making a Difference', *Professional Development in Education*, 38(4):663–78.

Bush, T. (2019), 'Distributed Leadership and Bureaucracy: Changing Fashions in Educational Leadership', *Educational Management, Administration and Leadership*, 47:3–4.

Bush, T. and Glover, D. (2014), 'School Leadership Models: What Do We Know?' *School Leadership and Management*, 34(5):553–71.

Busher, H. and Hodgkinson, K. (1996), 'Co-operation and Tension between Autonomous Schools: A Study of Inter-School Networking', *Educational Review*, 48(1):55–64.

Byrne, D. (1998), *Complexity Theory and the Social Sciences*, London: Routledge.

Caldwell, B. and Spinks, J. (2014), *The Self-Transforming School*, London: Routledge.

Callon, M. (1986), 'Some Elements of a Sociology of Translation: Domestication of the Scallops and the Fishermen of St Brieuc Bay', in J. Law (ed), *Power, Action and Belief: A New Sociology of Knowledge?* 196–233, London: Routledge.

Callon, M. and Latour, B. (1981), 'Unscrewing the Big Leviathan: How Actors Macrostructure Reality and How Sociologists Help Them to Do so', in K. D. Knorr-Cetina and A. V. Cicourel (eds), *Advances in Social Theory and Methodology: Toward an Integration of Micro- and Macro-Sociologies*, 277–303, Boston, MA: Routledge and Kegan Paul.

Castells, M. (2009), *The Rise of the Network Society*, 2nd edn, Oxford: Blackwell.

Chapman, C. (2015), 'From One School to Many: Reflections on the Impact and Nature of School Federations and Chains in England', *Educational Management Administration and Leadership*, 43(1):46–60.

Chapman, C. (2019), 'From Hierarchies to Networks: Possibilities and Pitfalls for Educational Reform of the Middle Tier', *Journal of Educational Administration*, 57(5):554–70.

Chapman, C., Muijs, D. and MacAllister, J. (2011), *A Study of the Impact of School Federation on Student Outcomes*, Nottingham: NCSL.

Charteris, J. and Smardon, D. (2018), 'Policy Enactment and Leader Agency: The Discursive Shaping of Political Change', *New Zealand Journal of Teachers' Work*, 15:28–45.

Chubb, J. E. and Moe, T. M. (1988), 'Politics, Markets, and the Organization of Schools', *The American Political Science Review*, 82(4):1065–87.

Cilliers, P. (2001), 'Boundaries, Hierarchies and Networks in Complex Systems', *International Journal of Innovation Management*, 5:135–47.

Cilliers, P. (2005), 'Complexity, Deconstruction and Relativism', *Theory, Culture & Society*, 22:255–67.

Clark, J. (2017), 'Commentary: From Beeby to Parata–the Continuing Problem of Inequality of School Achievement', *Waikato Journal of Education*, 22:113–23.

Cohen, D. K., Spillane, J. P. and Peurach, D. J. (2018), 'The Dilemmas of Educational Reform', *Educational Research*, 47(3):204–12.

Coldwell, M., Greany, T., Higgins, S., Brown, C., Maxwell, B., Stiell, B., Stoll, L., Willis, B. and Burns, H. (2017), *Evidence-Informed Teaching: An Evaluation of Progress in England: Research Report*, London: Department for Education.

Coleman, J. (1966), *Equality of Educational Opportunity*, Washington, DC: US Department of Health, Education and Welfare.

Coleman, J. (1988), 'Social Capital in the Creation of Human Capital', *American Journal of Sociology*, 94:supplement S95–120.

Coleman, J. (1990), *Foundations of Social Theory*, Cambridge, MA: Harvard University Press.

Collins, K. and Coleman, R. (2021), 'Evidence-Informed Policy and Practice', in T. Greany and P. Earley (eds), *School Leadership and Education System Reform*, 2nd edn, 19–28, London: Bloomsbury.

Cook, K., Hardon, R. and Levi, M. (2007), *Cooperation without Trust?* New York: Russell Sage Foundation.

Cormack, P. and Comber, B. (1996), 'Writing the Teacher: The South Australian Junior Primary English Teacher, 1962–1995', in B. Green and C. Beavis (eds), *Teaching the English Subjects: Essays on English Curriculum History and Australian Schooling* 118–144, Geelong: Deakin University Press.

Courtney, S. (2015), 'Mapping School Types in England', *Oxford Review of Education*, 41(6):799–818.

Courtney, S. (2016), 'Post-Panopticism and School Inspection in England', *British Journal of Sociology of Education*, 37(4):623–42.

Cousin, S. (2019), *System Leadership: Policy and Practice in the English Schools System*, London: Bloomsbury.

Cousin, S. and Crossley-Holland, J. (2021), *Developing a New Locality Model for English Schools: Summary Report*, AEC Trust/BELMAS.

Creemers, B. (2007), 'Educational Effectiveness and Improvement: The Development of the Field in Mainland Europe', in T. Townsend (ed), *International Handbook of School Effectiveness and Improvement*, 223–245, Dordrecht: Springer.

Creemers, B. and Kyriakides, L. (2008), *The Dynamics of Educational Effectiveness: A Contribution to Policy, Practice and Theory in Contemporary Schools*, London: Routledge.

Creemers, B. and Kyriakides, L. (2009), 'Situational Effects of the School Factors Included in the Dynamic Model of Educational Effectiveness', *South African Journal of Education*, 29:293–315.

Creemers, B. and Kyriakides, L. (2015), 'Process-Product Research: A Cornerstone in Educational Effectiveness Research', *Journal of Classroom Interaction*, 50:107–19.

Creese, B., Gonzalez, A. and Isaacs, T. (2016), 'Comparing International Curriculum Systems: The International Instructional Systems Study', *The Curriculum Journal*, 27:15–23.

Croft, J. (2015), *Collaborative Overreach: Why Collaboration Probably Isn't Key to the Next Phase of School Reform*, London: Centre for the Study of Market Reform of Education.

Crosby, B. C. and Bryson, J. M. (2005), *Leadership for the Common Good: Tackling Public Problems in a Shared Power World*, 2nd edn, San Francisco: Jossey-Bass.

Daly, A. and Chrispeels, J. (2008), 'A Question of Trust: Predictive Conditions for Adaptive and Technical Leadership in Educational Contexts', *Leadership and Policy in Schools*, 7(1):30–63.

Darling Hammond, L., LaPointe, M., Meyerson, D. and Orr, M. (2007), *Preparing School Leaders for a Changing World: Lessons from Exemplary Leadership Development Programs: Executive Summary*, Stanford, CA: Stanford Educational Leadership Institute.

Darr, C. (2017), *The National Monitoring Study of Student Achievement. Wānangatia te Putanga Tauira*. Set 2:57–60.

Davis, B. and Sumara, D. (2006), *Complexity and Education: Inquiries into Learning, Teaching, and Research*, Mahwah, NJ: Erlbaum.

Davis, B. and Sumara, D. (2008), 'Complexity as a Theory of Education', *Transnational Curriculum Inquiry*, DOI:10.14288/tci.v5i2.75.

Deleuze, G. and Guattari, F. (1987), *A Thousand Plateaus: Capitalism and Schizophrenia*, Minneapolis: University of Minnesota Press.

Denters, B. and Rose, L. (2005), *Comparing Local Governance: Trends and Developments*, Basingstoke: Palgrave.

Department of Education (1988), *Administering for Excellence: Report of the Taskforce to Review Education Administration*, Wellington, NZ: Department of Education.

Department for Education (2010), *The Importance of Teaching: The Schools White Paper*, London: DfE.

Department for Education (2014), *National Curriculum in England*, London: DfE.

Department for Education (2016), *Educational Excellence Everywhere*, London: DfE.

Department for Education (2017), 'Schools, Pupils and Their Characteristics: January 2017', SFR 28/2017. Available online: https://assets.publishing.service.gov.uk/government/uploads/system/uploads/attachment_data/file/650547/SFR28_2017_Main_Text.pdf (accessed 2 April 2020).

Department for Education (2020), *National Professional Qualification* (NPQ) - Executive Leadership Framework, London: DfE.

DeRue, D. S. and Myers, C. G. (2014), 'Leadership Development: A Review and Agenda for Future Research', in D. Day (ed), *The Oxford Handbook of Leadership and Organisations*, 832–858, Oxford: Oxford University Press.

Diani, M. (2003), 'Introduction: Social Movements, Contentious Actions and Social Networks: From Metaphor to Substance', in M. Diani and D. McAdam (eds), *Social

Movements and Networks: Relational Approaches to Collective Action, 1–20, Oxford: Oxford University Press.

Díaz-Gibson, J., Zaragoza, M. C., Daly, A. J., Mayayo, J. L. and Romaní, J. R. (2017), 'Networked Leadership in Educational Collaborative Networks', Educational Management Administration and Leadership, 45(6):1040–59.

DiMaggio, P. J. and Powell, W. W. (1983), 'The Iron Cage Revisited: Institutional Isomorphism and Collective Rationality in Organizational Fields', American Sociological Review, 48:147–60.

Dimmock, C. and Tan, C. Y. (2013), 'Educational Leadership in Singapore: Tight Coupling, Sustainability, Scalability, and Succession', Journal of Educational Administration, 51(3):320–40.

Durkheim, E. (1972), Selected Writings, Cambridge: Cambridge University Press.

Eacott, S. (2015), Educational Leadership Relationally: A Theory and Methodology for Educational Leadership, Management and Administration, Rotterdam: Sense.

Eacott, S. (2018), Beyond Leadership: A Relational Approach to Organizational Theory in Education, Singapore: Springer.

Earl, L., Katz, S., Elgie, S., Ben Jaafar, S. and Foster, L. (2006), How Networked Learning Communities Work, Nottingham: National College of School Leadership.

Earley, P. (2013), Exploring the School Leadership Landscape: Changing Demands, Changing Realities, London: Bloomsbury Academic.

Earley, P. (2021), 'Conceptions of Leadership and Leading the Learning', in T. Greany and P. Earley (eds), School Leadership and Education System Reform, 2nd edn, 81–92, London: Bloomsbury.

Easton, B. (1994), 'Economic and Other Ideas behind the New Zealand Reforms', Oxford Review of Economic Policy, 10:78–94.

Eddy-Spicer, D. (2019), 'Where the Action Is: Enactment as the First Movement of Sensemaking', in B. Johnson and S. Kruse (eds), Educational Leadership, Organizational Learning and the Ideas of Karl Weick: Perspectives on Theory and Practice, 94–118, London: Routledge.

Edmonds, R. (1979), 'Effective Schools for the Urban Poor', Educational Leadership, 37(1):15–24.

Education Council (2020), Educational Leadership Capability Framework, Wellington: Education Council.

Education Review Office (1999), School Governance and Student Achievement, Wellington: Education Review Office.

Education Review Office (2016), Collaboration to Improve Learner Outcomes: What Does the Evidence Tell us about What Works, Wellington: New Zealand Government.

Education Review Office (2017a), Communities of Learning | Kāhui Ako in Action: What We Know So Far, Wellington: Education Review Office.

Education Review Office (2017b), Communities of Learning | Kāhui Ako: Collaboration to Improve Learner Outcomes. Available Online: http://www.ero.govt.nz/

publications/communities-of-learning-kahui-ako-collaboration-to-improve-learner-outcomes/ (accessed 29 July 2021).

Ehren, M. and Baxter, J. (eds) (2021), *Trust, Accountability and Capacity in Education System Reform*, Abingdon: Routledge.

Ehren, M., and Perryman, J. (2017), 'Accountability of School Networks: Who Is Accountable to Whom and for What?' *Education Management, Administration and Leadership*, 46(6):942–59.

Evans, M. P. and Stone-Johnson, C. (2010), 'Internal Leadership Challenges of Network Participation', *International Journal of Leadership in Education*, 13(2):203–20.

Fancy, H. (2007), 'School Reform: Reflections on the New Zealand Experience', in T. Townsend (ed), *International Handbook of School Effectiveness and Improvement*, 325–340, Dordrecht: Springer.

Fenwick, T. (2010), '("Un") Doing Standards in Education with Actor-Network Theory', *Journal of Education Policy*, 25:117–33.

Fenwick, T. and Edwards, R. (2010), *Actor-Network Theory in Education*, London: Routledge.

Fickel, L., Mackey, J. and Fletcher, J. (2019), 'The Changing Spaces of Education in Aotearoa New Zealand', in A. Kamp (ed), *Education Studies in Aotearoa: Key Disciplines and Emerging Directions*, 254–69, Wellington: NZCER Press.

Fielding, M., Bragg, S., Craig, J., Cunningham, I., Eraut, M., Gillinson, S., Horne, M., Robinson, C. and Thorn, J. (2004), *Factors Influencing the Transfer of Good Practice*, London: Department for Education and Skills.

Fiske, E. B. and Ladd, H. F. (2000), *When Schools Compete: A Cautionary Tale*, Washington, DC: Brookings Institution Press.

Fleishman, E. A., Mumford, M. D., Zaccaro, S. J., Levin, K. Y., Korotkin, A. L. and Hein, M. B. (1991), 'Taxaonomic Efforts in the Description of Leader Behaviour: A Synthesis and Functional Interpretation', *Leadership Quarterly*, 2(4):245–87.

Fluckiger, B., Lovett, S. and Dempster, N. (2014), 'Judging the Quality of School Leadership Learning Programmes: An International Search', *Professional Development in Education*, 40(4):561–75.

Frankowski, A., van der Steen, M., Bressers, D. and Schulz, M. (2018), *Dilemmas of Central Governance and Distributed Autonomy in Education: Three Education Policies in the Netherlands*, Education Working Paper 189, Paris: OECD.

Freeman, C., Nairn, K. and Gollop, M. (2015), 'Disaster Impact and Recovery: What Children and Young People Can Tell Us', *Kōtuitui: New Zealand Journal of Social Sciences Online*, 10:103–15.

Fullan, M. (2001), *Leading in a Culture of Change*, San Francisco: Jossey-Bass.

Fullan, M. (2005), Leadership across the System', Available online: http://www.michaelfullan.ca/media/13396061760.pdf (accessed 27 June 2021).

Fullan, M. (2015), *Leadership from the Middle: A System Strategy*, Canada: Canadian Education Association.

Galdames, S. and Gonzalez, A. (2016), 'The Relationship between Leadership Preparation and the Level of Teachers' Interest in Assuming a Principalship in Chile', *School Leadership & Management*, 36:435-51.

Gerritsen, J. (2020), 'Call to Axe Kahui Ako Scheme and Redirect Funding', *New Zealand Herald*, 3 August.

Gewirtz, S., Ball, S. and Bowe, R. (1995), *Markets, Choice and Equity in Education*, Buckingham: Open University Press.

Giddens, A. (1984), *The Constitution of Society*, Cambridge: Polity.

Giddens, A. (2002), *Runaway World: How Globalisation Is Reshaping Our Lives*, London: Profile.

Gilbert, C. (2017), *Optimism of the Will: The Development of Local Area-Based Partnerships*, London: LCLL.

Glassman, R. B. (1973), 'Persistence and Loose Coupling in Living Systems', *Behavioural Science*, 18:83-98.

Glatter, R. (2003), 'Collaboration, Collaboration, Collaboration: The Origins and Implications of a Policy', *Management in Education*, 17(5):16-20.

Glatter, R. (2008), *Of Leadership, Management and Wisdom: A Brief Synthesis of Selected Reports and Documents on Leadership Development*, Nottingham: NCSL.

Glatter, R., Woods, P. and Bagley, C. (1997), *Choice and Diversity in Schooling: Perspectives and Prospects*, London: Routledge.

Glazer, J. and Peurach, D. (2015), 'Occupational Control in Education: The Logic and Leverage of Epistemic Communities', *Harvard Educational Review*, 85(2):172-202.

Glazer, J., Greany, T., Duff, M. and Berry, W. (2022), 'Networked Improvement in the US and England: A New Role for the Middle Tier', in D. J. Peurach, J. L. Russell, L. Cohen-Vogel and W. R. Penuel (eds), *Handbook on Improvement-Focused Educational Research*, Lanham, MD: Rowman & Littlefield.

González, A., Ehren, M. and Montecinos, C. (2020), 'Leading Mandated Network Formation in Chile's New Public Education System', *School Leadership and Management*, 40(5):425-43.

Gorard, S. (2010), 'Serious Doubts about School Effectiveness', *British Educational Research Journal*, 36:745-66.

Gorard, S. ed. (2020), *Getting Evidence into Education: Evaluating the Routes to Policy and Practice*, Abingdon: Routledge.

Gordon, L. (2015), '"Rich" and "Poor" Schools Revisited', *New Zealand Journal of Educational Studies*, 50:7-21.

Gordon, L., Boyask, D. and Pearce, D. (1994), *Governing Schools: A Comparative Analysis*, Christchurch, NZ: University of Canterbury.

Gorur, R. (2015), 'Situated, Relational and Practice-Oriented: The Actor-Network Theory Approach', in K. Gulson, M. Clarke and E. Bendix Petersen (eds), *Education Policy and Contemporary Theory. Implications for Research*, 87-98, Abingdon: Routledge.

Granovetter, M. (1973), 'The Strength of Weak Ties', *American Journal of Sociology*, 78:1360–80.

Granovetter, M. (1983), 'The Strength of Weak Ties: A Network Theory Revisited', *Sociological Theory*, 1:201–33.

Greany, T. (2018a), *Sustainable Improvement in Multi-School Groups*, London: Department for Education.

Greany, T. (2018b), 'Balancing the Needs of Policy and Practice while Remaining Authentic: An Analysis of Leadership and Governance in Three National School Leadership Colleges', *Wales Journal of Education*, 20(2):63–98.

Greany, T. (2019), 'Approaches to Scaling Innovations across Schools: An Analysis of Key Theories and Models', in M. Peters and R. Heraud (eds), *Encyclopedia of Educational Innovation*, Singapore: Springer.

Greany, T. (2020a), 'Place-Based Governance and Leadership in Decentralised School Systems: Evidence from England', *Journal of Education Policy*, DOI: 10.1080/02680939.2020.1792554.

Greany, T. (2020b), 'Self-Policing or Self-Improving?: Analysing Peer Reviews between Schools in England through the Lens of Isomorphism', in D. Godfrey (ed), *School Peer Review for Educational Improvement and Accountability: Theory, Practice and Policy Implications*, 71–94, London: Springer.

Greany, T. and Allan, T. (2014), *School Improvement Networks and System Leadership in Coventry: Evaluating Progress, Areas for Development and Possible Next Steps*, London: Institute of Education.

Greany, T. and Brown, C. (2015), *Partnerships between Teaching Schools and Universities*, London: Centre for Leadership in Learning, UCL IOE.

Greany, T. and Earley, P. (2017), 'Introduction', in P. Earley and T. Greany (eds), *School Leadership and Education System Reform*, 1–14, London: Bloomsbury.

Greany, T. and Higham, R. (2018), *Hierarchy, Markets and Networks: Analysing the 'Self-Improving School-led System' Agenda in England and the Implications for Schools*, London: UCL IOE Press.

Greany, T. and Maxwell, B. (2017), 'Evidence-Informed Innovation in Schools: Aligning Collaborative Research and Development with High Quality Professional Learning for Teachers', *International Journal of Innovation in Education*, 4(2/3):147–70.

Greany, T. and McGinity, R. (2021), 'Structural Integration and Knowledge Exchange in Multi-Academy Trusts: Comparing Approaches with Evidence and Theory from Non-Educational Sectors', *School Leadership and Management*, DOI: 10.1080/13632434.2021.1872525

Greany, T. and Waterhouse, J. (2016), 'Rebels against the System: Leadership Agency and Curriculum Innovation in the Context of School Autonomy and Accountability in England', in *School Autonomy and 21st Century Learning: Special Issue - International Journal of Education Management*, 30(7):1188–206.

Greany, T., Gu, Q., Handscomb, G. and Varley, M. (2014), *School-University Partnerships: Fulfilling the Potential – Summary Report*, Bristol: Research Councils UK and National Co-ordinating Centre for Public Engagement.

Greany, T., Thomson, P., Martindale, N. and Cousin, S. (2021), *Leading in Lockdown: Research on School Leaders' Work, Wellbeing and Career Intentions*, Nottingham: University of Nottingham.

Grimaldi, E. (2011), 'Governance and Heterachy in Education: Enacting Networks for School Innovation', *Italian Journal of Sociology of Education*, 3(2):114–50.

Gronn, P. (2002a), 'Distributed Leadership as a Unit of Analysis', *Leadership Quarterly*, 13:423–51.

Gronn, P. (2002b), 'Designer-Leadership: The Emerging Global Adoption of Preparation Standards', *Journal of School Leadership*, 10(1):552–78.

Gronn, P. (2003), *The New Work of Educational Leaders: Changing Leadership Practice in an Era of School Reform*, London: Sage Publications.

Gronn, P. (2008), 'The Future of Distributed Leadership', *Journal of Educational Administration*, 46:141–58.

Gronn, P. (2016), 'Fit for Purpose No More?, *Management in Education,* 30(4):168–72.

Gulson, K., Clarke, M. and Bendix Petersen, E. (2015), 'Introduction: Theory, Policy, Methodology', in K. Gulson, M. Clarke and E. Bendix Petersen (eds), *Education Policy and Contemporary Theory: Implications for Research*, 1–12, Abingdon: Routledge.

Gulson, K. N. (2011), *Education Policy, Space and the City: Markets and the (in)visibility of Race*, New York: Routledge.

Gumus, S., Bellibas, M. S., Esen, M. and Gumus, E. (2018), 'A Systematic Review of Studies on Leadership Models in Educational Research from 1980 to 2014', *Educational Management Administration and Leadership*, 46:25–48.

Hadfield, M. (2007), 'Co-leaders and Middle Leaders: The Dynamic between Leaders and Followers in Networks of Schools', *School Leadership and Management*, 27(3):259–83.

Hadfield, M. and Jopling, M. (2012), 'How Might Better Network Theories Support School Leadership Research?' *School Leadership and Management*, 32(2):109–21.

Hager, P. and Beckett, D. (2019), *The Emergence of Complexity: Rethinking Education as a Social Science*, Cham: Springer International Publishing.

Hall, J., Lindorff, A. and Sammons, P. (2020), 'Introduction', in J. Hall, A. Lindorff and P. Sammons (eds), *International Perspectives in Educational Effectiveness Research*, 1–8, Switzerland: Springer.

Hallgarten, J., Hannon, V. and Beresford, T. (2015), *Creative Public Leadership: How School System Leaders Can Create the Conditions for System-wide Innovation*, Doha: WISE.

Hallinger, P. ed. (2003), *Reshaping the Landscape of School Leadership Development: Contexts of Learning*, Lisse: Swets and Zeitlinger.

Hallinger, P. (2018), 'Bringing Context Out of the Shadows of Leadership', *Educational Management Administration and Leadership*, 46(1):5–24.

Hallinger, P. and Hammad, W. (2017), 'Knowledge Production on Educational Leadership and Management in Arab Societies: A Systematic Review of Research', *Educational Management, Administration and Leadership*, 47(1):20–36.

Hallinger, P and Walker, A. (2017), 'Leading Learning in Asia – Emerging Empirical Insights from Five Societies', *Journal of Educational Administration*, 55(2):30–146.

Ham, V., Cathro, G., Winter, M and Winter, J. (2012), *Evaluative Study of Co-located Schools Established Following the Christchurch Earthquake*, Wellington: Ministry of Education.

Hannon, V. and Peterson, A. (2020), *Thrive: Schools Reinvented for the Challenges We Face*, Cambridge: Cambridge University Press.

Hargreaves, A. and Fullan, M. (2012), *Professional Capital: Transforming Teaching in Every School*, New York: Teachers College Press.

Hargreaves, A. and Shirley, D. (2020), 'Leading from the Middle: Its Nature, Origins and Importance', *Journal of Professional Capital and Community*, 5(1):92–114.

Hargreaves, A., Parsley, D. and Cox, E. K. (2015), 'Designing Rural School Improvement Networks: Aspirations and Actualities', *Peabody Journal of Education*, 90(2):306–21.

Hargreaves, D. H. (2001), 'A Capital Theory of School Effectiveness and Improvement', *British Educational Research Journal*, 27:487–503.

Hargreaves, D. H. (2010), *Creating a Self-Improving School System*, Nottingham: National College for School Leadership.

Hargreaves, D. H. (2011), *Leading a Self-Improving School System*, Nottingham: National College for School Leadership.

Hargreaves, D. H. (2012a), *A Self-Improving School System: Towards Maturity*, Nottingham: National College for School Leadership.

Hargreaves, D. H. (2012b), *A Self-Improving School System in International Context*, Nottingham: National College for School Leadership.

Harman, G. (2009), *Prince of Networks: Bruno Latour and Metaphysic*, Melbourne: re.press.

Harris, A. (2013), 'Distributed Leadership: Friend or Foe?' *Educational Management, Administration and Leadership*, 41:545–54.

Harris, A. and Jones, M. (2015), 'Transforming Education Systems: Comparative and Critical Perspectives on School Leadership', *Asia Pacific Journal of Education*, 35(3):311–8.

Harris, A., Jones, M. and Adams, D. (2016), 'Qualified to Lead? A Comparative, Contextual and Cultural View of Educational Policy Borrowing', *Educational Research*, 58(2):166–78.

Harris, A., Jones, M. and Hashim, N. (2021), 'System Leaders and System Leadership: Exploring the Contemporary Evidence Base', *School Leadership & Management*, DOI: 10.1080/13632434.2021.1889492.

Harris, J., Zhao, Y. and Caldwell, B. (2009), 'Global Characteristics of School Transformation in China', *Asia Pacific Journal of Education*, 29(4):413–26.

Hartley, J. and Benington, J. (2006), 'Copy and Paste, or Graft and Transplant? Knowledge Sharing through Inter-Organizational Networks', *Public Money and Management*, 26(2):101–8.

Hatcher, R. (2008), 'System Leadership, Networks and the Question of Power', *Management in Education*, 22(2):24–30.

Hatcher, R. (2014), 'Local Authorities and the School System: The New Authority-Wide Structures', *Educational Management Administration and Leadership*, 42(3):355–71.

Hattie, J. (2008) *Visible Learning*, London: Routledge.

Hawkins, M. and James, C. R. (2018), 'Developing a Perspective on Schools as Complex, Evolving, Loosely Linking Systems', *Educational Management, Administration and Leadership*, 46:729–48.

Henry, G., Pham, L., Kho, A. and Zimmer, R. (2020), 'Peeking into the Black Box of School Turnaround: A Formal Test of Mediators and Suppressors', *Educational Evaluation and Policy Analysis*, 42(2):232–56.

Heifetz, R. (1994), *Leadership without Easy Answers*, Cambridge, MA: Harvard University Press.

Heitfetz, R. and Linsky, M. (2002), *Leadership on the Line: Staying Alive through the Dangers of Leading*, Cambridge, MA: Harvard University Press.

Hickman, G. (2010), *Leading Change in Multiple Contexts*, Thousand Oaks, CA: Sage Publications.

Higgins, S., Katsipataki, M., Coleman, R., Henderson, P., Major, L. and Coe, R. (2015), *The Sutton Trust-Education Endowment Foundation Teaching and Learning Toolkit*, London: Education Endowment Foundation.

Higham, R. (2021), 'Ethical Leadership', in T. Greany and P. Earley (eds), *School Leadership and Education System Reform*, 2nd edn, 253–262, London: Bloomsbury.

Higham, R., Hopkins, D. and Matthews, P. (2009), *System Leadership in Practice*, Maidenhead, UK: Open University Press.

Hill, R. (2008), *Achieving More Together: Adding Value through Partnership*, Leicester, UK: ASCL.

Hill, R. (2010), *Chain Reactions: A Thinkpiece on the Development of Chains of Schools in the English School System*, London: National College for Leadership of Schools and Children's Services.

Hill, R. (2011), *The Importance of Teaching and the Role of System Leadership: A Commentary on the Illuminas Research*, Nottingham: National College for School Leadership.

Hipkins, C. (2019), *Supporting All Schools to Succeed*. Available online: https://www.beehive.govt.nz/release/supporting-all-schools-succeed (accessed 29 July 2021).

Hitt, D. and Tucker, P. (2016), 'Systematic Review of Key Leader Practices Found to Influence Student Achievement: A Unified Framework', *Review of Educational Research*, 86(2):531–69.

Ho, J. M. and Koh, T. S. (2018), 'Historical Development of Educational Leadership in Singapore', in T. S. Koh and D.W. Hung (eds), *Leadership for Change: The Singapore Schools' Experience*, 29–84, Singapore: World Scientific.

Holmqvist, M. (2003), 'A Dynamic Model of Intra-and Interorganizational Learning', *Organization Studies*, 24(1):95–123.

Hood, C. (1991), 'A Public Management for all Seasons', *Public Administration*, 69:3–19.
Hopkins, D. (2007), *Every School a Great School*, New York: McGraw-Hill.
Hopkins, D. (2015), 'School Improvement and Education System Reform', in C. Chapman, D. Muijs, D. Reynolds and S. Taylor (eds), *The Routledge International Handbook of Educational Effectiveness and Improvement*, 124–48, London: Taylor and Francis.
Hopkins, D. and Higham, R. (2007), 'System Leadership: Mapping the Landscape', *School Leadership and Management*, 27:147–66.
Hopkins, D., Stringfield, S., Harris, A., Stoll, L. and Mackay, T. (2014), 'School and System Improvement: A Narrative State of the Art Review', *School Effectiveness and School Improvement*, 25:257–81.
House of Commons Education Select Committee (2013), *Fourth Report: School Partnerships and Cooperation*. Available online: https://publications.parliament.uk/pa/cm201314/cmselect/cmeduc/269/26902.htm (accessed 27 July 2021).
Hoxby, C. (2006), *School Choice: The Three Essential Elements and Several Policy Options*, Auckland: The Education Forum.
Hubers, M. D., Moolenaar, M, Schildkamp, K., Daly, A., Handelzalts, A. and Pieters, J. (2018), 'Share and Succeed: The Development of Knowledge Sharing and Brokerage in Data Teams' Network Structures', *Research Papers in Education*, 33(2):216–38.
Hudson, G. (2007), 'Governing the Governance of Education: The State Strikes Back?' *European Educational Research Journal*, 6(3):266–82.
Hung, D., Jamaludin, A., Toh, Y., Lee, S. S., Wu, L. and Shaari, I. (2016), 'A System's Model of Scaling: Leveraging upon Centralised and Decentralised Structures for Diffusion', *Learning: Research and Practice*, 2(2):143–59.
Jackson, D. and Temperley, J. (2006), *From Professional Learning Community to Networked Learning Community*. Conference Paper for International Congress for School Effectiveness and Improvement (ICSEI) Fort Lauderdale, USA, January 3–6.
Jacobson, M. J., Levin, J. A. and Kapur, M. (2019), 'Education as a Complex System: Conceptual and Methodological Implications', *Educational Researcher*, 48:112–19.
Jacobson, M. J. and Wilensky, U. (2006), 'Complex Systems in Education: Scientific and Educational Importance and Implications for the Learning Sciences', *Journal of the Learning Sciences*, 15:11–34.
Jansen, C. and Wall, G. (n.d.), *Grow Waitaha: Educational Transformation through a Co-Designed Collaborative Approach in a Complex Public-Sector Context*, Christchurch: Grow Waitaha.
Janssens, F. G. and Ehren, M. (2016), 'Toward a Model of School Inspections in a Polycentric System', *Journal of Evaluation and Program Planning*, 56:88–98.
Jencks, C., Smith, M., Acland, H., Bane, M. J., Cohen, D. and Gintis, H. (1972), *Inequality: A Reassessment of the Effects of Family and Schooling in America*, New York: Basic Books.
Jensen, B., Downing, P. and Clark, A. (2017), *Preparing to Lead: Lessons in Principal Development from High-Performing Education Systems*, Washington, DC: National Center on Education and the Economy.

Jessop, B. (2011), 'Metagovernance', in M. Bevir (ed), *The Sage Handbook of Governance*, 106–23, London: Sage Publications.

Jessop, B., Brenner, N. and Jones, M. (2008), 'Theorizing Sociospatial Relations', *Environment and Planning D: Society and Space*, 26:389–401.

Johnson, B. and Kruse, S. (2019), *Educational Leadership, Organizational Learning and the Ideas of Karl Weick: Perspectives on Theory and Practice*, London: Routledge.

Jupp, B. (2000), *Working Together: Creating a Better Environment for Cross-Sector Partnerships*, London: DEMOS.

Kadushin, C. (2012), *Understanding Social Networks: Theories, Concepts and Findings*, New York: Oxford University Press.

Kamp, A. (2006), *A Study of the Geelong Local Learning and Employment Network*, Geelong: Deakin University.

Kamp, A. (2012), 'Experimentation in Contact with the Real': Networking with Deleuze & Guattari', *International Journal of the Humanities*, 9:165–76.

Kamp, A. (2013a), 'Policy, Paradigms, and Partnership Potential: Rethinking the Governance of Learning Networks', in *American Educational Research Association Annual Meeting*, San Francisco: AERA.

Kamp, A. (2013b), *Rethinking Learning Networks: Collaborative Possibilities for a Deleuzian Century*, Bern: Peter Lang.

Kamp, A. (2017), 'Assembling the Actors: Exploring the Challenges of "System Leadership" in Education through Actor-Network Theory', *Journal of Education Policy*, 33(6):778–92.

Kamp, A. (2019a), 'Case-study of VET/PCET in Aotearoa New Zealand', in J. Tummons (ed), *Handbook for PCET*, 248–262, London: Sage Publications.

Kamp, A. (2019b), 'Kāhui Ako and the Collaborative Turn in Education: Emergent Evidence and Leadership Implications', *New Zealand Annual Review of Education*, 24:177–91.

Kapucu, N. (2006), 'New Public Management: Theory, Ideology, and Practice', in A. Farazmand and J. Pinkowski (eds), *Globalization: Issues in Public Management*, London: Routledge.

Kelly, A. (2020), 'The Fifth Phase of Educational Effectiveness Research: The Philosophy and Measurement of Equity', in J. Hall, A. Lindorff and P. Sammons (eds), *International Perspectives in Educational Effectiveness Research*, 71–100, Switzerland: Springer.

Kelsey, J. (1995), *The New Zealand Experiment*, Auckland: Auckland University Press.

Kenny, L. (2020), 'Christchurch Schools Rebuild Plan Still Years from Completion', Available online: https://www.stuff.co.nz/national/education/123149328/christchurch-schools-rebuild-plan-still-years-from-completion (accessed 29 July 2021).

Kickert, W., Klijn, E. H. and Koppenjan, J. F. M. (eds) (1997), *Managing Complex Networks: Strategies for the Public Sector*, London: Sage Publications.

Klar, H. and Brewer, C. (2013), 'Successful Leadership in High-Needs Schools: An Examination of Core Leadership Practices Enacted in Challenging Contexts', *Educational Administration Quarterly*, 49(5):768–808.

Koh, T. S. and Hung, D. W. (eds) (2018), *Leadership for Change: The Singapore Schools' Experience*, Singapore: World Scientific.

Kools, M. and Stoll, L. (2016), 'What Makes a School a Learning Organisation?' Education Working Papers 137, Paris: OECD Publishing.

Koyama, J. (2011), 'Principals, Power, and Policy: Enacting "Supplemental Educational Services"', *Anthropology & Education Quarterly*, 42:20–36.

Kyriakides, L., Creemers, B. and Panayiotou, A. (2020), 'Developing and Testing Theories of Educational Effectiveness Addressing the Dynamic Nature of Education', in J. Hall, A. Lindorff and P. Sammons (eds), *International Perspectives in Educational Effectiveness Research*, 33–70, Switzerland: Springer.

La Rocque, N. (2005), *School Choice: Lessons from New Zealand. Briefing Papers: The Education Forum*, May:12.

Landri, P. (2021), *Educational Leadership, Management, and Administration through Actor-Network Theory*, London and New York: Routledge.

Lange, D. (1988), *Tomorrow's Schools: The Reform of Educational Administration in New Zealand*, Wellington: New Zealand Government Printer.

Latour, B. (1987), *Science in Action: How to Follow Engineers in Society*, Milton Keynes: Open University Press.

Latour, B. (1991), 'Technology Is Society Made Durable', in J. Law (ed), *A Sociology of Monsters: Essays on Power, Technology and Domination*, 103–131, Florence: Routledge.

Latour, B. (1999), 'On Recalling ANT', in J. Law and J. Hassard (eds), *Actor Network Theory and After*, 15–25, Oxford: Blackwell.

Latour, B. (2004a), 'Why Has Critique Run Out of Steam?: From Matters of Fact to Matters of Concern', *Critical Inquiry*, 30:225–48.

Latour, B. (2004b), 'The Social as Association', in N. Gage (ed), *The Future of Social Theory*, 77–90, London: Continuum.

Latour, B. (2007), *Reassembling the Social: An Introduction to Actor-Network-Theory*, Oxford: Oxford University Press.

Lauder, H., Hughes, D., Watson, S., Waslander, S., Thrupp, M., Strathdee, R., Simiyu, I., Dupuis, A., McGlinn, J. and Hamlin, J. (1999), *Trading in Futures: Why Markets in Education Don't Work*, Buckingham: Open University Press.

Law, J. (1992), 'Notes on the Theory of the Actor-Network: Ordering, Strategy, and Heterogeneity', *Systemic Practice and Action Research*, 5:379–93.

Law, J. (1999), 'After ANT: Complexity, Naming and Topology', in J. Law and J. Hassard (eds), *Actor Network Theory and after*, 1–14, Oxford: Blackwell.

Law, J. (2009), 'Actor Network Theory and Material Semiotics', in B. S. Turner (ed), *The New Blackwell Companion to Social Theory*, 141–158, Chichester: Wiley-Blackwell.

Law, J. and Hassard, J. (1999), *Actor Network Theory and after*, Oxford: Blackwell.

Lee, S., Ho, J. and Yong, T. L. (2021), 'Hierarchical Structures with Networks for Accountability and Capacity Building in Singapore: An Evolutionary Approach', in M. Ehren and J. Baxter (eds), *Trust, Accountability and Capacity in Education System Reform*, 164–81, Abingdon: Routledge.

Lee, S. and Hung, D. (2016), 'A Socio-Cultural Perspective to Teacher Adaptivity: The Spreading of Curricular Innovations in Singapore Schools', *Learning: Research and Practice*, 2(1):64–84.

Lee, S. K., Lee, W. O. and Low, E. L. (eds) (2014), *Education Policy Innovations: Levelling Up and Sustaining Educational Achievement*, Singapore: Springer.

Leithwood, K. (2019), 'Characteristics of Effective Leadership Networks: A Replication and Extension', *School Leadership and Management*, 39(2):175–97.

Leithwood, K., Harris, A. and Hopkins, D. (2008), 'Seven Strong Claims about Successful School Leadership', *School Leadership and Management*, 28:27–42.

Leithwood, K., Harris, A. and Hopkins, D. (2020), 'Seven Strong Claims about Successful School Leadership Revisited', *School Leadership and Management*, 40:5–22.

Lemke, J. L. and Sabelli, N. H. (2008), 'Complex Systems and Educational Change: Towards a New Research Agenda', *Educational Philosophy and Theory*, 40:118–29.

Levin, B. (2011), 'Chile, Latin America, and Inequality in Education', *Phi Delta Kappan*, 93:74–5.

Lewis, M. W. (2000), 'Exploring Paradox: Toward a More Comprehensive Guide', *The Academy of Management Review*, 25:760–76.

Levin, B. (2012), *System-wide Improvement in Education*, jointly published by UNESCO, Paris and The International Academy of Education: Brussels.

Liebowitz, D. and Porter, L. (2019), 'The Effect of Principal Behaviors on Student, Teacher, and School Outcomes: A Systematic Review and Meta-Analysis of the Empirical Literature', *Review of Educational Research* 89(5):785–827.

Lin, N. (1999), 'Building a Network Theory of Social Capital', *Connections*, 22(1):28–51.

Lindorff, A., Sammons, P. and Hall, J. (2020), 'International Perspectives in Educational Effectiveness Research: A Historical Overview', in J. Hall, A. Lindorff and P. Sammons (eds), *International Perspectives in Educational Effectiveness Research*, 9–32, Switzerland: Springer.

Lipshitz, R., Friedman, V. J. and Popper, M. (2007), *Demystifying Organizational Learning*, California: Sage Publications.

Lubienski, C. (2009), *Do Quasi-markets Foster Innovation in Education? A Comparative Perspective*, OECD Education Working Papers, No. 25. Paris: OECD.

Lubienski, C. (2014), 'Re-making the Middle: Dis-Intermediation in International Context', *Educational Management Administration and Leadership*, 42:423–40.

Lubienski, C., Lee, J. and Gordon, L. (2013), 'Self-Managing Schools and Access for Disadvantaged Students: Organizational Behaviour and School Admissions', *New Zealand Journal of Educational Studies*, 48:82–98.

Lucas, B., Stoll, L., Greany, T., Tsakalaki, A. and Nelson, R. (2017), *Independent-State School Partnerships: An Initial Review of Evidence and Current Practices*, Windsor: Eton College.

Lumby, J. (2018), 'Distributed Leadership and Bureaucracy', *Educational Management Administration and Leadership*, 47:5–19.

Lupton, R. and Thomson, S. (2015), *The Coalition's Record on Schools: Policy, Spending and Outcomes 2010–2015*, Working Paper 13, London: Joseph Rowntree Foundation/Nuffield Foundation/Trust for London.

MacBeath, J. (2007), 'Improving School Effectiveness: Retrospective and Prospective', in T. Townsend (ed), *International Handbook of School Effectiveness and Improvement*, 57–74, Dordrecht: Springer.

Macfarlane, S. and Macfarlane, A. (2019), 'Indigenous and Sociocultural Imperatives for Educational Practice', in A. Kamp (ed), *Education Studies in Aotearoa New Zealand: Key Disciplines and Emerging Directions*, 9–24, Wellington: NZCER Press.

MacLure, M. (2010), 'The Offence of Theory', *Journal of Education Policy*, 25:277–86.

McCarthy, H., Miller, P. and Skidmore, P. (2004), *Network Logic: Who Governs in an Interconnected World?* London: DEMOS.

McCormick, R., Fox, A., Carmichael, P. and Procter, R. (2011), *Researching and Understanding Educational Networks*, London: Routledge.

McKibben, S. (2014), *Leading Lateral Learning: Learning and Change Networks and The Social Side of School Reform*, Wellington: Fulbright New Zealand.

Malone, M., Groth, L., & Glazer, J. (2021) 'Leading in complex environments: the role of leadership in multi-school organization improvement', *School Leadership & Management*, 41:4–5, 352–369.

Marks, H. and Printy, S. (2003), 'Principal Leadership and School Performance: An Integration of Transformational and Instructional Leadership', *Educational Administration Quarterly*, 39(3):370–97.

Mason, M. (2008), 'What Is Complexity Theory and What Are Its Implications for Educational Change?' *Educational Philosophy & Theory*, 40:35–49.

Mason, M. (2016), 'Complexity Theory and Systemic Change in Education Governance', in T. Burns and F. Köster (eds), *Governing Education in a Complex World*, 41–54, Paris: OECD Publishing.

Massumi, B. (1992), *User's Guide to Capitalism and Schizophrenia: Deviations from Deleuze and Guattari*, Cambridge, MA: MIT Press.

Matthews, P. and Berwick, G. (2013), *Teaching Schools: First among Equals?* Nottingham: National College for Teaching and Leadership.

Maturana, H. and Varela, F. (1980), *Autopoiesis and Cognition: The Realization of the Living*, London: Reidl.

Michael, M. (2017), *Actor-Network Theory: Trials, Trails and Translations*, Thousand Oaks: Sage Publications.

Middlewood, D., Abbott, I. and Robinson, S. (2018), *Collaborative School Leadership: Managing a Group of Schools*, London: Bloomsbury Publishing.

Milward, H. and Provan, K. (2006), *A Manager's Guide to Choosing and Using Collaborative Networks*, Washington, DC: IBM Center for the Business of Government.

Ministry of Education (2014), *Investing in Educational Success – Report of the Working Group*, Wellington: Ministry of Education.

Ministry of Education (2015a), *Community of Schools Investing in Educational Success Tips and Starters: Working Together*, Wellington: Ministry of Education.

Ministry of Education (2015b), *The New Zealand Curriculum*, Wellington: Ministry of Education.

Ministry of Education (2016a), *Communities of Learning Guide for Schools and Kura*, Wellington: Ministry of Education.

Ministry of Education (2016b), *A Guide to Support the Development of Collaborative Practice in Communities of Learning | Kāhui Ako*. Available online: https://www.education.govt.nz/assets/Documents/col/Development-map-Version-3.pdf

Ministry of Education (2017), *Uptake and Early Implementation: Communities of Learning | Kāhui Ako*, Wellington: Research and Evaluation, Ministry of Education.

Ministry of Education (2018a), *Communities of Learning | Kāhui Ako 2017 Survey*, Wellington Ministry of Education.

Ministry of Education (2018b), *Summary of Education System in Singapore*, Wellington, Ministry of Education.

Ministry of Education (2019), *Supporting All Schools to Succeed: Reform of the Tomorrow's Schools System*, Wellington: Ministry of Education.

Ministry of Education (n.d.), *Community of Learning Leader*. Available online: https://www.education.govt.nz/communities-of-learning/leadership-and-governance/community-of-learning-leader/ (accessed 7 October 2020).

Mintrop, R. (2017), *Design-Based School Improvement: A Practical Guide for Education Leaders*. Cambridge, MA: Harvard Education Press.

Montecinos, C., González, A. and Ehren, M. (2021), 'From Hierarchy and Market to Hierarchy and Network Governance in Chile', in M. Ehren and J. Baxter (eds), *Trust, Accountability and Capacity in Education System Reform*, 201–21, Abingdon: Routledge.

Morgan, G. (2006), *Images of Organization*, Thousand Oaks, CA: Sage Publications.

Morrison, K. (2002), *School Leadership and Complexity Theory*, London: Taylor and Francis.

Morrison, K. (2005), 'Structuration, Habitus and Complexity Theory: Elective Affinities or New Wine in Old Bottles?' *British Journal of Sociology of Education*, 26:311–26.

Morrison, K. (2008), 'Educational Philosophy and the Challenge of Complexity Theory', *Educational Philosophy & Theory*, 40:19–34.

Muijs, D. (2015a), 'Improving Schools through Collaboration: A Mixed Methods Study of School-to-School Partnerships in the Primary Sector', *Oxford Review of Education*, 41(5):563–86.

Muijs, D. (2015b), 'Collaboration and Networking among Rural Schools: Can It Work and When? Evidence from England', *Peabody Journal of Education*, 90(2):294–305.

Muijs, D. and Rumyantseva, N. (2014), 'Coopetition in Education: Collaborating in a Competitive Environment', *Journal of Educational Change*, 15(1):1–18.

Muijs, D., Ainscow, M., Chapman, C. and West, M. (2011), *Collaboration and Networking in Education*, Netherlands: Springer.

Muijs, D., West, M. and Ainscow, M. (2010), 'Why Network? Theoretical Perspectives on Networking', *School Effectiveness and School Improvement*, 21(1):5–26.

Munby, S. (2021), 'Imperfect Leadership', in T. Greany and P. Earley (eds), *School Leadership and Education System Reform*, 2nd edn, 263–272, London: Bloomsbury.

Munby, S. and Fullan, M. (2016), *Inside-Out and Downside-Up: How Leading from the Middle Has the Power to Transform Education Systems*, Berkshire, UK: Education Development Trust/Motion Leadership.

Murphy, J. (1991), *Restructuring Schools: Capturing and Assessing the Phenomena*, New York: Teachers College Press.

Musset, P. (2012), *School Choice and Equity: Current Policies in OECD Countries and a Literature Review*, Paris: OECD Publishing.

NAHT (2020), *Improving Schools: A Report of the School Improvement Commission*, West Sussex, UK: NAHT.

Nederhand, J., Bekkers, V. and Voorberg, W (2016), 'Self-Organization and the Role of Government: How and Why Does Self-Organization Evolve in the Shadow of Hierarchy?' *Public Management Review*, 18(7):1063–84.

Nespor, J. (2002), 'Networks and Contexts of Reform', *Journal of Educational Change*, 3:365–82.

New Zealand Government (2001), *Education Standards Public Act 2001 No 88*, Wellington.

Ng, P. T. (2007), 'Quality Assurance in the Singapore Education System in an Era of Diversity and Innovation', *Educational Research for Policy and Practice*, 6:235–47.

Ng, P. T. (2010), 'The Evolution and Nature of School Accountability in the Singapore Education System', *Educational Assessment, Evaluation and Accountability*, 22(44):275–92.

Ng, P. T. (2017), *Learning from Singapore: The Power of Paradoxes*, New York: Routledge.

Northouse, P. G. (2009), *Leadership: Theory and Practice*, 5th edn, London: Sage Publications.

Nowotny, H. (2005), 'The Increase of Complexity and Its Reduction: Emergent Interfaces between the Natural Sciences, Humanities and Social Sciences', *Theory, Culture & Society*, 22:15–31.

O'Callaghan, J. (2015), 'Linwood College Roll Continues to Drop', *Stuff*. Available online: https://www.stuff.co.nz/the-press/news/68696108/linwood-college-roll-continues-to-drop (accessed 3 March 2021).

OECD (2011), *PISA in Focus* 2011/9 (October), Paris: OECD Publishing.

OECD (2015), *Schooling Redesigned: Towards Innovative Learning Systems*, Educational Research and Innovation, Paris: OECD Publishing.

OECD (2018), *Singapore Student Performance (PISA 2018)*, Paris: OECD Publishing.

OECD (2019), *Trends Shaping Education 2019*, Paris: OECD Publishing.

Ofsted (2003), *Excellence in Cities and Education Action Zones: Management and Impact*, London: Ofsted.

Ofsted (2008), *Implementation of 14–19 Reforms: An Evaluation of Progress*, London: Ofsted.

Ofsted (2013), *Unseen Children; Access and Achievement 20 Years on*, London: Ofsted.

Oliver, C. and Elbers, M. (1998), 'Networking Network Studies: An Analysis of Conceptual Configurations in the Study of Inter-Organisational Relationships', *Organisation Studies*, 19(4):549–83.

Olsson, P., Folke, C. and Berkes, F. (2004), 'Adaptive Co-Management for Building Social-Ecological Resilience', *Environmental Management*, 34:75–90.

O'Neill, J. (1996), 'Inter-School Collaboration', *The High School Journal*, 79(2):129–33.

O'Neill, J. and Snook, I. (2015), 'What Will Public Education Look Like in the Future and Why?' *New Zealand Journal of Educational Studies*, 50:195–209.

O'Reilly, D and Reed, M. (2011), 'The Grit in the Oyster: Professionalism, Managerialism and Leaderism as Discourses of UK Public Services Modernization', *Organization Studies*, 32(8):1079–101.

Osberg, D. and Biesta, G. (2010), *Complexity Theory and the Politics of Education*, Rotterdam: Sense Publishers.

O'Toole, V. (2018), '"Running on Fumes": Emotional Exhaustion and Burnout of Teachers Following a Natural Disaster', *Social Psychology of Education*, 21:1081–112.

O'Toole, V. and Martin, R. (2019), 'The Role of Emotions in Education in Aotearoa', in A. Kamp (ed), *Education Studies in Aotearoa New Zealand: Key Disciplines and Emerging Directions*, 179–200, Wellington: NZCER Press.

Ozga, J. (2011), 'Governing Narratives: "Local" Meanings and Globalising Education Policy', *Education Inquiry*, 2(2):305–18.

Paquin, R. and Howard-Grenville, J. (2013), 'Blind Dates and Arranged Marriages: Longitudinal Processes of Network Orchestration', *Organization Studies*, 34(11):1623–53

Page, S., Stone, M., Bryson, J. and Crosby, B. (2015), 'Public Value Creation by Cross-Sector Collaborations: A Framework and Challenges for Assessment', *Public Administration*, 93:715–32.

Paniagua, A. and Istance, D. (2018), *Teachers as Designers of Learning Environments: The Importance of Innovative Pedagogies*, Educational Research and Innovation, Paris: OECD Publishing.

Papanastasiou, N. (2017), 'The Practice of Scalecraft: Scale, Policy and the Politics of the Market in England's Academy Schools', *Environment and Planning A*, 49(5):1060–79.

Parliament of New Zealand (2020), *Education and Training Act 2020 No 38*, Wellington: Parliamentary Counsel Office.

Parry, K., and Bryman, A. (2006), 'Leadership in Organizations', in S. Clegg, C. Hardy, T. Lawrence and W. Nord (eds), *The SAGE Handbook of Organization Studies*, 447–468, London: Sage Publications.

Patterson, R. (2014), *No School Is an Island: Fostering Collaboration in a Competitive System*, Wellington: The New Zealand Initiative.

Pearce, C. and Conger, J. (2003), 'All Those Years Ago: The Historical Underpinnings of Shared Leadership', in C. L. Pearce and J. A. Conger (eds), *Shared Leadership: Reframing the Hows and Whys of Leadership*, Thousand Oaks, 1–12, CA: Sage Publications.

Pearce, D. and Gordon, L. (2005), 'In the Zone: New Zealand's Legislation for a System of School Choice and Its Effect', *London Review of Education* 3:145–57.

Pendleton, D. and Furnham, A. (2012), *Leadership: All You Need to Know*, London: Palgrave Macmillan.

Penuel, W. R. and Gallagher, D. J. (2017), *Creating Research-Practice Partnerships in Education*, Cambridge, MA: Harvard Education Press.

Perry, B. L., Pescosolido, A. and Borgatti, S. P. (2020), *Egocentric Network Analysis: Foundations, Methods and Models*, Cambridge, UK: Cambridge University Press.

Peurach, D. and Glazer, J. (2012), 'Reconsidering Replication: The Structure and Function of School Improvement Networks', *Journal of Educational Change*, 13.

Piattoeva, N. (2020), 'How can Transnational Connection Hold? An Actor Network Theory Approach to the Materiality of Transnational Governance', in A. Wilkins and A. Olmedo (eds), *Education Governance and Social Theory: Interdisciplinary Approaches to Research*, 103–122, London: Bloomsbury.

Pillans, G. (2015), *Leadership Development – Is It Fit for Purpose?*, London: Corporate Research Forum.

Pino-Yancovic, M. and Ahumada, L. (2020), 'Collaborative Inquiry Networks: The Challenge to Promote Network Leadership Capacities in Chile', *School Leadership and Management*, 40(2/3):221–41.

Pino-Yancovic, M., Parrao, C., Ahumada, L. and Gonzalez, A. (2019), 'Promoting Collaboration in a Competitive Context: School Improvement Networks in Chile', *Journal of Educational Administration*, 58(2):208–26.

Pino-Yancovic, M., Torres, A. G., Figueroa, L. A. and Chapman, C. (2020), *School Improvement Networks and Collaborative Enquiry: Fostering Systemic Change in Challenging Contexts*, London: Emerald Publishing.

Pollitt, C. (2014), '40 Years of Public Management Reform in UK Central Goverment: Promises, Promises ... Rethinking Policy and Politics', in S. Ayres (ed), *Reflections on Contemporary Debates in Policy Studies*, 7–28, Bristol: Policy Press.

Pollitt, C. and Bouckaert, G. (2011), *Public Management Reform: A Comparative Analysis – New Public Analysis, Governance and the Neo-Weberian State*, Oxford: Oxford University Press.

Pont, B. and Hopkins, D. (2008), *Approaches to System Leadership: Lessons Learned and Policy Pointers*, Paris: OECD Publishing.

Pont, B., Nusche, D. and Moorman, H. (2008), *Improving School Leadership. Vol 1 Policy and Practice*, Paris: OECD Publishing.

Pont, B., Figueroa, D., Zapata, J. and Fraccola, S. (2013), *Education Policy Outlook, New Zealand*, Paris: OECD Publishing.

Popp, J., MacKean, G., Casebeer, A., Milward, H. and Lindstrom, R. (2014), *Inter-Organizational Networks: A Critical Review of the Literature to Inform Practice*, Washington, DC: IBM Centre for the Business of Government.

Preedy, M., Bennett, N. and Wise, C. (2012), *Educational Leadership: Context, Strategy and Collaboration*, Milton Keynes: Open University.

Professional Development Advisory Group (2014), *Report of the Professional Learning and Development Advisory Group*, Wellington: Ministry of Education.

Provan, K., and Kenis, P. (2008), 'Modes of Network Governance: Structure, Management, and Effectiveness', *Journal of Public Administration Research and Theory*, 18(2):229–52.

Putnam, R. D. (1993), 'The Prosperous Community. Social Capital and Public Life', *The American Prospect*, 4(13):1–6.

Qian, H. and Walker, A. (2019), 'Reconciling Top-Down Policy Intent with Internal Accountability: The Role of Chinese School Principals', *Educational Assessment, Evaluation and Accountability*, 31:495–517.

Rabinow, P. (2009), 'Foucault's Untimely Struggle: Toward a Form of Spirituality', *Theory, Culture & Society*, 26:25–44.

Radford, M. (2008), 'Prediction, Control and the Challenge to Complexity', *Oxford Review of Education*, 34:505–20.

Rae, K. (2002), '"Education Market" or "Network of Schools": Competing Paradigms in School Enrolment Scheme Policy in Aotearoa – New Zealand', *International Studies in Educational Administration*, 30(1):36.

Raikes, L., Giovannini, A. and Getzel, B. (2019), *Divided and Connected: Regional Inequalities in the North, the UK and the Developed World – State of the North Report*, Manchester: IPPR.

Raffo, C., Dyson, A. and Kerr, K. (2014), 'Lessons from Area-Based Initiatives in Education and Training', NESET. Available online: https://nesetweb.eu/wp-content/uploads/2019/06/LessonsfromareabasedinitiativesJuly2014.pdf (accessed 30 March 2020).

Rameka, L. (2018), 'A Māori Perspective of Being and Belonging', *Contemporary Issues in Early Childhood*, 19:367–78.

Ramsey, P. and Poskitt, J. M. (2019), 'Understanding Leadership Dynamics "Within" and "Across School" Roles – and Moving Forward', *New Zealand Principals' Federation Magazine*, 34:10–12.

Révai, N. (2020), *What Difference Do Networks Make to Teachers' Knowledge? Literature Review and Case Descriptions*, Education Working Paper 215, Paris: OECD.

Reynolds, D. (2010), *Failure-Free Education? The Past, Present and Future of School Effectiveness and Improvement*, London: Routledge.

Rhodes, M., Murphy, J., Muir, J. and Murray, J. A. (2011), *Public Management and Complexity Theory*, New York: Routledge.

Rhodes, R. (1996), 'The New Governance: Governing without Government', *Political Studies*, XLIV:652–67.

Rhodes, R. (1997), *Understanding Governance: Policy Networks, Governance, Reflexivity and Accountability*, Philadelphia: Open University Press.

Riley, K. A. (2009), 'Reconfiguring Urban Leadership: Taking a Perspective on Community', *School Leadership and Management*, 29:51–63.

Rincón-Gallardo, S. and Fullan, M. (2016), 'Essential Features of Effective Networks in Education', *Journal of Professional Capital and Community*, 1(1):5–22.

Rittel, H. and Webber, M. (1973), 'Dilemmas in a General Theory of Planning', *Policy Sciences*, 4(2):155–69.

Robinson, V. and Gray, E. (2019), 'What Difference Does School Leadership Make to Student Outcomes?' *Journal of the Royal Society of New Zealand*, 49(2):171–87.

Robinson, V., Hohepa, M. and Lloyd, C. (2009), *School Leadership and Student Outcomes: Identifying What Works and Why: Best Evidence Synthesis Iteration*, Wellington: Ministry of Education.

Robinson, V., McNaughton, S. and Timperley, H. (2011), 'Building Capacity in a Self-Managing Schooling System: The New Zealand Experience', *Journal of Educational Administration*, 49:720–38.

Robinson, V. and Timperley, H. (2004), *Strengthening Education in Mangere and Otara Evaluation: Final Evaluation Report*, Wellington: Ministry of Education.

Robinson, V. and Ward, L. (2005), 'Lay Governance of New Zealand's Schools: An Educational, Democratic or Managerialist Activity?' *Journal of Educational Administration*, 43(2):170–86.

Rudd, P., Holland, M., Sanders, D., Massey, A. and White, G. (2004), *Evaluation of the Beach Schools Initiative – Final Report*, Slough: NfER.

Rutter, M., Maughan, B., Mortimore, P. and Ouston, J. (1979), *Fifteen Thousand Hours*, London: Open Books.

Ruwhiu, D. and Elkin, G. (2016), 'Converging Pathways of Contemporary Leadership: In the Footsteps of Māori and Servant Leadership', *Leadership*, 12:308–23.

Sahlberg, P. (2012), 'How GERM Is Infecting Schools around the World', Available online: https://pasisahlberg.com (accessed 27 July 2021).

Salomão Filho, A. and Kamp, A. (2019), 'Performing Mundane Materiality: Actor-Network Theory, Global Student Mobility and a Re/formation of "Social capital"', *Discourse: Studies in the Cultural Politics of Education*, 40:122–35.

Saltman, K. (2020), 'Foreword', in A. Wilkins and A. Olmedo (eds), *Education Governance and Social Theory: Interdisciplinary Approaches to Research*, xviii–xxiv, London: Bloomsbury.

Sartory, K., Jungermann, A. and Jarvinen, H. (2017), 'Support for School to School Networks: How Networking Teachers Perceive Support Activities of a Local Co-ordinating Agency', *British Journal of Educational Studies*, 65(2):143–65.

Scharpf, F. (1994), 'Games Real Actors Could Play: Positive and Negative Coordination in Embedded Negotiations', *Journal of Theoretical Politics*, 6(1):27–53.

Scheerens, J. (2013), 'The Use of Theory in School Effectiveness Research Revisited', *School Effectiveness and School Improvement*, 24:1–38.

Sherer, D., Paquin-Morel, R., Larbi-Cherif, A. and Russell, J. L. (2021), 'Conceptualizing, Evaluating, and Measuring Improvement Networks', in *Oxford Bibliographies: Series on Improvement-Focused Educational Research*, New York: Oxford University Press.

Scott, D., Posner, C., Martin, C. and Guzman, E. (2016), *Interventions in Education Systems: Reform and Development*, London: Bloomsbury.

Schwartz, B. and Sharpe, K. (2010), *Practical Wisdom*, New York: Riverhead.

Senge, P. M. (1990), *The Fifth Discipline: The Art and Practice of the Learning Organization*, New York: Doubleday.

Sharp, C., Pye, D., Blackmore, J., Brown, E., Eames, A., Easton, C., Filmer-Sankey, C., Tabary, A., Whitby, K., Wilson, R. and Benton, T. (2006), *National Evaluation of Creative Partnerships Final Report*, Slough: NfER.

Silvia, C. and McGuire, M. (2010), 'Leading Public Sector Networks: An Empirical Examination of Integrative Leadership Behaviors', *The Leadership Quarterly*, 21:264–77.

Skelcher, C. (2000), 'Changing Images of the State: Overloaded, Hollowed-Out, Congested', *Public Policy and Adminstration*, 15(3):3–19.

Skidmore, P. (2004), 'Leading between', in H. McCarthy, P. Miller and P. Skidmore (eds), *Network Logic: Who Governs in an Interconnected World*, 89–102, London: DEMOS.

Skyttner, L. (1996), *General Systems Theory: An Introduction*, London: MacMillan Press.

Smith, W. and Lewis, M. (2011), 'Toward a Dynamic Theory of Paradox: A Dynamic of Equilibrium Model of Organizing', *The Academy of Management Review*, 36:381–403.

Spillane, J. (2006), *Distributed Leadership*, San Francisco: Jossey-Bass.

St. Pierre, E. A. (2004), 'Deleuzian Concepts for Education: The Subject Undone', *Educational Philosophy and Theory*, 36:283–96.

Standing, G. (2011), *The Precariat: The New Dangerous Class*, London: Bloomsbury Academic.

StatsNZ (2016), *Well-Being Statistics: 2016*, Wellington: StatsNZ | Tatauranga Aotearoa.

Streek, W. and Thelen, K. (eds) (2005), 'Introduction', in *Beyond Continuity: Institutional Change in Advanced Political Economies*, Oxford: Oxford University Press.

Stubbs, T. and Strathdee, R. (2012), 'Markets in Education: The Impact of School Choice Policies in One Market Context in New Zealand', *International Studies in Sociology of Education*, 22(2):97–124.

Suggett, D. (2014), *Networking as System Policy: Balancing Vertical and Horizontal Dimensions*, Paris: OECD Centre for Educational Research and Innovation.

Supovitz, J. (2014), *Building a Lattice for School Leadership: The Top to Bottom Rethinking of Leadership Development in England*, Philadelphia: Consortium for Policy Research in Education.

Tan, O. S., Low, E. and Hung, D. (eds) (2017), *Lee Kuan Yew's Educational Legacy: The Challenges of Success*, Singapore: Springer.

Taylor, C. (1999), 'To Follow a Rule…', in R. Shusterman (ed), *Bourdieu: A Critical Reader*, 29–44, Oxford: Blackwell.

Tenbensel, T. (2005), 'Multiple Modes of Governance', *Public Management Review*, 7(2):267–88.

Tenbensel, T. (2017), 'Bridging Complexity Theory and Hierarchies, Markets, Networks, Communities: A "Population genetics" Framework for Understanding Institutional Change from Within', *Public Management Review*, 24(4):1–20.

Theisens, H. (2016), 'Hierarchies, Networks and Improvisation in Education Governance', in T. Burns and F. Koster (eds), *Governing Education in a Complex World*, 55–70, Paris: OECD.

Thomson, K. (2010), 'Externalities and School Enrolment Policy: A Supply-Side Analysis of School Choice in New Zealand', *Journal of School Choice* 4(4):418–49.

Thomson, P., Gunter, H. and Blackmore, J. (2021), 'Series Editor Introduction', in P. Landri (ed), *Educational Leadership, Management, and Administration through Actor-Network Theory*, ix–xv, London: Routledge.

Thomson, P. and Heffernan, A. (2021), 'Using Theory in Educational Leadership, Management and Administration Research', in S. Courtney, H. Gunter, R. Niesche and T. Trujillo (eds), *Understanding Educational Leadership: Critical Perspectives and Approaches*, 155–170, London: Bloomsbury.

Thrift, N. (2005), *Knowing Capitalism*, London: Sage Publications.

Thrupp, M. (2001a), 'Sociological and Political Concerns about School Effectiveness Research: Time for a New Research Agenda', *School Effectiveness and School Improvement*, 12:7–40.

Thrupp, M. (2001b), 'School-level Education Policy under New Labour and New Zealand Labour: A Comparative Update', *British Journal of Educational Studies*, 49(2):187–212.

Thrupp, M. (2010), 'Choice and Zoning', in M. Thrupp and R. Irwin (eds), *Another Decade of New Zealand Education Policy: Where to Now?* 47–55, Hamilton: Wilf Malcom Institute of Educational Research.

Thrupp, M. (2013), *Research, Analysis and Insight into National Standards (RAINS) Project: Second Report: Understanding New Zealand's Very Local National Standards*, Hamilton: University of Waikato.

Thrupp, M. (2018), 'To Be "In the Tent" or Abandon it? A School Clusters Policy and the Responses of New Zealand Educational Leaders', in J. Wilkinson, R. Niesche and S. Eacott (eds), *Challenges for Public Education: Reconceptualising Educational Leadership, Policy and Social Justice as Resources for Hope*, 132–44, Abingdon, UK: Routledge.

Thrupp, M., Powell, D., O'Neill, J., Chernoff, S. and Seppänen, P. (2021), 'Private Actors in New Zealand Schooling: Towards an Account of Enablers and Constraints since the 1980s', *New Zealand Journal of Educational Studies*, 56:23–39.

Timperley, H., Hohepa, M., Keegan, P., Parr, J., Lai, M. and McNaughton, S. (2010), *Building Evaluative Capability in Schooling Improvement: Milestone Report, Part A: Strand One and Strand Three*, Wellington: Ministry of Education.

Timpson, E. (2019), *Timpson Review of School Exclusion*, London: HMG.

Toh, Y., Hung, D., Chua, P. and Jamaludin, S. (2016), 'Pedagogical Reforms within a Centralised-Decentralised System: A Singapore's Perspective to Diffuse 21st Century Learning Innovations', *International Journal of Educational Management*, 30(7):1247–67.

Toh, Y., Jamaludin, A., Hung, W. and Chua, P. (2014), 'Ecological Leadership: Going beyond System Leadership for Diffusing School-Based Innovations in the Crucible of Change for 21st Century Learning', *Asia-Pacific Education Researcher*, 23:835–50.

Tomorrow's Schools Independent Taskforce (2018), *Our Schooling Futures: Stronger Together: Report by the Tomorrow's Schools Independent Taskforce*, Wellington: Ministry of Education.

Townsend, T. (2007), '20 Years of ICSEI: The Impact of School Effectiveness and School Improvement on School Reform', in T. Townsend (ed), *International Handbook on School Effectiveness and Improvement*, 1–26, Dordrecht: Springer.

Townsend, T. (2015), 'Leading School Networks, Hybrid Leadership in Action?' *Educational Management Administration and Leadership*, 43(5):719–37.

Trujillo, T. (2013), 'The Reincarnation of the Effective Schools Research: Rethinking the Literature on District Effectiveness', *Journal of Educational Administration*, 51(4):426–52

Urry, J. (2003), *Global Complexity*, Cambridge: Polity Press/Blackwell Publishing.

Urry, J. (2005), 'The Complexities of the Global', *Theory, Culture & Society*, 22:235–54.

van Dijck, J. and Poell, T. (2018), 'Social Media Platforms and Education', in J. Burgess, A. Marwick and T. Poell (eds), *The SAGE Handbook of Social Media*, 579–91, London: Sage Publication.

Vangen, S. (2017), 'Developing Practice-Oriented Theory on Collaboration: A Paradox Lens', *Public Administration Review*, 77:263–72.

Vangen, S. and Huxham, C. (2003), 'Enacting Leadership for Collaborative Advantage: Dilemmas of Ideology and Pragmatism in the Activities of Partnership Managers', *British Journal of Management*, 14:61–76.

Vangen, S. and Huxham, C. (2012), 'The Tangled Web: Unraveling the Principle of Common Goals in Collaborations', *Journal of Public Administration Research & Theory*, 22(4):731–60.

Varpio, L., Paradis, E., Uijtdehaage, S. and Young, M. (2020), 'The Distinctions between Theory, Theoretical Framework, and Conceptual Framework', *Academic Medicine*:989–94.

Verger, A. and Parcerisa, L. (2020), 'Test-Based Accountability and the Rise of Regulatory Governance in Education: A Review of Global Drivers', in A. Wilkins and A. Olmedo (eds), *Education Governance and Social Theory: Interdisciplinary Approaches to Research*, 139–158, London: Bloomsbury.

von Bertalanffy, L. (1972), 'The History and Status of General Systems Theory', *The Academy of Management Journal*, 15:407–26.

Waldrop, M. (1993), *Complexity: The Emerging Science at the Edge of Order and Chaos*, New York: Touchstone Books.

Walker, A., Bryant, D. and Lee, M. (2013), 'International Patterns in Principal Preparation: Commonalities and Variations in Pre-Service Programmes', *Educational Management Administration and Leadership*, 41:405–34.

Walker, A. and Qian, H. (2020), 'Developing a Model of Instructional Leadership in China', *Compare: A Journal of Comparative and International Education*, DOI: 10.1080/03057925.2020.1747396.

Waltz, S. B. (2006), 'Nonhumans Unbound: Actor-Network Theory and the Reconsideration of "Things" in Educational Foundations', *Educational Foundations*, 20:51–68.

Ward, L. and Henderson, A. (2011), *An Evaluation of Network Learning Communities*, Wellington: Ministry of Education.

Waslander, S., Pater, C. and van der Weide, M. (2010), *Markets in Education: An Analytical Review of Empirical Research on Market Mechanisms in Education*, Education Working Paper 52, Paris: OECD.

Wasserman, S. and Faust, K. (1994), *Social Network Analysis: Methods and Applications*, Cambridge: Cambridge University Press.

Watson, C. (2014), 'Effective Professional Learning Communities? The Possibilities for Teachers as Agents of Change in Schools', *British Educational Research Journal*, 40:18–29.

Weick, K. E. (1976), 'Educational Organizations as Loosely Coupled Systems', *Administrative Science Quarterly*, 21:1–19.

Weick, K. E. (2011), 'Organized Sensemaking: A Commentary on Processes of Interpretive Work', *Human Relations*, 65(1):141–53.

Wellman, B. (1983), 'Network Analysis: Some Basic Principles', *Sociological Theory*, 1(1):155–200.

Wenger, E. (1998), 'Communities of Practice: Learning as a Social System', *Systems Thinker*, 9:1–5.

Wenger, E. (2000), 'Communities of Practice and Social Learning Systems', *Organizational Articles*, 7:225–46.

Western, S. (2019), *Leadership: A Critical Text*, 3rd edn, London: Sage Publications.

Wheatley, M. and Frieze, D. (2011), 'Leadership in the Age of Complexity: From Hero to Host', *Resurgence Magazine*, Winter.

Wilkins, A. and Olmedo, A. (2020), 'Introduction: Conceptualizing Education Governance: Framings, Perspectives and Theories', in A. Wilkins and A. Olmedo (eds), *Education Governance and Social Theory: Interdisciplinary Approaches to Research*, 1–20, London: Bloomsbury.

Williams, P. (2012), *Collaboration in Public Policy and Practice: Perspectives on Boundary Spanners*, Bristol: Policy Press.

Woods, P., Bagley, C. and Glatter, R. (1998), *School Choice and Competition: Markets in the Public Interest?* London: Routledge.

Wu, W. Y., Chan, D. W. K. and Forrestor, V. (2005), 'Quality Education Initiatives in Hong Kong: School Networks in Transition', in W. Veugelers and M. O'Hair (eds), *Network Learning for Educational Change*, 159–71, Maidenhead: Open University Press.

Wylie, C. (2012a), *Challenges around Capability Improvements in a System of Self-Managed Schools in New Zealand*, Washington: US Department of Education.

Wylie, C. (2012b), *Vital Connections: Why We Need More than Self-Managing Schools*, Wellington: NZCER Press.

Wylie, C. (2016), *Communities of Learning | Kāhui Ako: The Emergent Stage*, Wellington: NZCER.

Zhao, Y. (2017), 'What Works May Hurt: Side Effects in Education', *Journal of Educational Change*, 18:1–19.

Index

Locators followed by "n." indicate endnotes

Academies Act (2010) 59
Academy of Singapore Teachers (AST) 24
actor-network theory (ANT) 5, 31, 142,
  145, 158–9, 184, 207 n.1
  agency 50
  defining 49
  empirical approach 52
  human actors 49–50, 147, 152, 155, 159
  mediation 51–2, 157
  network 147, 155–8
  sources of uncertainty 52–3
  symmetry 49, 147–52, 159
  translation 50–1, 147, 152–5
adaptive work 162, 167
Adler, P. 41
Administering for Excellence report 77
Ainscow, M. 11–13, 32
Amagoh, F. 46
ancillary staff system 45, 128
Aotearoa New Zealand 73, 106, 135, 139,
    148, 150, 156, 187, 189, 200
  decentralized system 76–81
  economic rationalism 76, 112
  Education Act 1877 76
  education in 124
  education policy context 76–81
  Education Reform Office's inspection
    95
  ethnic identity of school-aged children
    75
  evaluations 97
  formal education 74
  funding 75
  hierarchical accountability framework
    124
  leadership 137
  New Zealand Experiment 76
  Picot taskforce 77
  policy-driven networking initiatives 83
  policy strands 114
  pre-existing partnerships 120
  school autonomy in 114
  snapshot (2021) 74
  Teaching Council 194
  Transparency International 73
  Treaty of Waitangi/Tiriti o Waitangi
    73, 113, 124–5, 148, 169, 185
Ardern, J. 73, 86, 112–13, 118
Armstrong, P. 14, 20
assessment 79, 93–7, 168, 192
Aupaki Kāhui Ako (New Zealand) 4, 97,
    124, 171, 190
  achievement challenges 87–9, 97,
    102–3, 124, 130, 140, 153
  Bays Cluster 87, 103, 125, 130, 189
  Linwood College 87–9, 103, 130, 153,
    170, 206 n.17
Averch, H. A. 52
Avonside Girls' High School 150, 206 n.17

Bampton Alliance (England) 4, 62–3,
    132–3, 154, 169, 171, 189, 204 n.7,
    206 n.2
  Bampton Education Partnership 64–5,
    68, 96–7, 121, 126, 141, 149, 206 n.2
  commitment and community 134
  fragmentation and reformation (after
    2010) 64–6
  new place-based 'school-led' network
    68–70
  Opportunity Area (OA) 63, 65, 68, 96,
    105, 122–4, 133–4, 138, 154–5, 171
  as place-based meta-partnership 123
  school-to-school networks 66–8
  strategy group 63–4, 68, 70–1, 122,
    126, 133–4, 136, 154–5, 171
  Teaching Schools 67, 122, 133, 156,
    206 n.3

Bananarama principle 106
Bauer, S. 173, 208 n.2
Bays Cluster 87, 103, 125, 130, 189
Beckett, D. 138-9
Beeby, C.E. 86, 206 n.15
behaviours, leadership 167
Bernstein, B. 145
Bevir, M. 38. *See also* governance theory
black box models 34, 51, 138, 156-7
Blackmore, J. 163
Bogotch, I. 208 n.2
bottom up community governance 122, 125
Bourdieu, P. 12, 44, 154
Brown, C. 14, 20-1
Bryant, D. 193
Bryman, A. 164
Bryson, J. M. 10
Bunt, L. 190
Byrne, D. 45

Callon, M. 49, 51, 152
capacity for improvement, school 94
    across non-homogenous partnerships 99
    assessments 96-7
    funding 98-9
    inspections 95-6
    limitations, assessing 99
    self-evaluation 94-5
capital theory
    of school effectiveness and improvement 37
    social (*see* social capital)
Carnegie Foundation for the Advancement of Teaching 21-2
Castells, M. 7
centralized-decentralization 23-4, 111
Chapman, C. 14, 20, 202 n.3
Charter Management Organisations (CMOs) 208 n.2
Chile
    Education Conflict 148-9
    mandated networks 156, 169
    policies and practices 4, 8, 23, 28
    publicly funded schools 156
    reforms 112, 194
    school inspections 95-6
    school networks in 25-8
    SLEs 187-8
    voucher system 117

China, school principals interview report 22-3
Cilliers, P. 140
Clark, J. 86
co-design approach 69, 101, 105, 190, 196
coevolution, concept of 46
Coleman, J. 12
collaborative leadership theory 164-5
collaborative thuggery 20, 171
collective sense-making 143, 173-4
Comber, B. 50
commitment and contribution 16-17, 98, 157
community 42, 110, 118, 120-5
complexity theories 5, 54, 169, 184
    boundaries 140-1
    conditions 128-9
    connectivity and interdependence 46
    critique 44
    decentralized/dispersed control 48-9, 137-8
    defining 42-3
    dissipative structures 46
    economy of concepts 45
    emergence 46
    implications of emergence 138-41
    internal diversity 47, 129-31, 171
    internal/external connectedness 128
    internal redundancy 47-8, 131-5
    learning 45
    neighbour interactions 48, 135-6, 171
    nesting, concept of 47
    nonlinearity and feedback 46
    organization-environment system 47
    policymakers 46
    'praise and blame' culture 142
    self-organization and adaptation 46
    strategies for emergence, hierarchy 46
    subsystems, school 45, 128
Conger, J. 166
constructivist theory 11, 13
content 18
conventional concept 37
co-present group 139-40
Cormack, P. 50
Cousin, S. 168
Covid-19 pandemic 1, 13, 64, 70, 73, 84, 136, 152, 201
CPDL 203 n.1

Creative Action Project (CAP), Singapore 194–5
Creemers, B. 32, 35
Crosby, B. C. 10

Davis, B. 5, 47–8, 129, 135, 138
decentralization 111, 113, 187
decentralized/dispersed control, complexity 5, 48–9, 137–8
deep partnerships 17, 37, 93–4
democratic-populist strand 114, 187
design and delivery model 193
Development Map and Toolkit, New Zealand 106
digital platforms 149–51
DiMaggio, P. J. 106
Dimmock, C. 195
distributed leadership 5, 163, 166–7, 170. *See also* system leadership/leaders
diversity, embrace of 172
Durkheimian theory 12, 13
dynamic model 35

eco-leadership 174–5
ecological whole system approach 126, 143, 159
ecosystem 24, 44, 101, 165, 174
Education Act (1989) 79, 113
Education Endowment Foundation (EEF) Teaching and Learning Toolkit 202–3 n.1
education policy context 4
  Aotearoa New Zealand 76–81
  England 57–8
education production models 34
Education Reform Act (ERA, 1988), England 57
Education Review Office (ERO), New Zealand 79, 85, 106, 206 n.1
Education Service Agency, New Zealand 113, 115
Education & Training Act 76
Edwards, R. 49–50
effectiveness and improvement, educational 4, 11, 13, 16, 18, 48, 52–4, 108–9, 162, 185, 200
  capacity to improve 94–9 (*see also* capacity for improvement, school)
  capital theory 37
  conventional model 36–7

critiques and evidence 34, 36
development of theories 32
dynamic model 35
educational outcomes 93
external networks, role 36
intellectual and social capital 99–103
legacy of work 33
leverage and outcomes 103–7
policy and practice 35
RCTs 35–6
school autonomy and 193
scientific management 33
teaching and learning 35
theories of 36–7
Egocentric Network analysis 10
Ehren, M. 26, 28, 112, 187
Elizabeth II, Queen 73
El Mercurio 148
emergence, concept of 46, 138–41
  attractors and boundaries 140
  co-present group 139–40
  and governance 140
  of system leadership 165–70
England 55–7
  Bampton Alliance (*see* Bampton Alliance (England))
  challenges 69
  educational groups in 101
  education policy context 57–8
  evidence of networking 32
  learning links network 16
  markets on collaboration 119
  MATs (*see* Multi-Academy Trusts (MATs), England)
  National Curriculum 56, 59
  networking initiatives 112
  New Labour initiatives 58, 60
  Ofsted 56–7, 64, 67, 96–7, 106, 118, 121, 150
  parental choice of school 118
  primary schools 55–6
  RSCs 69, 204 n.11
  school inspections 95–6
  school networks 60–3
  school-to-school support partnerships 14, 61, 105, 168, 185
  secondary schools 55–6
  'self-improving, school-led system' agenda 59–61, 132
  state-funded schools 56

system leadership models 121,
  167–8 (*see also* system leadership/
  leaders)
enrolment moment, translation 51, 153, 159
epistemic carryovers 25, 101
epistemic community 97, 100–2, 104, 107,
  131, 135, 142, 173, 184, 196
Equality of Educational Opportunity
  (Coleman) 33
equally prevalent tendency 138–9
equitable partnerships 15
evidence on networks 20–3, 29, 32, 131
exploration and exploitation 19, 99
externally funded partnerships 98

Fancy, H. 76
Faust, K. 202 n.1
Fenwick, T. 49–50, 207 n.1
Fiske, E. B. 76, 79. See also *When Schools
  Compete: A Cautionary Tale* (Fiske
  & Ladd)
fixed quantum approach 41
Fullan, M. 21, 128–9, 167, 170, 202 n.2
function 18
Furnham, A. 165

general systems theory 43–4
Giddens, A., structuration theory 44
Gilbert, C. 123
Glassman, R. B. 43
Glatter, R., partnership 61
Glazer, J. 100–1
global educational networks 20–3
Global Education Reform Movement
  (GERM) 39–40
goal-directed networks 10, 202 n.2
González, A. 26, 28, 112, 187
Gordon, L. 78
Gorur, R. 49
governance and management structures
  18, 158
governance theory 5, 54, 109, 140, 184
  community 42, 120–5
  defining 38–40
  GERM 'infections' 39–40
  heuristics 41
  hierarchy 41, 110–17
  instruments of 39
  markets 41, 117–20
  meta-governance 39, 109, 117

networks 41, 120–5
NPM (*see* new public management
  (NPM))
policy-makers 40
soft governance 39, 150
wicked problems 38, 109
Greany, T. 41, 59, 61, 63, 106, 110, 111–12,
  117–20, 122, 133, 157, 168
  contrasting interpretations of 'middle
    tier' in literature 188
  improvement approaches in
    collaborative groups 100
  middle tier 186
Grimaldi, E. 14
Gronn, P. 166
Gross Domestic Product (GDP), UK 55
groupthink 15, 179
Gunter, H. 163

habitus, concept 44
Hadfield, M. 202 n.3
Hager, P. 138–9
Hallinger, P., principal instructional
  leadership 22–3
hallmark education policy 81
Hargreaves, A. 170, 188
Hargreaves, D. H. 5, 31, 36–7, 93, 99, 103,
  107–8, 168, 170
  capital theory 37
  deep partnerships 17, 37, 93–4
  educational model 31
  full 'maturity model' 203 n.3
  joint practice development 19, 37, 62,
    93, 100, 102–3, 108, 132, 151, 154,
    156, 191
  peer evaluation and challenge 102
  theory-based model 108
Harris, A. 165–6, 168–9, 190
Hawkins, M. 43, 45, 128
Heffernan, A. 32
Heifetz, R. 162
hierarchical leadership 90, 137, 191
hierarchy 41, 110, 124, 139, 180
  decentralization 111, 113
  forms of coordination 113, 116–17
  meta-governance 117
  public funding and accountability 111
  school autonomy, shifts 113
  strategies for fostering networks 115–16
  'traditional' bureaucracies 111, 113, 116

Higham, R. 41, 59, 61, 110, 112, 117–20, 122, 133, 157, 166–8, 174
high-autonomy-high-accountability system 57
high/higher-performing school 58–9, 62–4, 105–6, 120–1, 132, 204 n.8
   new economy of knowledge 122–3
   and school leaders 60
Ho, J. 24–5, 95, 104
homogenization 106
Hopkins, D. 34–5, 165–7
human capital 23, 40, 129, 139, 175
human/non-human actors 147, 149–52, 154–5, 157–9, 184, 192, 201
Hung, D. 25, 121
Huxham, C. 20, 171–2. *See also* collaborative thuggery
hybrid leadership 167

immutable mobiles 149
informal learning 13
Information Communications Technology (ICT) 58, 101
information technologies 127
innovation promotion networks 21
intellectual capital 37, 99–100, 203 n.2
   development and movement of 100, 108
   as ICT pioneers 101
   and joint practice development 103
   shared 105
interessement moment, translation 51, 153
internal diversity, complexity 5, 47, 129–31, 133, 142, 171
   maintenance of 131
   trust 130
internal redundancy, complexity 5, 47–8, 131–5, 142
   educational spaces 132
   partnerships and collaboratives 133
   social learning system 131
inter-organizational networks 3–5, 9, 11, 32, 36, 41, 54, 199
   deep partnerships 37
   educational outcomes 93
   and partnerships 15, 17
   types of 9
inter-school networks 3, 54, 110–11, 115, 119, 170, 179
   co-opetition 119
   and partnerships 94

Investing in Educational Success (IES), New Zealand 81, 84, 96, 106, 130, 152, 169
Istance, D. 20–1

James, C. R. 43, 45, 128
Jensen, B. 194
Jessop, B. 38, 109
join-the-dots approach 146
joint practice development 19, 37, 62, 93, 100, 102–3, 108, 132, 151, 154, 156, 191
Jopling, M. 202 n.3

Kadushin, C., intrinsic needs 15–16
Kāhui Ako 81–4, 129–30, 156, 205 n.12, 207 n.2. *See also* Aupaki Kāhui Ako (New Zealand)
   collaborative roles 82, 166
   Community of Learning Role Selection and Appointment Information 85
   development 84–6
   domains of work 83
   Education Support Agency 153
   Education Work Programme 84, 86, 153
   fully-functioning 107
   funding 82
   IES (*see Investing in Educational Success* (IES), New Zealand)
   instruments 81–2, 136
   Kōrero Mātauranga (Education Conversation) 82–4, 86
   negotiation 153
   policy 81
Kamp, A. 46, 50, 75, 85, 146, 175
   ANTian sensibility 50, 146
   governing collaborative goals, strategies 46, 85, 175
Kapucu, N., traditional to post bureaucratic paradigm 38
Kenis, P. 3, 9, 13, 18
knowledge and diffusing innovations 158
knowledge sharing 19, 27, 41, 187, 189
Kyriakides, L. 32, 35

Labour government, New Zealand 76, 82–4, 112, 205 n.5, 205 n.8
Ladd, H. F. 76, 79. *See also When Schools Compete: A Cautionary Tale* (Fiske & Ladd)

Landri, P. 146–7, 156
    ANTian analysis 5
    network stabilization 147
    non-human actors 147, 149–50, 152
Latour, B. 49, 51–2
Law, J. 49
leadership 2, 10, 19, 29, 132, 161
    characteristics of 162–3
    collaboration 164–5
    implications for 94
    inter-school networks and 3
    leader as hero 164, 178
    leader as host 178
    and management 158
    networks and network (*see* networks and network leadership)
    paradigms 162
    school, imagining 1–2, 7 (*see also* schools and school leaders)
    system orientation to 163
    transnational leadership package 163–5
    without authority 162
leadership development 5, 169, 178–80, 186
    approaches to 192–5
    implications for 192–5
    for networked leadership 195–6
    policymakers and 196–7, 199
Leadership Strategy and Educational Leadership Capability Framework 194
Leaders in Education Programme (LEP), Singapore 194–5
lead organization networks 18
lead practitioners 19
Learning and Change Networks (LCN), New Zealand 80–1
learning links network (England) 16
Lee, M. 193
Lee, S. 24–5, 95, 104
Leithwood, K. 13, 165–6
Lemke, J. L. 43
leverage and outcomes 37, 92, 103, 203 n.2
    Development Map and Toolkit 106
    domains 107
    evidence-based interventions 107
    scope for 104
Lin, N. 12
Local Management of Schools (LMS), England 57

Local Public Education Services (SLEs), Chile 26–8, 115, 187
local solutions 190–2, 195–7
lower-performing schools 14, 121
Lubienski, C. 79

managerialist strand 114, 187
Māori medium education 74
market(s) 41, 110, 117, 125–6
    -based approach 124
    generational shifts 112
    marketization reforms 148
    mechanisms 26, 40, 117
    -oriented strand 187
    overarching findings 119
    school zones 118
    social mobility 117
Mason, M. 134
Massumi, B. 46, 175
'maths mastery' approaches 148
McCormick, R. 202 n.3
mediation, concept of 51–2, 147, 157, 164
meta-governance 39, 109, 117
meta-networks 9, 41, 62, 204 n.7. See also Bampton Alliance (England)
middle tier 5, 39, 113–15, 122, 125, 179–80, 184, 186–92, 196–7, 199, 208 n.2
Ministry of Education (MOE), Singapore 24–5, 111
mobilization moment, translation 51, 154, 159
moments of translation 51, 152–5, 159
Montecinos, C. 26, 28, 112, 187
Morrison, K. 43–4, 128
    School Leadership and Complexity Theory 127–8
Muijs, D. 11–13, 20, 32, 61, 105
Multi-Academy Trusts (MATs), England 4, 9, 58–9, 63–6, 71–2, 99, 104, 114, 121–3, 132–3, 150, 168, 189, 204 n.7, 204 n.8, 206 n.2, 207 n.3
    collaboration, schools 204 n.7
    system 133
Munby, S. 174
Murphy, J. 33

National Administration Guidelines, New Zealand 75, 205 n.3
National Certificate of Educational Achievement (NCEA), New Zealand 74–5

National College for School Leadership, England 167
National Institute of Education (NIE), Singapore 111–12, 194–5
National Leaders of Education (NLEs) programme, England 58, 60, 63, 67, 104–5, 121–2, 168–9, 206 n.3
National Literacy and Numeracy Strategy, England 167
National Professional Qualification for Headteachers (NPQH), England 193–4
National Qualifications Framework, New Zealand 75
National Standards, New Zealand 80–1, 88–9, 205 n.8
neighbour interactions, complexity 5, 48, 135–6
Nespor, J. 50
nesting, concept of 48
Network Administrative Organizations (NAO) 18
network governance 41–2, 111, 146, 187. *See also* governance theory
networking initiatives 21, 83, 112
network learning architectures 196
network learning communities (NLCs) 24–5, 58, 80, 188
networks, features 15, 98, 157, 196
   commitment and contribution 16–17, 98, 157
   exploration and exploitation 19, 99
   governance and management structures 18, 158
   implications 175–6
   inter-organizational networks/partnerships 15–16
   knowledge and diffusing innovations 158
   leading and managing networks 19–20, 158, 170
   mediation 157
   network effectiveness, principles 18–19
   share values, practices and attributes 17, 98, 157
   social networks, inter-organizational partnerships 17–18
   societal contexts 157

networks and network leadership 2, 4–5, 32, 41, 120–5, 146, 161, 167, 170–1, 197, 199–200. *See also* system leadership/leaders
   ANT 147, 155–8
   and collaboration 22
   characteristics, leaders 162–3
   defining 3, 9–10
   ecological perspective on 156
   emergence and innovation 5
   features and barriers to achievement 15–20 (*see also* networks, features)
   hybrid 167, 172
   implications 2, 8, 108, 110, 125, 142, 147, 180, 184
   leading and managing 19–20, 158, 170
   and networking 2
   outcomes and benefits 201
   'shared-power world' of 10
   system orientation to 163
   theoretical perspectives on 11–12
   typology of 20
network society 7, 9–10, 141
network theories, rationales and benefits 10–15
new leadership theories 164
new public management (NPM) 39, 109, 112–13, 125, 131, 162, 168, 184, 191
   reforms 109, 117
   Transnational Leadership Package 192
new social movements 11, 13, 41
New Zealand. *See* Aotearoa New Zealand
New Zealand Council for Educational Research (NZCER) 206 n.15
The New Zealand Curriculum 74, 80, 204–5 n.2
Ng, P. T. 111
non-goal-directed networks 9–10
Northouse, P. G. 10
Nowotny, H. 42
NZEI 80

Office for Standards in Education, Children's Services and Skills (Ofsted) 56–7, 59, 64, 67, 96–7, 106, 118, 121, 150
online network 21
Ontario, system leadership 168
O'Reilly, D. 172

organic leadership 165
organizational theory 19, 43, 162, 173
organizations and organizing 173
Ōtākaro Community of Learning 150

Panayiotou, A. 32
Paniagua, A. 20-1
paper-based forms 149
parent-assistants 127-8
parent system 45, 128
Parry, K. 164
partner-specific communication 172
Patterson, R. 81
Pearce, C. 166
pedagogical approach networks 21
pedagogy and innovation 21
peer reviews 67, 96-7, 102, 105-6
Pendleton, D. 165
Peurach, D. 100
Picot Report 205 n.6
Pino-Yancovic, M. 18
  government-funded evaluation 26-7
place-based collaboration 189
place-based 'middle tier' 5, 186, 192
place-based partnerships 133-4, 189
Poell, T. 149
policies and practices 2, 4-5, 8, 20-1, 23, 28-9, 35, 95, 109, 164-5, 178, 186, 199
  application to 199-200
  frameworks 180
  implications for 179-80, 200
  and leadership development 196-7
  'middle tier' arrangements 187
policymakers 4, 8-9, 40, 46, 83, 107, 109, 116, 119, 168, 186-7, 199
  England 168
  and leadership development designers 196-7
  middle tier 190, 192, 196
  and practitioners 185
  systems 115, 119
policymaking and policy-implementation 109
policy strands (New Zealand) 114
Popp, J. 9, 13, 19, 145, 170
Powell, W. W. 106
practice-oriented theory 172
principal instructional leadership 22-3

problematization moment, translation 51, 152-3, 155
professional learning 13, 54, 194, 205 n.7
  and development 89
  funding 89, 98
  networks 21
  for staff 36, 106
professional learning communities (PLCs) 24-5, 80
Programme of International Student Assessment (PISA) 23, 40, 50, 78, 147-8, 207 n.2
Provan, K. 3, 9, 13, 18
publicly funded schools 3, 9, 25, 55, 110, 125, 156
Putnam, R. D. 12

Qian, H. 22

Radford, M. 142
RAND Corporation 34
Randomised Controlled Trials (RCTs) 35-6
Reed, M. 172
Regional Schools Commissioners (RSCs), England 69, 204 n.11
return time 206 n.1
Révai, N. 20
Riley, K. A. 161
Rincon-Gallardo, S. 21, 202 n.2
Rittel, H. 38
Rush, P. 89

Sabelli, N. H. 43
safety 16
Sahlberg, P. 39
Saltman, K. 40
Sartory, K. 21
Scheerens, J. 35-6
scholarship, role of 31
school cluster system 24
school effectiveness and school improvement (SESI) 184-5. *See also* effectiveness and improvement, educational
School Excellence Model (SEM), Singapore 95, 104, 149
School Improvement Network (SIN) strategy, Chile 26-7

'school-led' partnership 72
school management teams 95, 104
school principals interview report (China) 22
schools and school leaders 4, 8, 22, 24, 42, 57, 60–1, 65, 70, 72, 90, 95, 97, 106, 108–9, 119, 121, 125, 132–4, 151–2, 165, 169, 180, 194, 196, 203 n.1
   complexity of 43
   effectiveness and improvement (*see* effectiveness and improvement, educational)
   leader, imagining 1–2, 7, 199
   partnership-building skills 37
   partnerships with organizations 9
   questions 191–2
   self-management of 77
   subsystems 45
school-to-school support partnerships 14, 60, 105, 168, 185
self-evaluation, school 25, 95, 149
self-funded partnerships 98
'self-improving, school-led system' agenda 59, 61, 112, 132, 168, 187, 203 n.3
Senge, P. M., systemic thinking 45
sense-making 103–4, 196
   collective 126, 143, 171, 173–4
   structures 131, 135
Serres, M. 50. *See also* translation, concept of
Seven Strong Claims about Successful School Leadership (Leithwood, Harris, and Hopkins) 165
shared governance networks 18
shared intellectual capital 100, 103, 105
'shared-power world' of networks 10
shared social capital 105
share values, practices and attributes 17, 98, 157
Shirley, D. 188
Shirley Boys' High School 150, 206 n.17
significant other systems 45, 128
Singapore
   centralised-decentralisation 111
   innovation hub schools 121
   nodal schools in 101
   partnerships, differences 121
   policies and practices 4, 8, 23
   school inspections 95–6
   school networks in 23–5

system leadership as system change 168
systems thinking 169
Skidmore, P. 162–3, 169
skills and qualities 19, 37, 61, 94, 108, 170, 201
snowball effect 134
social capital 11, 16, 37, 94, 99–100, 102–3, 105, 108, 129, 139, 151, 154, 195, 203 n.2
Social Network Analysis (SNA) 10
social process of learning together 173
socio-cultural theory 13, 202 n.3
splendid isolation, school in 1
status 16
strategies for achieving collaborative goals 175–6
strength 18
Strengthening Education In Mangere and Otara project 79
structural-pluralist perspective 202 n.3
structure 18, 45
structured structures 44
student system 45, 128
Suggett, D. 18, 21
Sumara, D. 5, 47–8, 129, 135, 138
Supporting All Schools to Succeed. Reform of the Tomorrow's Schools System (report) 83
Swan Partnership 67, 96–8, 102, 105, 122, 133
symmetry, ANT 49, 147–52, 159
   Covid-related challenges 152
   human/non-human actors 52, 147, 149–51, 155
   standards 147–8
synthesis 5, 179–86
system leadership/leaders 5, 36, 61, 94, 104, 121–2, 163, 185
   within and beyond schools 165–70
   collective sense-making 173–4
   domains 165
   eco-leadership 174–5
   questions 191–2
   schools 60, 62, 71, 96, 105, 206 n.3
   working with paradox 172–3

Tamai Kāhui Ako 88, 153
Tan, C. Y. 195
teachers and teaching 14, 35, 37, 39, 60, 87, 99–100, 107, 137, 167, 203 n.1

teaching school alliance (TSA) 62, 67–8, 120–2, 125, 157
Teaching School Hubs 204 n.8
teaching staff system 45, 128
Teach Less Learn More (TLLM) agenda, Singapore 23
te Ao Māori 185
Te Marautanga o Aotearoa 74
Tenbensel, T. 41–2
Theisens, H. 8, 45
theory of agency 146
Thinking Skills Learning Nation (TSLN) agenda, Singapore 23–4
Thomson, K., static universe 118
Thomson, P. 32, 163
A Thousand Plateaus (Deleuze & Guattari) 46
Thrupp, M.
  Investing in Educational Success 84
  networks in Aotearoa 86
Toh, Y. 24, 101, 131, 174
Tomorrow's Schools 77–80, 83–4, 88, 112–13, 117, 120, 124, 152, 187
Tomorrow's Schools Taskforce 205 n.12
Townsend, T. 167, 172
trait theory 164
transformations, network society 7
translation, concept of 50–1, 147, 152–5, 184
  intermediaries and mediators 51
  moments of 51, 152–5 (*see also specific translation moments*)
transnational leadership package (TLP) 163–5, 174, 185

Trends in International Maths and Science Study (TIMSS) 23
trust and social capital 136, 184, 195

United States
  educational groups in 101
  networking initiatives 21
  One Best System 208 n.2

value-adding change 194
van Dijck, J. 149
Vangen, S. 20, 171–2. *See also* collaborative thuggery
Varpio, L. 4
Vote Education budget 153

Waldrop, M. 134
Walker, A. 193
  principal instructional leadership 22–3
Waltz, S. B. 50
Wasserman, S. 202 n.1
Webber, M. 38
Weick, K. E., loosely coupled systems 43, 173
well-functioning collaborative networks 14
West, M. 11–13, 32
When Schools Compete: A Cautionary Tale (Fiske & Ladd) 76
wicked problems 38, 109
Williams, P. 164–5
Wylie, C. 79

Yong, T. L. 24–5, 95, 104

www.ingramcontent.com/pod-product-compliance
Lightning Source LLC
Chambersburg PA
CBHW062133300426
44115CB00012BA/1907